WARSAW BEFORE THE FIRST WORLD WAR: POLES AND JEWS IN THE THIRD CITY OF THE RUSSIAN EMPIRE 1880–1914

by

STEPHEN D. CORRSIN

EAST EUROPEAN MONOGRAPHS, BOULDER

DISTRIBUTED BY COLUMBIA UNIVERSITY PRESS, NEW YORK
1989

EAST EUROPEAN MONOGRAPHS, NO. CCLXXIV

Copyright © 1989 by Stephen D. Corrsin
ISBN 0-88033-166-6
Library of Congress Card Catalog Number 89-85205

Printed in the United States of America

Contents

Preface and Acknowledgements	v
Introduction	1
Chapter 1. Russian Rule in Warsaw	7
Chapter 2. The People of Warsaw	21
Chapter 3. The Faces of the City	39
Chapter 4. Patterns of Employment	51
Chapter 5. The Periodical Press	66
Chapter 6. The Elections to the Russian State Duma and the "Jewish Question," 1906–12	78
Conclusions	107
Map	110
Notes	112
List of Tables	139
Tables	140
Employment Categories	152
Selected Bibliography	168
Index	175

Preface and Acknowledgements

My work on the history of Warsaw first took shape as a doctoral dissertation at the University of Michigan. In the process of preparing subsequent articles and papers, I added a great deal of new material and increasingly focused on the theme which was of greatest interest to me and which, I felt, was surprisingly neglected: the development of Warsaw as *both* a Polish and a Jewish city under Russian rule.

I have many people to thank, particularly Roman Szporluk, who guided my dissertation, and then encouraged me to continue my research into this topic; the readers, auditors, and critics, anonymous and otherwise, of the original dissertation and my subsequent articles, public lectures, and conference papers; the Library Department and administration of Brooklyn College, for research leave time in 1987 and 1988; and all those friends and colleagues who have encouraged me along the way.

I would also like to thank Michael F. Hamm, who, several years ago, gave me the opportunity to publish a summary of my research on Warsaw as a chapter in *The City in Late Imperial Russia* (published in 1986 by the Indiana University Press). This made it possible for me to go on to complete this much longer study. My thanks also go to my colleagues in the library field—Slavicists, archivists, and interlibrary loan staff—at the University of Michigan, Columbia University, the New York Public Library (especially the Slavonic and Jewish Divisions), the Yivo Institute for Jewish Research, the City University of New York, the National Library of Israel, and in Warsaw, at the Biblioteka Narodowa, the Biblioteka Uniwersytecka, and the Archiwum Państwowe miasta stołecznego Warszawy.

But it is to my wife, Lori, who has watched me work on this topic since the beginning, that this is dedicated. To quote the preface to my dissertation: "No one is happier than she to see this work completed."

As usually happens in Eastern European and Russian studies, dates and names create problems. The Russian Empire was officially on the Julian calendar, while Poland, with the rest of Catholic Europe, had operated under the Gregorian calendar for several centuries.

Both dates were often given in Congress Poland (in the nineteenth century, the Gregorian calendar was twelve days in advance of the Julian; the difference is thirteen days in the twentieth). I have used the Gregorian calendar, except for the dates of the 1897 Russian imperial census, and of Russian laws.

In general, I have followed spelling and capitalization practices of the time when citing names, titles, etc. Polish names and periodical and book titles appear in the form used at the turn of the century, which are sometimes slightly different from modern spellings (*kurjer* instead of today's *kurier*, for example) and often are inconsistent (*kuryer* can also appear). In transliterating Russian, I have used the Library of Congress system. For transliterations of Hebrew-derived words in Yiddish (*kheyder, khadorim*), I have used the spellings that appear in Uriel Weinreich's *Modern English-Yiddish Yiddish-English Dictionary* (New York, 1968).

Jewish names can be particularly troublesome, and it is practically impossible to apply a system that is both consistent and appropriate. I have tried to follow the principle of using those forms of names which can be found most readily in American library catalogs or reference works, especially the catalogs of the Library of Congress and the New York Public Library, and the *Encyclopedia Judaica* (1971–72 edition). The names of assimilationist Jewish leaders generally appear in Polish forms as found in the *Polski słownik biograficzny* (Polish Biographical Encyclopedia), however. In regard to variations in the spellings of periodical titles, Yiddish, like Polish and Russian, has experienced a great deal of orthographic change, as well as considerable inconsistency. I have tried to use the spellings under which they appear most often in the historical literature. I have also tried to follow this principle with Hebrew periodical titles.

All translations from Polish, Russian, Yiddish, German, and French are mine unless otherwise indicated.

Introduction

The city of Warsaw—Varshava to the Russians—was the third city of the Russian Empire in the nineteenth and early twentieth centuries, trailing only St. Petersburg and Moscow in size and importance. But Warsaw was not a Russian city. Russia had gained control of it and the surrounding Polish territories after Napoleon's disastrous Russian campaign of 1812, and ruled there until the Central Powers drove the Russians out in 1915. Warsaw was the chief city and administrative and military center of the Russian Empire's Polish provinces, which were known officially, from the 1870s on, as the Vistula Region (*Privislinskii krai*, in Russian), but more commonly as Congress Poland or the Polish Kingdom.

Warsaw–Warszawa in Polish—had been the capital of the vast Polish–Lithuanian Commonwealth since the late sixteenth century, until the Commonwealth was partitioned by its increasingly powerful and aggressive neighbors, Russia, Prussia, and Austria, at the end of the eighteenth century. Still, Warsaw remained far and away the greatest city of divided Poland, symbolizing the hopes of nationalistic Poles everywhere that there would someday be a reunited and independent Poland.

Warsaw was, as well, one of the greatest of Jewish cities. In the nineteenth and twentieth centuries, no European city could match the size and diversity of its Jewish community; elsewhere, only New York surpassed it in the 1880s, as a result of the massive migration of the Eastern European and Russian Jews to America. The city was known as Varshe in Yiddish, the daily language of most of the Jews of Eastern Europe.

Varshava in Russian, Warszawa in Polish, and Varshe in Yiddish: all these aspects of Warsaw must be included to produce a balanced view of the city in the late nineteenth and early twentieth centuries.[1]

From the middle of the nineteenth century, the city exploded in size. In the early 1860s, Warsaw had, according to official estimates, less than a quarter of a million people. By the eve of World War I, Warsaw was a city of close to nine hundred thousand people, ranking among the ten largest cities of Europe. Warsaw had been in the mid-nineteenth century the largest city and leading political, cultural, and economic center of the Polish provinces of the Russian Empire, as well as of all the divided Polish lands. It retained this position. However, in the several decades before World War I, large scale socioeconomic change had a profound impact on many spheres of life. Industrialization, the revolutions in transportation and communication, commercial development, and the huge in-migration from the surrounding countryside and towns of Congress Poland helped to transform Warsaw from a regional center into a great city on a European scale.

There were significant political developments as well. The middle decades of the nineteenth century saw two unsuccessful Polish uprisings against Russian rule, the November Insurrection of 1830–31 and the January Insurrection of 1863–64. Russian rule was especially oppressive in the late nineteenth century. Congress Poland was a conquered land, with a sizable Russian army of occupation and many Russian officials. The imperial government followed a policy of intensive Russification of the region's administrative, legal, and educational systems.

Despite this, by the end of the century independent political life was reviving in Warsaw, at first chiefly taking the form of underground nationalist and socialist movements, either Polish or Jewish in their ethnic orientations. From late 1904 through 1907, there was massive unrest in Congress Poland, as in the rest of the Empire. The 1905 revolution shook, albeit temporarily, the hold of the Russian government, and forced it to make significant concessions. Major areas of political and cultural life were notably freer after late 1905 than they had been before. Popular energies were funneled into social and cultural as well as political causes; this could be seen clearly in the rapid development of the periodical press, of groups promoting education outside of the established school system, and also in the excitement generated by local elections.

One of the most important factors in Warsaw's history was its ethnically mixed population. In our period, Poles made up a little more than half of the city total, and the Jews one-third to two-fifths. These two peoples, although they had lived side by side in Poland for centuries, led largely separate lives. There was little sense of community between them; they were essentially alien to one another. This remained the case during the socioeconomic transformations and political upheavals of the nineteenth and early twentieth centuries.

The Polish and Jewish "questions" ranked near the top of the list of problems which beset the Empire and profoundly troubled its rulers and citizens. The Empire was both deeply Polonophobic and Judeophobic. Moreover, Polish–Jewish relations were of great importance to both the Polish and the Jewish peoples. No ethnic issue was more important than the "Jewish question" in Polish politics, except for the general question of Polish survival under foreign rule; and relations with Poles of Congress Poland, the part of the Empire which had the largest concentrations of both Poles and Jews, were crucial in the history of the Jews of the Russian Empire.

This ethnic theme became particularly important with the rise of mass political movements, in Poland as well as elsewhere in Eastern Europe, in the late nineteenth and early twentieth centuries. Ethnicity became a key political issue. The most obvious result of this was the rise of nationalist movements. Even in internationalist socialist groups, however, which supposedly held that class, not ethnicity, was the decisive point, ethnic political polarization was clearly visible; socialist groups in the Polish lands generally became either heavily Polish in orientation and membership, or Jewish.

The "Jewish question" (*sprawa* or *kwestia żydowska*, in Polish) became one of the crucial issues of Polish politics.[2] This "question" actually covered a range of issues: How should Poles deal with the large, and increasingly political assertive, Jewish population? What role should the Jews play in Poland's economy, culture, and society? What voice should the Jews have in the politics of Poland? Should Poles accept, or reject, Jewish acculturation and assimilation? Some Polish groups, including socialists and liberals, looked to the assimilation of Jews to Polish identity as the answer. But what did assimilation mean to them? Normally, the model of assimilation that Polish liberal leaders looked to was intolerant of Jewish distinctiveness, and coercive towards the Jews. Moreover, many Polish nationalists did not believe that assimilation was possible or acceptable, and some extremists reached the point of near–racist obsession with the Jews. In the early years of the twentieth century, anti-Semitism became an increasingly important component of the Polish nationalist movement, just as it was becoming stronger in other European nationalist movements.

The Jews themselves were also debating issues of their present situation and future prospects. This was the time of the rise of political Zionism and of Jewish socialist movements, as well as of debates among advocates of the adoption of the Polish language (or Russian, or German), supporters of Yiddish, and those who called for a Jewish national culture using Hebrew.

Nowhere in the Polish lands did these issues become more pressing and complex than in Warsaw, the third city of the Russian Empire, the unofficial capital of partitioned Poland, and the greatest Jewish city in Europe.

This study examines selected aspects of the shared and separate development of Warsaw's Polish and Jewish communities in the crucial decades before World I. The starting point of my research is the model of Warsaw as an ethnically mixed city of the Russian Empire, one with a largely Polish and Jewish population. The significance of this, of these intertwined themes, requires clarification. Warsaw's development as a whole cannot be understood without studying in some depth the Jews, the city's second largest group, as well as the majority Polish population. Polish (and general) developments, political, cultural, and socioeconomic, remain inexplicable if the Jewish community and Polish responses to the Jewish presence are ignored or inadequately covered. Despite this, almost all Polish studies on the history of Warsaw—and there has been a flood of them in recent decades—underestimate and undervalue the role of the Jews. They seem to regard Warsaw as though it was always, as it is now, an overwhelmingly Polish city. In the nineteenth century, and in the twentieth up to the destruction in World War II of Warsaw's Jewish community, the city's ethnic character was decidedly not so uniform as it is today. Rather, considering the size, importance, and separate development of the Jewish community, in many respects Warsaw was a "bi-ethnic" city. Meanwhile, traditional Jewish research has focused on the Jews alone, which has produced a somewhat out-of-context picture of Warsaw's Jews.

The other important point—that the city was ruled by the Russians—has been harder to avoid. Nonetheless, very little has been written on Warsaw's and Congress Poland's place in the Russian Empire. Scholars of the Russian Empire, westerners as well as Russian and Soviet writers, have normally left Congress Poland out of their considerations, except to refer to the insurrections against Russian rule. In the light of the importance of the region and its two largest cities, Warsaw and Łódź, to the Empire, this is unfortunate, to say the least.

This study examines selected aspects of demographic, social, and political change in Warsaw in the late nineteenth and early twentieth centuries, specifically from the early 1880s to World War I, focusing on the above-mentioned ethnic themes in the city's development. The first chapter surveys the city's history under Russian rule; the nature of Russian rule in Warsaw; and touches on key local issues with which the government was concerned, particularly education. It places the city within the imperial context, in its role as the third city of the Empire.

Introduction 5

The next three chapters concern themselves with demographic and socioeconomic processes. Chapter 2 discusses the city's population, including such specific issues as the growth of the population and of the Catholic and Jewish communities, the interactions of ethnic identity, faith, and language use, and Jewish acculturation and assimilation. Chapter 3 examines the social characteristics of the major parts of the city, and also the distribution of Catholics and Jews around the neighborhoods of Warsaw; chapter 4 covers the employment structure of the population, thereby shedding light on the different economic roles played by Polish and Jewish communities.

Taken together, chapters 2–4 present a picture of key facets, with emphasis on ethnicity, of the city's population and society. They rely heavily on the two censuses which were taken in the city, the local census of 1882 and the imperial census of 1897. Other statistical data, plus a great deal of non-quantitative material (contemporary descriptions, literature, memoirs, polemics, and Russian reports), are used as well.

Chapters 5 and 6 move into the sphere of political concerns and actions, concluding with the "Jewish question" in Polish politics. Chapter 5 surveys the rise of both the Polish and Jewish periodical presses, which served as the first means of mass communications, and as instruments central to the political and cultural developments of the two peoples and the city and region. Chapter 6 examines Polish attempts to respond to the "Jewish question" during the elections to the Russian State Duma, the Empire's quasi-parliament, in 1906–12. More than any other single events, these elections marked the politicization of the "Jewish question" in Warsaw and Congress Poland, strengthened the place of anti-Semitism in the Polish nationalist movement there, and saw the end of serious hopes for extensive interethnic political cooperation. The discussion of these elections concentrates on Polish perceptions and actions, and does not present Jewish activities in depth. Jewish positions in the elections were largely reactive in relation to Polish ones; moreover, examination of Jewish politics in pre-1914 Warsaw is deserving of a separate monogrphic study. Chapters 5 and 6 employ the press, archival records, memoirs, and contemporary and subsequent polemics and studies as their main sources.

I have not attempted a comprehensive survey history of Warsaw. Nor have I tried to write a history of either Polish or Jewish, or, for that matter, Russian Warsaw. I have selected certain topics to illuminate major demographic, social, and political themes in the light of the model of Warsaw as a "bi-ethnic" city under the rule of a "foreign" Empire. Many important areas are not covered in detail, for example, the city's economy, religious developments, and specifically Jewish politics. I have chosen to combine social and political themes, not only because extensive social and demographic changes formed the background against which Polish attempts to answer the "Jewish question" were made, but also because in many respects the political issues were really social and demographic ones: the rapidly growing Jewish population, Jewish in-migration, the concentration of Jews in certain parts of the local economy and in certain quarters of the city, and Jewish acculturation and assimilation were all crucial facets of the larger "Jewish question."

The decades which I have chosen to examine, from the early 1880s to 1914, represent a distinct period in the city's history. By the early 1880s, the Russian system which was implemented after the 1863 uprising and was to continue to the war was largely in place, and Russification of the educational and administration systems was well under way; the political revival which culminated in the mass movements of the early twentieth centuries, both Polish and Jewish, was beginning; and the city was entering the period of intensive social, economic, and demographic change which led to the rise of Warsaw as a modern city.[3]

Chapter 1

Russian Rule in Warsaw

The Historical Background

The circumstances surrounding Warsaw's founding and its early decades remain obscure. The site of Warsaw, on the middle reaches of the Vistula River, was in Mazovia, to the north and east of the medieval Polish heartland. Mazovia was a minor principality under the loose suzerainty of the Polish crown. Around the year 1300, a fortress was built on the river's western bank; a town was established nearby, which received a chapter from the Mazovian princes. Until the first half of the sixteenth century, Warsaw grew slowly. It was no more than a regional governmental center and minor princely residence, with some economic significance due to its location on the Vistula. By the 1520s, when the Polish Kingdom fully absorbed Mazovia, the city had perhaps five thousand residents.[1]

Warsaw soon replaced Kraków as the capital of the vast Polish–Lithuanian Commonwealth. The most important factor in Warsaw's rise was its location, near the Lithuanian Grand Duchy, the Commonwealth's eastern half. The joint Diet first met in Warsaw in the 1550s; from 1573, the kings were elected there; and in 1611 it officially became the royal residence. Through the seventeenth and eighteenth centuries, Warsaw experienced significant growth; about 110,000 people lived in the city by the time of the 1792 census, right after all parts of the Warsaw urban region (including both the Old and New Cities, the suburbs, and Praga, on the river's east bank) were united into a single large city.[2] This remarkable growth was chiefly in the eighteenth century, a time of decline for the Commonwealth, as Russia, Prussia, and Austria increasingly dominated Poland–Lithuania. They partitioned the Commonwealth in 1772 and 1793, and finally wiped it off the map in 1795.

The period of the Four–Year Diet (1788–92) was one of national political revival and reform; due to this extraordinary Diet's presence, Warsaw became more than ever before the focus of national political life. However, strong groups opposed the constitution which the Diet produced, and with Russian backing they gained control of the country. In the spring of 1794, a bloody uprising began in the city, but the Russians suppressed it within a few months and took Warsaw in November.

The 1795 partition reduced Warsaw to the status of a provincial city within the Prussian state. In 1807, after Napoleon crushed Prussia, he established the Grand Duchy of Warsaw, which included the central part of the old Polish Kingdom. Following the failure of Napoleon's 1812 campaign, the Russians again occupied Warsaw.

In 1815, Warsaw and the surrounding Polish provinces became, under Russian rule, the Congress Kingdom of Poland. The Kingdom had in theory extensive autonomy with its own constitution, administration, Diet, and army, and was tied to Russia in the person of the tsar as king of Poland. This autonomy was much weaker in practice than in theory, and the constitutional period ended with the Polish uprising of November 1830 against Russia. The Poles drove the Russians from Warsaw, and had some initial successes in the field. The Russian army defeated the Poles and reoccupied Warsaw in the fall of 1831.

Over the next quarter of a century, the Russians swept away most separate Polish governmental institutions, and tied the Kingdom more tightly to the Empire. Tsar Nicholas I's repressive rule was exemplifed by the construction of the fearsome Citadel on the city's northern edge, and by his statement to Polish notables that, "at the least unrest I will destroy the city, I will destroy Warsaw, and . . . it will not be I who will rebuild it."[3]

The accession of Alexander II in 1855 and the death of Nicholas's viceroy in Poland, Ivan Paskevich, in 1856, revived Polish hopes for liberalization, renewed autonomy, and for many nationalists, eventual independence and reunification. Warsaw in 1861–62 was the scene of extensive political activity, both in the open and underground. Patriotic demonstrations, and shootings by police and soldiers, rocked the city. Open insurrection broke out in January 1863, in the form of a guerrilla war directed by a secret National Government in Warsaw. The Russians crushed the rebellion in 1864, and began a program of renewed and increased, and far more systematic repression. The vestiges of Polish autonomy were eliminated, and far-reaching Russification took place, most notably in the legal, administrative, and educational systems.

Warsaw's population had dropped after the 1795 partition, to about 65,000 by 1797. The next six decades saw substantial but uneven growth; the population was approximately 230,000 in 1861.

For centuries Warsaw had been a multiethnic city, albeit with a Polish majority. Since the Middle Ages there had been a small German community, which was important in the city's commercial and industrial development; the Protestant population, which included many Germans, was less than 7 percent of the total in the early 1860s. Russians began to come to Warsaw in large numbers only after 1863, chiefly for official or military service; the Russian Orthodox (not counting the garrison) made up a little over 1 percent of the population in 1864.[4]

The Jews became the second largest group in Warsaw. They had begun to settle in the city by the early fifteenth century. The next four centuries saw repeated attempts by the local citizenry to restrict the Jewish presence, often with the support of the Mazovian princes and the Polish crown. These attempts were not consistently successful, as is shown by the fact that they were repeated every few decades. Jews made up 8.3 percent of the population counted in 1792.[5]

After the fall of the Commonwealth, Warsaw began to develop into one of Europe's most important Jewish centers. The Prussian government legally sanctioned the Jewish presence in the city. Thenceforth, the Jewish share rose significantly to 18 percent in 1810 and 33 percent in 1861. These are official estimates; it is likely that the real share was higher, especially in the earlier decades.

The Congress Kingdom inherited a system of discriminatory laws against the Jews.[6] While the Grand Duchy's 1807 constitution in theory granted equal rights to all, supplementary legislation exempted the Jews. After 1815, the government retained and in some cases extended anti-Jewish laws and regulations. Jews paid heavy additional taxes, and could live only in certain parts of cities and work only in certain trades. They were not allowed to live in villages, in many towns, and near the borders of the Kingdom. These rules were often circumvented, but they remained burdens on the Jewish population and perpetuated its isolation.

Jews were not allowed to live or own property on many of Warsaw's main streets. By 1842, 47 of Warsaw's 223 streets were in this way "exempted" from Jewish residence. A few families—those that were wealthy, secularly educated, and did not speak Yiddish or wear traditional Jewish clothing—could live on these streets. Only 131 such families had taken advantage of this by 1842. Thus, while Jews were not forced into a closed ghetto in Warsaw, the result of government policies was to concentrate them in less desirable sections, including the northwest side and Praga.[7]

Various government committees endlessly debated possible ameliorations of laws directed against the Jews, but nothing significant was done until the early 1860s. The "Jewish question" became a matter for public debate during the thaw after the deaths of Nicholas I and Paskevich. Jews and liberal Poles pushed for full Jewish legal emancipation. Jews also took part in the Polish patriotic movement of 1861–62. Assimilationists, such as the wealthy Mathias Rosen and liberal rabbis Marcus Jastrow and Isaac Kramsztyk, were active, but so was the orthodox chief rabbi of Warsaw, Dov Berush Meisels.

The Russian government finally introduced extensive reforms in the laws affecting Jews, largely in an attempt to prevent the possibility of a Polish–Jewish united front. Count Aleksander Wielopolski, a conservative Pole who looked to gain substantial Polish autonomy when he was head of the Kingdom's civil administration in 1861–62, forced the issue. The decree of June 5, 1862, eliminated most rules restricting Jewish residence and economic activities, and also special taxes. It did not, however, create full legal equality for the Jews.

Shortly afterward, the Polish revolutionaries appealed directly to the Jews for support; those of 1830–31 had made no serious attempt to deal with the "Jewish question." In a statement addressed to "Brother Poles of the Mosaic faith," dated June 22, 1863, the underground National Government said:

> You and your children will enjoy all civil rights without exceptions and restrictions, while the National Government will ask, not about faith or descent, but about place of birth, are you a Pole? And they will say about Poland: '. . . that this man was born there. Selah.' (Psalms 87:6)."[8]

The hopes of the early 1860s, for full Jewish emancipation and improved Polish–Jewish relations, were not, in the long run, fulfilled.

The Character of Russian Rule

The population of Warsaw and of all Congress Poland had no voice in local government. The Russian authorities made concessions in the early 1860s to local self–government in Warsaw, in particular an elected city council, but the January Insurrection convinced the Russians that they could not allow the Poles any political room to maneuver. Henceforth, Russia made no bones about the fact that it was in Poland as a conqueror. The short–lived city council was eliminated; local self–government bodies that were subsequently established elsewhere in the Empire, including both city councils and rural zemstvos, were never introduced in Congress Poland; the imperial municipal statutes of 1870 and 1892 were never applied here. Many of the trappings of Polish autonomy which had survived into the 1860s were abolished. For example, the name "Polish Kingdom"

(*Tsarstvo Pol'skoe*, in Russian) largely disappeared from official use, and was replaced by "Vistula Region" (*Privislinskii krai*).

Warsaw remained the Russian administrative and military capital of Congress Poland. It was the seat of the last man to hold the title of Viceroy of the Polish Kingdom, General Fedor Berg, and after his death in 1874, of the governors–general of the region. Berg followed a policy of harsh repression. His successors, among whom General Gurko served the longest (1883–94), ruled in quieter times, except for General Skalon (1905–14), who faced the 1905 revolution and its aftermath.

The imperial government followed a policy of Russification with respect to most of its ethnic minorities and borderlands. The term "Russification" has been used to cover a number of developments,[9] including efforts to integrate the non–Russian territories into the administrative structure of the Empire, and also the government's introduction of Russian as the primary language of administration and education in these regions, at the expense of other languages, such as Polish, German, and Ukrainian. It is crucial to understand that Russification was not a unified, well planned, and coordinated drive, but a complicated and changing series of efforts, which varied considerably by time and place. The responses of particular elements of local populations, to whom it was variously applied, also differed.

After the failure of the January Insurrection, the Russian authorities in the 1860s and 1870s followed a policy of integrating Congress Poland fully into the Empire. The use of Russian as the primary language of administration, law, and education was a central facet of this. Congress Poland was officially recognized as a distinct entity within the Empire in negative ways; special restrictive legislation was applied, and some limited reforms elsewhere, particularly in the area of local rural and urban self–government, were never introduced.

Nonetheless, it does not appear that the government's policy was to turn Poles and Jews into ethnic Russians, nor to make the Polish, Yiddish, and Hebrew languages disappear. The goals were more specific: to tighten administrative control over this dangerous region; to make it more easily governed, by making Russian more its dominant language than had been the case before; to prevent the Polonization of local minorities (including the Jews); and to neutralize the rebellious Polish elite. These goals were often pursued in brutal and arbitrary fashion, in Warsaw as in the Polish countryside.

Congress Poland was an occupied land. At the turn of the century there were two hundred thousand soldiers among the nine million people of the country. Forty thousand soldiers were stationed in and around Warsaw. Cossack patrols were regular sights on the city's streets. The ring of fortifications around the city was ostensibly directed against Germany, but there could be no doubt that the Citadel existed solely to intimidate the local population.[10]

After the governor-general, the city president was by title the most important official, but he actually had little power. Sokrates Starynkevich (president in 1875-92) was the city president best and most kindly remembered by Polish writers (indeed, he was the only Russian official in Warsaw for whom they consistently had kind words). Starynkevich, in contrast to many of his colleagues, was not an extreme Russian chauvinist and was favorably inclined towards the Poles. He was involved in such beneficial projects as the construction of water and sewer lines, transportation improvements, and the extension of the city's boundaries into its rapidly growing suburbs. The city government was subordinated both to the governor-general and the Ministry of Internal Affairs in St. Petersburg. City outlays over five thousand rubles needed the approval of the governor-general, and those of thirty thousand had to be approved by St. Petersburg.[11]

More powerful than the city president was the *oberpolitseimeister*, the "high chief of police." His duties went far beyond ordinary criminal matters, and included censorship, the supervision of private organizations and institutions, the fire department, and the control of internal passports; he reported directly to St. Petersburg.[12]

All of the most important official posts in Warsaw and Congress Poland were held by Russians, often Russian chauvinists. Russian civil servants were brought in to fill the upper and middle ranks of the administration, and received special pay and privileges. Russian Warsaw, including the families of officers, bureaucrats, judges, teachers, and educational officials, existed as a sheltered and isolated island in an alien, and occasionally hostile, Polish and Jewish sea. The families went to separate, Russian Orthodox churches; the children, to special schools.[13]

The Issues of Urban Life

Local publicists expressed considerable dissatisfaction with the quality of life in Warsaw; they compared city services and administration to those of Central and Western European cities, rather than to other cities of the Russian Empire, and found their own wanting. But in the context of the Empire, Warsaw did well. From 1883 to 1914, the city budget grew almost seven-fold, from 2.4 to 16.1 million rubles, while the population a little more than doubled; by 1914, the budget came to approximately eighteen rubles per resident, close to triple what it had been three decades before. These figures compared well to other cities of the Empire, but concerned citizens of Warsaw saw that it was considerably less than the per capita allotment of Vienna, Berlin, or Prague.[14] Table 1-1 shows the distribution of government expenditures in 1883 and 1914. The city was carrying a huge load of debt payments in 1914, thanks to the public works projects begun in the 1880s. Also, the budget share for charitable efforts and hospitals increased enormously. These two areas, plus "general administration," the water and sewer lines, cleaning and maintenance of streets, parks, and buildings, and the police, courts, and fire protection, accounted for approximately five-sixths of the "ordinary expenditures" in the 1914 budget.

Warsaw was a very compact city; it was about eight kilometers from the west bank's northern to its extreme southern edges, and it averaged three kilometers from the Vistula to the western boundaries. By the early twentieth century Warsaw was four times more densely populated than St. Petersburg, three times more than Moscow or Paris, and two and a half times more than Berlin, according to a 1913 report.[15] The basic cause of the crowding was the belt of fortifications surrounding the city. Until 1911, the authorities allowed no construction there, so the rapidly growing population crammed itself ever more tightly into the narrow city boundaries and inner suburbs. Housing became an issue of great importance. Large tenements, often built around several busy courtyards, provided housing for much of the middle classes as well as the poor and working classes. In 1911, Warsaw averaged 116 residents per residential building, compared to 40 in Łódź, 52 in St. Petersburg, and 38 in Moscow.[16] In 1868, 46 percent of the residential buildings had just one floor, 47 percent had two or three, and 7 percent four or more. Five decades later, these figures were 13 percent, 27 percent, and 60 percent.[17] The small, separate wooden houses that had once characterized the outlying neighborhoods were disappearing. By 1910, over four-fifths of the buildings in the city were stone or brick, chiefly built within the preceding few decades.

Housing for the poor, whether in the form of enormous tenements, workers' barracks in the factory districts, or wooden shacks in the suburbs, was dreadful; in addition, the poor generally lived in buildings and neighborhoods which were the worst provided with public services of all sorts, from pavement to plumbing. Jewish slums were notoriously crowded, but were relatively centrally located and thus closer to services; Polish slums were more likely to be on the city edges or in the suburbs, with more space and greenery but very primitive services.

For the destitute, there were night shelters and cheap kitchens.

In 1895, the Society for Lodging Houses, Cheap Kitchens and Tea Rooms, and Work Houses (*Towarzystwo Domów Nocległowych, Tanich Kuchni-Herbaciarni i Domów Pracy*) was founded, under the joint auspices of the police and leading businessmen. By 1899, it had four shelters with a year-round average of 700 people per night, plus a number of cheap kitchens providing six to seven thousand meals daily.[18]

More prosperous residents also had difficulties due to the high cost and scarcity of adequate housing. A 1911 report noted that it was getting easier to find larger, more luxurious five-room apartments, but that it was still very had to find two- or three-room, moderately priced dwellings.[19] For the city's wealthy, the spacious villas and palaces that had once been popular lost ground to smaller residences, especially large apartments with central locations. In the last years before the war, the *oberpolitseimeister* referred regularly to the city's housing crisis in his reports to the tsar.

Public works and services improved a great deal from the 1880s to World War I, thanks to large public investments, but observers agreed that there was a long way to go. Improvements came to wealthy and centrally located sections well before they reached poorer or suburban neighborhoods, and some areas did not get comprehensive, basic public services at all. Important services, including telephones, water mains and sewers, gas, and electricity, were usually entrusted to foreign firms.

Cleanliness of the city was a crucial issue. Polish writer Bolesław Prus wrote in 1877: "Warsaw stands on garbage, its residents eat, drink, and breathe garbage, and when one of them dies, he rests among garbage for all eternity."[20] (But a Russian, recalling the first years of the twentieth century, mentioned Warsaw's "irreproachable cleanliness."[21] Either the situation improved drastically in three or four decades, or Polish and Russian conceptions of urban cleanliness were markedly different.)

Warsaw was an unhealthy place to live. In the early 1880s, the city's water supply was poor in quality, unreliable, and unfiltered. Earlier efforts had given the city water mains only in a few sections, and scattered and inadequate sewer lines and other methods of waste disposal. Sociologist Ludwik Krzywicki recalled that, in his student days in the late 1870s, there was no running water in his building, and that water was brought in from a wooden well in the courtyard.[22] Outdoor privies were the rule for much of the population; sewage often overflowed courtyards and streets. In the early 1880s, the city turned for both water mains and sewer lines to an English firm, that of engineer William Lindley. The improvements that followed were significant but uneven. By 1911, 87 percent of Warsaw's properties were tied to water mains, and 61 percent to sewer lines; there were over 273 kilometers of water mains. Sewage was pumped far down the Vistula.[23] The west bank was better served than Praga, and Praga better than the suburbs. Running water or sewer lines often did not reach individual apartments, but rather single places on each floor, or a single place in a building, or indeed just the courtyard of a tenement. Even these modest improvements were sometimes resisted by property owners.[24]

This was a time of transition in the use of fuels. Coal was used extensively, and in 1899 the *oberpolitseimeister* reported that the poor were suffering due to shortages and high prices.[25] The first gas works were build in the 1850s by a German firm, but twenty years later many people still used wood stoves, and residences with gas lighting were the exception.[26] Gas was used mostly for public places, although after 1900 it was reported that the poor had become the chief users of gas, which was relatively expensive, and were thereby subsidizing the city's first steps towards large scale electrification.[27] After the turn of the century, electricity became increasingly common in public places, wealthier homes, and industry and public transport. In 1919, one-third of all properties (areas within the 1914 boundaries) lacked gas, and almost one-half lacked electricity.[28]

The telephone arrived in Warsaw shortly after its invention, but only came into wide use after the turn of the century, when a Swedish firm got the concession. In 1910 Warsaw had 37 residents per telephone, compared to averages of 54 in Moscow, 60 in St. Petersburg, and 238 residents per telephone in industrial Łódź.[29]

Horses remained until the eve of World War I the city's main means of public transport. They pulled carts, cabs, and buses and trams as well. From 1865, horse trams connected the new railroad stations on the Praga side with the Warsaw–Vienna station in west-central Warsaw. In 1880, a concession to build more extensive lines was awarded to a Belgian firm. In the first years of the new century, long and difficult negotiations over the development of electric lines took place. By 1901, the number of passenger trips on the horse trams had risen to twenty-two million, an average of only thirty trips per year for every resident. The electric lines, which opened in 1908 with great ceremony, were a success, and in 1913 a total of eighty-six million passenger rides were counted (an average of about one hundred trips per year per person.) On the busiest streets, such as Marszałkowska or Krakowskie Przedmieście and Nowy Świat, trams passed every minute or even more often.[30]

Historians rarely mention Warsaw's underworld, but it flourished in this period. Its mainstay was prostitution. In 1883, Prus wrote, no doubt with some exaggeration, "There seems to be nowhere in Europe a city as dissolute as Warsaw."[31] The city's west side, a high crime area, by the turn of the century had two major criminal gangs, one Polish and one Jewish, whose livelihoods came from controlling prostitution.[32] Isaac Bashevis Singer, who spent part of his boyhood (ca. 1910–17) in Warsaw, lived near "ill-famed Krochmalna Square, where pickpockets and hoodlums loitered and dealers in stolen goods carried on with their trade. The houses facing the square also harbored a number of brothels."[33]

Violent crime was rising. The annual reports of the *oberpolitseimeisters* referred to the prevalence of knives among the poor, and their growing willingness to use them in robberies or quarrels; this was termed the *nozhevshchina* in Russian, or *nożownictwo* in Polish (which means, roughly, the "knife problem"). Other areas of great concern were public drunkenness, and the use by adult criminals of bands of youthful thieves and pickpockets. Warsaw had a famous pre–war "school for thieves," directed by one Abraham Celender (Tselender), whose students were notorious not only in Poland, but in Russia and Germany as well.[34] Still, the *oberpolitseimeister* claimed in his 1894 report: "All crimes which were out of the ordinary were uncovered along with the guilty, who were handed over to the hands of justice."[35] In later years, reports to St. Petersburg were filled with pleas for more police, especially after the heavy casualties of the 1905 revolution.

The years 1905–07 were particularly violent, a time not only of great political unrest but also of rising violent crime. It was difficult to tell where political action ended and ordinary crime began, as street crime, bombings, shootings and knifings, and official retaliations and acts of violence, proliferated. *Oberpolitseimeister* Meier expressed his concern about the "extremely perverse attitude of the lower orders to the property of others," and noted that attacks on the police and the robberies of state liquor stores had become especially common.[36] (It is interesting to speculate about the extent to which many immigrant gangsters in American cities in the first part of the century picked up their training in the cities of the Russian Empire. Odessa's underworld is well known today because of the stories of Isaac Babel, but Warsaw's, which never found a chronicler of Babel's stature, should not be overlooked.)

Education: Russification and Response

Few issues were of greater concern to the government and society alike than education. The Russian government put substantial resources into its attempts to control, and to Russify, large sectors of education, and this became a major area of contention between the government and Polish society.

Polish education was a particular target of Russian policies.[37] In the government's view, Polish schools, using Polish as their medium of instruction and teaching Polish subjects, could only serve to keep Polish nationalism alive. Polish schools had provided important bases for nationalist activity in the "thaw" of the late 1850s–early 1860s. Polish leaders, meanwhile, promoted the re-establishment of Polish educational institutions, or greater use of Polish in existing schools. There was also considerable support in the Polish community for underground or unofficial Polish education and scholarship.

The Russian government had made some concessions in the area of education in the early 1860s. Particularly important was the Main School (*Szkoła Główna*), founded in 1862, which served as a Polish university in all but name. (The original Warsaw University had been closed after the 1830 uprising.) Intensive Russification of the schools began in the wake of the January Insurrection. The Imperial University of Warsaw, which was thoroughly Russian in programs, faculty, and spirit, replaced the Main School in 1869.[38] Russian was made the chief language of instruction in secondary and higher education, in all schools, including private ones. Russian history, geography, and literature replaced Polish subjects. Russian later became the first (though not exclusive) language of instruction in primary instruction as well. The penalties for resistance were severe. Students were punished for speaking Polish at school; some private schools (including Jewish ones) were closed for allowing students to speak Polish or for having too much Polish content in their programs. Aleksandr Apukhtin, curator of the Warsaw Educational District in 1879–97, won special notoriety as a fervent Russifier.

An important part of the Russification of education was providing special pay, pensions, and other benefits to Russian teachers and educational officials, in order to attract them to the Kingdom. Poles working in state education did not advance beyond the lower and middle ranks, and almost no Jews were employed there. More non-Russians taught in primary and non-state schools, but many Russian directors and teachers worked in them as well.

The level of educational attainment suffered, as schools were inadequate in number and quality as well as foreign in character and in tongue. Options open to prosperous families included home tutoring or sending their children to institutions in Central or Western Europe or even to Russia proper, which were generally of higher quality than schools in the Kingdom.

Underground educational efforts in Warsaw became a huge secret industry. Self-education groups appeared in the Imperial University and in secondary schools. One of the most important undertakings was the "Flying University" (*Latajqcy Uniwersytet*). Its origin was in secret education groups in girls' secondary schools in the 1880s. There were a great many programs to promote basic adult literacy and workers' education. It is noteworthy that assimilationist Jews were prominent in many underground or unofficial efforts, and Jewish girls' schools played important roles in attempts to preserve Polish education; this led to the closing of some of these schools under Apukhtin.[39] After the 1905 revolution, many legal private programs to promote education were founded. In the area of higher education, the Association for Scholarly Courses (*Towarzystwo Kursów Naukowych*), provided a number of programs on a university level, but was not allowed to grant degrees or otherwise become a full substitute for a Polish university. Its programs were often innovative, and the majority of its registered students (who normally numbered in the hundreds) consisted of women.[40]

Jewish schools were treated somewhat differently by the authorities, and the responses of elements of the Jewish community were varied and complex. Assimilationist Jews, again, were often leaders in Polish educational efforts, both in attempts to keep Polish education alive (legally or underground), and in very significant efforts to spread Polish and secular learning among the Jewish community. The *kehile* (Jewish communal organization) board, the great synagogue on Tłomacka Street, and the Association of Jewish Commercial Employees, all of which were controlled by assimilationists, were among the leaders in supporting Polish education for Jews.

Significant numbers of Jews went to Russified state or private schools, although quotas imposed in the state schools in the 1880s sharply limited their numbers (quotas also existed in Polish private schools). Few Jews among those who had Yiddish as their native language had gone very far in such schools by the 1897 census; only 1.3 percent had attained a formal education "beyond the primary level," compared to 10 percent of Polish-speakers of all faiths.[41]

The government's Russification policy was less thorough in the area of Jewish religious education than in state schools or secular private schools. Traditional Jewish education relied on the *khadorim*, the religious elementary schools, through which most Jewish boys passed. Most *khadorim* were tiny and their hygienic circumstances were notoriously bad. The purpose of these schools was to teach the reading of prayers and traditional religious literature.[42] The government attempted to bring these under some sort of control, for example requiring the registration of both schools and teachers, as well as some teaching of Russian, and trying to improve the physical conditions of the schools. Many schools and teachers alike found ways to avoid compliance with registration, and the teaching of Russian might be limited to memorization of the tsar's titles and the names of members of the imperial family, plus a bribe to the Russian school inspector.[43]

The *khadorim* declined to some extent in this period. It appears that the share of boys who attended them fell.[44] Also, by the eve of World War I the lack of Jewish education for girls had become an issue in the Jewish press.[45] One response to the decline of traditional religious schools was attempts to reform and expand *kheyder* programs, to make them more like general primary schools.[46]

Jewish unofficial and clandestine education was at least as varied as Polish efforts. An enormous amount of religious study went on in the traditional Jewish community, in yeshivas and *bote-midroshim* (houses of study) as well as in advanced *khadorim*, even though Warsaw had never been a leading center for Jewish religious education (such as, for example, Vilnius). At the same time, assimilationist Jews, including the leaders of the *kehile*, promoted the study of Polish in the larger Jewish community, and nationalist and socialist groups sponsored education circles and programs. There were basic adult literacy programs aimed specifically at the Jewish poor. These often had the express goal of "productivization" of the allegedly unproductive Jewish poor, moving them from petty commerce into manufacturing and crafts.[47]

Warsaw's educational environment changed radically with the 1905 revolution. In early 1905, a student strike began. Later in the year, it became legal to establish private schools and educational programs with languages of instruction other than Russian. Many new private schools, both Polish and Jewish, were founded; they provided considerable competition for state schools, even though the government discouraged them through such measures as limiting access to higher education in the Empire to their graduates, and by general harassment.[48] The new educational possibilities opened up a whole new area of debate over Jewish language use; should programs in Yiddish be encouraged, or in Hebrew, or only in Polish? The *kehile* was particularly active in promoting Polish, but it faced opposition both from the Russian authorities and from anti-assimilationist Jews.[49]

How successful was the Russification of the schools? The main result was depressed levels of literacy and educational attainment, as many people avoided Russified schools and the government limited private initiatives. Russification of the schools certainly did not neutralize Polish nationalism, nor prevent the rise of socialist movements or Jewish nationalism. To be sure, a significant part of the local population learned at least some Russian in the schools. The further one's schooling went, the better one was likely to have learned Russian; many Polish and Jewish intellectuals knew the language well. But it is hardly likely that this was as great a factor in maintaining effective Russian rule as two hundred thousand Russian soldiers or close economic ties between Congress Poland and the larger Empire.

Warsaw was the third city of the Russian Empire, a major governmental, military, and economic center. It also served as the base for the two most threatening nationalist insurrections of late Russian imperial history. Warsaw's appearance and state of urban development represented a mix of Central European and Russian elements, but there is no doubt that Warsaw's residents generally saw themselves as Europeans rather than as Russians. The city's ethnic character remained Polish and Jewish; Warsaw was the largest of Polish cities, and (in Europe) of Jewish ones. It is to the examination of selected characteristics of the population and society that we turn in the next three chapters.

Chapter 2

The People of Warsaw

From the early 1880s to World War I, the population of Warsaw more than doubled, from less than four hundred thousand to almost nine hundred thousand people. Through this entire period a little more than half of the population consisted of Polish Catholics and one-third to two-fifths were Jews.[1] This chapter examines the growth of the population, changes in its composition, and the interactions of language, faith, and ethnic identity, including Jewish acculturation and assimilation. Warsaw's importance to the Russian Empire and to the Polish and Jewish peoples insured that changes in the city's population would create issues of great political significance. The key issues that developed were tied to the growth of and changes in the Jewish population. The great growth of Warsaw's Jewish community led both Russian officials and Polish leaders to express concern about the "Judaization" of the city. Further, Jewish acculturation and assimilation complicated an already tangled ethno-political environment and confronted Poles and Jews alike with new problems and choices.

The primary sources for the study of the city's population are the two censuses which were taken on February 9, 1882, and January 28, 1897.[2] They are in many respects difficult to use for comparative purposes. The 1882 count was locally organized and studied primarily the resident population. The 1897 imperial census was chiefly concerned with the population actually present at the time of the census. The two censuses often asked different questions, and organized their results differently. It is impossible to state with assurance how accurate the two censuses were; such evaluations cannot be made without extensive outside data to check the results against. Other sources, which used vital statistics gathered by the local authorities on a routine basis, were less trustworthy and considerably less detailed than the censuses.

Significant difficulties in interpretation and differences between the two censuses are dealt with as they arise in this and the following chapters. Despite many criticisms of the censuses, and the need to reject their results on certain points (for example, the 1882 data on ethnic identity), most scholars regard them as reasonably trustworthy, and the best that could be expected in the given time and place. Moreover, they are the only detailed population sources which exist for Warsaw in this period, and for this reason at least must not be dismissed out of hand.

Population Growth

Table 2-1 shows the growth in Warsaw's population in 1882, 1897, and 1914. The 1882 data cover the resident population. The 1897 census gave the population actually present as 624,189. Persons temporarily present in the city were included (7,585); absent residents were not (4,194).[3] This census also counted the entire garrison including troops living in barracks in the city, about twenty thousand men. The city's Statistical Department used the census data to state that the population, excluding soldiers in barracks, was 601,408.[4] The 1914 total was compiled from ongoing data on births and deaths and officially registered migrants, and represents an official estimate rather than a census.

Part of the increase in Warsaw's population resulted from the extension of its boundaries. The city covered 2,740 hectares in 1882, and 3,273 in 1913. The largest single suburban annexation took place in 1889, when Praga approximately doubled in size. Warsaw's population density rose substantially, from 140 to 258 persons per hectare in 1882-1913. The density of the Vistula's west bank increased from 164 to 321; in less developed Praga, from 35 to 99.[5]

The city's suburbs grew at a rapid pace from the mid-1890s on. A number of factories were established in them, and many recent in-migrants settled there. The annual population estimates for the suburbs are even less reliable than those for the city, but they still show the approximate course of growth. In the four communes around the city which were most affected by urbanization (Mokotów, Czyste, Młociny, and Bródno), the population more than tripled in 1890-1913, from 57,000 to 191,000.[6]

The most rapid population increases in Warsaw and its suburbs took place in the 1890s and in the last few years before World War I, which were periods of great economic expansion. The first decade of the twentieth century saw slower growth and, for several years after 1904, apparent population decline. This was a result both of the economic depression which the Empire underwent starting at the turn of the century, and the extensive political unrest and violence in Warsaw from late 1904 to 1907. Probably in-migration from the surrounding provinces slowed down, and many recent arrivals returned again to their home villages. The 1904 population total was not reached until 1910, when the city was entering a new period of economic growth.

A large part of Warsaw's population increase resulted from heavy in-migration. According to both censuses, only a little more than half of Warsaw's population had been born in the city. The rest consisted chiefly of persons born in the provinces of the Polish Kingdom, with the largest group coming from Warsaw province. Smaller numbers came from other parts of the Empire, Germany, and Austria-Hungary.

Serious problems of interpretation arise in comparing birthplace data from the two censuses. Again, the 1882 census dealt with the resident population while the 1897 count covered persons actually present. Further, the later census included over twenty thousand soldiers living in barracks, most of whom were Russians or Ukrainians who had been born outside the Congress Kingdom. Both these factors would decrease the locally born share in 1897 relative to the 1882 count. Table 2-2 presents the data on the birthplaces of Warsaw's population in 1882 and 1897, respectively.

Of Warsaw's residents in February 1882, just over half, 52.6 percent, had been born in the city, and another 11.3 percent had been born elsewhere in Warsaw province. Over a quarter of the population came from the nine other provinces of Congress Poland, so that 90 percent of the total could be termed locally born.

In-migrants from other parts of the Empire made up 5.6 percent of city residents, and the foreign born 4.4 percent. In all, 4.5 percent of Warsaw's residents were foreign citizens, chiefly from Austria-Hungary (1.6 percent) and Germany (2.6 percent).[7] Many of these came from Austrian Galicia and Prussian Poland, former parts of the Commonwealth which had large Polish populations; Galicia had a sizable Jewish minority as well.

Of the present population in 1897, 50.4 percent had been born in the city; 14 percent in the surrounding province; and 22.9 percent elsewhere in the Kingdom. Thus, 87.3 percent of the population were locally born. The relatively large share of men born in the Empire but outside the Kingdom, 15.8 percent of the male total, was due to the inclusion of the garrison.

Of Warsaw's present population, only 1.4 percent (8,446) were foreign citizens. Most came from Austria-Hungary and Germany: 0.5 percent (3,214) and 0.7 percent (4,355), respectively.[8] Slightly higher percentages had been born in these states, 0.7 percent and 0.9 percent. There was a substantial drop in 1882-97 in absolute numbers as well as percentages of persons born in, or who were citizens of, these neighboring empires. It seems likely that with the increasingly oppressive official Russification of Congress Poland, Warsaw was becoming less attractive to citizens of Galicia and Prussia.

The obvious issue to cover now would be natural increase in the city, and to compare its effects on the population with those of migration. However, the ongoing registration of births and deaths in the city (as elsewhere in the Empire) was very unreliable, especially for the Jews. Instead, we will rely on the censuses to examine the growth as well as the differing demographic structures of the city's major groups.

Demographic Differences between the Polish and Jewish Communities

Faith was the primary indicator of ethnic boundaries in Congress Poland. The differential growth of the city's two major religious groups, the Roman Catholics and the Jews, whose boundaries largely coincided with those of the Polish and Jewish ethnic communities, was of great significance for the social, cultural, and political development of the city. The Catholics in Warsaw were almost all Poles, and most Jews were Jewish in both a religious and an ethnic sense. There was also an important Jewish minority that had adopted many aspects of Polish culture, most obviously language; the assimilationists among them—those who had gone beyond acculturation to self-identification with the Polish ethnic group—often identified themselves by such terms as Jewish Poles (*Żydzi-Polacy* in Polish), and Poles of Mosaic faith or descent (*Polacy mojżeszowego wyznania, pochodzenia*). A few Jews converted to Christianity, often because of strong self-identification with Polish culture and ethnic identity. Among the city's smaller religious groups, the Orthodox were chiefly Russians or Ukrainians, many of them soldiers, and the Lutherans and other Protestants consisted mainly of ethnic Poles and Germans. Table 2-3 presents data on the composition of Warsaw's population in 1882–1914.[9]

The religious composition of the population did not change a great deal in these decades. Still, the growth of the Jewish community was significantly greater than that of the Catholic. In 1882–1914, the total population rose by 131 percent; the Catholic by 118.7 percent; and the Jewish by 163.5 percent. The data show a stable Jewish share of approximately one-third, and a Catholic share of three-fifths, through the late nineteenth century. Subsequent official estimates from 1910–1914 indicate that Jewish growth was accelerating relative to the rest of the city, reaching 36 to 39 percent of the total, while the Catholic share fell to 54 to 57 percent. (An alternative or supplementary explanation is that the Jewish population declined less than the Catholic during the turmoil of 1904–07; again, the accuracy of the data, especially for later years when no census was taken, cannot be pushed very far.)

The data will always remain sparse and uncertain. For example, low Jewish numbers in the early and middle decades of the nineteenth century, when Jewish in-migration to the city was restricted and Jews had to pay additional taxes, certainly understate the actual totals.[10] Scholars have assumed, nonetheless, that the available data from the last several decades of Russian rule provide a fair approximation of the city's population, and thus that the Jewish share was growing significantly by the early twentieth century. It is also noteworthy that contemporary observers saw an increasing Jewish presence in the city.

Examination of the demographic data from the censuses, particularly those on the age and sex structures of the population, shows striking differences between the Jewish and Catholic communities. This would have had important effects on their differential growth. In 1882, the resident population of Warsaw had 90 men per 100 women, as did the present population in 1897 (excluding soldiers living in barracks). In 1882, there were 86 Catholic men per 100 women; in 1897 there were 85. For Jews these ratios were 90 to 100 in 1882 and 92 to 100 in 1897. In the Congress Kingdom as a whole in 1897 there were 96 men to 100 women among the Catholics, and among Jews 95.[11]

Table 2–4 shows that Catholic–Jewish differences in the age breakdowns were even more striking. The Jewish community had many more children, and the Catholic had a significant bulge among young and middle-aged adults. As in the sexual division of the population, there was a greater similarity between the age structures of the Jewish populations of the city and Kingdom than was the case for the Catholics, as the third section of Table 2–4 reveals.

The sharply different demographic structures of the city's Jewish and Catholic communities, and the greater similarity between the age and sex structures of the Jewish populations of the city and Kingdom as compared to the Catholic populations, are best explained by assuming different patterns of in-migration to Warsaw. Evidently, Jews came to the city more often as families with children, and Catholics as individual adults, leading to more "normal" (for Congress Poland) age and sex structures for the Jewish community of the city. It is probable that Catholic women were more likely to come to Warsaw when they left their native villages and towns, and Catholic men to bypass Warsaw and to seek work in Germany or even overseas. This led to the high percentages of Catholic women and of Catholic adults in general in the city relative to the Kingdom.

It would be best at this point to examine in detail the separate factors behind the differential growth of the Catholic and Jewish communities, and in particular the influence of the three ways by which the city's population changed: migration, natural increase, and the extension of boundaries. Unfortunately, the available data are such that it is not possible to examine clearly and directly the roles each of these factors played in the changes in Warsaw's composition or, indeed, in the overall growth of the population. The censuses do not discuss in-migrants by faith, for example, nor faith or language by birthplace. The ongoing registration of births, deaths, and migration was not reliable, especially in the case of the Jews, and scholars cannot with confidence make significant use of the resulting data to consider important demographic issues, such as the different roles played by natural increase and migration in the development of either the Jewish or the Catholic population.[12]

Data from the censuses, however, are detailed and reliable enough to be used to examine certain important topics indirectly. One such topic is fertility and infant and child mortality among Warsaw's Jews and Catholics. This can be done by calculating ratios between the totals of children and women of child-bearing age in each group, which "indirectly reflect both the fertility of women and the survival of their offspring, and gives us a rough but usable way of measuring the comparative success of the various ethnic groups in rearing children."[13] For the 1882 census, women born in 1842–61 are considered here to be representative of all women of child-bearing age; for 1897, women aged twenty to thirty-nine are so regarded.

Major differences between Catholics and Jews are apparent. In 1882, for every 100 Catholic women born in 1842–61, there were 84 Catholic children (born in 1872–82); among Jews there were 183 children per 100 women of this age group. In 1897, for every 100 Catholic women aged twenty to thirty-nine, there were 13 infants up to one year and 86 small children from one to nine; among Jews there were 17 infants and 142 small children.[14] These data could indicate a combination of several factors: higher Jewish fertility, lower child mortality, or migration by families. We have already noted the differences in migration patterns. Information from various sources, as well as the greater Catholic–Jewish difference in the child–woman ratios for children aged one to nine than for infants in 1897, suggests that lower mortality among Jews was crucial, and that differences in fertility were not a factor. The data also indicate that the child–woman ratio "gap" between the Jewish and Catholic communities narrowed somewhat in 1882–97. One study done in Łódź before World War I supports the view that differences in mortality were crucial. (It is reasonable to assume that similar trends in birth and death patterns were taking place in Warsaw and Łódź.) Władysław Schoenaich, a physician at the hospital of Anna–Maria in Łódź, published this study in 1914 in the scholarly quarterly *Ekonomista* (Economist). This hospital served chiefly the poor of the city, both Christians and Jews. Schoenaich kept records as to how many children each woman who came to the hospital to give birth had already had, and also noted the age of the mothers, and whether they were Christians or Jews. (Łódź had a large Protestant minority, which was relatively prosperous, and it is likely that most Christian women who came to a hospital for the poor would be Catholics.) In all, he noted 11,324 Christian mothers who had had 49,221 children, and 3,833 Jewish mothers, who had had 17,216 children. On the average, each Christian mother had given birth to 4.35 children, and each Jew to 4.49; this indicates that there was not much difference in fertility. At the time that they were questioned, 35.4 percent of the children born to Christian mothers had died, compared to 24.7 percent of the Jewish children.

Schoenaich ascribes lower infant and child mortality among Jews to such factors as better care, longer periods of breastfeeding, and less alcoholism and lower incidence of venereal disease.[15] Other writers, from Poland and elsewhere, have also noted traditionally lower Jewish child mortality and mentioned a number of additional factors, for example: Jews were more likely to seek medical care than were Catholics; Jewish women were more likely to stay home with small children, rather than to work outside the home; and as a population which had been relatively urbanized for some time, Warsaw's Jews were more acclimated to the health problems of urban life than the Polish Catholics, many of whom were from peasant families.[16]

Other factors would also have helped keep Jewish child mortality low. Jews migrated to Warsaw, as noted, relatively often as families, and Catholics as individual adults. This would not only have added to the number of Jewish children in the city by means of in-migration, but would also have reinforced lower Jewish infant and child mortality, because families would have had greater success in keeping children alive in the city than would single parents (or foundling homes, where many illegitimate babies were left), considering the deep poverty in which many of Warsaw's residents lived.

A common contemporary opinion was that Jewish fertility was very high, but now the usual scholarly view is that it was lower than that of the general population in the Empire as a whole. The existing data from Warsaw on births, which are, again, not very reliable, particularly for the Jews, show a significantly lower Jewish than Catholic birth rate.[17]

It is probable that a major factor in low Jewish infant and child mortality was the very low rate of illegitimate births among Jews, especially compared to the Catholics. This would have had a profound effect on infant and child mortality rates, because illegitimate children had higher death rates than legitimate ones. While the data are no more reliable than those on births in general, they reveal such striking differences between the Jewish and Catholic communities that they cannot be ignored. Official figures from 1882 state that one in five Catholic births was illegitimate, compared to less than 1 percent of Jewish births. The wide difference between Catholic and Jewish rates of illegitimacy had begun to narrow slightly by the turn of the century (15 percent of officially registered Catholic births were illegitimate in 1901, and 2 percent of Jewish births).[18]

It is clear that several factors were involved in differential Jewish and Catholic population growth and demographic change in Warsaw. These factors—particularly differences in migration patterns, and in infant and child mortality due to social and cultural differences—are, because of the inadequacy of the data, extraordinarily difficult to disentangle, and it is not possible to separate out a "first cause" underlying the differences.

The Censuses on Ethnic Identity and Native Language

The 1882 census, in addition to information on faith, provides data on ethnic identity (*narodowość* in Polish, *natsional'nost'* in Russian). The 1897 count has data on native language (*rodnoi iazyk* in Russian). The 1882 results are useful for what they reveal about the attitudes of the Jewish assimilationist leaders of the day rather than for the data themselves. The 1897 language data tell us much more; they appear to be reasonably trustworthy, and are cross tabulated with figures on faith, which makes them helpful in considering the relations between faith and language use.

The data from 1882 contradict standard views of ethnicity in nineteenth century Poland: 90.7 percent of the population were listed as Polish, 4 percent as Russian, 2.7 percent as Jewish, 2 percent as German, and 0.7 percent as members of other groups. The mystery is that only 10,031 out of 127,917 Jews evidently claimed Jewish ethnic identity, while the overwhelming majority appeared as Polish. These figures cannot be accepted at face value.

In the published census this result is explained by stating that Jews "born in the provinces of the Polish Kingdom consider themselves to be Poles."[19] This view has survived in Polish historiography. A 1961 study of Warsaw's population stated:

> In the year 1882 strong assimilationist trends dominated among the Jewish population, the memory of joint demonstrations by the whole population of Warsaw [during the early 1860s] was still alive, and the ethnic consciousness of the Jews had not been awakened; for these reasons only a small number of Jews claimed Jewish ethnic identity in the census. We feel that persons who did not really understand the question of their ethnic identity often identified themselves as Poles by virtue of the fact that they had been born and lived in the Congress Kingdom.
>
> Besides this, the way the census takers explained things had to have a great influence on the results of the census. It can be assumed that in many cases the census taker advised people to claim Polish ethnic identity.[20]

The first part of this explanation is extremely improbable. In fact, Polish–Jewish ethnic boundaries were quite strong, and the assimilation of individual Jews or Jewish families to strong self-identification with "Polishness" (*polikość*), as distinct from the more widespread phenomenon of Jewish acculturation, that is the adoption of Polish cultural traits such as language and dress, affected only a small minority. Joint demonstrations twenty years before had indeed had positive effects on ethnic relations, but had not involved the greater part of the Jewish community, and the positive memories had faded with time and as a consequence of the 1881 pogrom, which took place just six weeks before the census. One Jew answered the census question by saying that until the pogrom he would have called himself a Pole, but no longer.[21] Jewish ethnic consciousness was very strong, even though as yet it was not politically directed into organized nationalist or autonomist movements; while few Jews in Warsaw in 1882 thought of themselves as members of a Jewish political nationality, they knew very well that they were Jews, not Poles.

The second part of the explanation, concerning the census takers, has a far more likely ring to it. Jewish historian Jacob Shatzky provides more useful evidence:

> In 1881 the Warsaw statistician Zalewski requested Dr. Natanson to see to it that the Jews declared themselves as Poles in the census. Natanson presented the proposal of the Polish statistician at a session of the Kehilla board, where it was agreed to support it. The resolution added that those who did not wish to declare their nationality as Polish should,

at least, refrain from registering as members of any other—including the Jewish—nationality.[22]

The idea was no doubt to lend support to the view that despite religious differences, Warsaw was an overwhelming Polish city, and that the Jews identified with the Poles. The assimilationist Jews who had controlled the *kehile* board since 1871—led by Dr. Ludwik Natanson, member of an influential and wealthy family, who headed the board until his death in 1896—regarded themselves as Poles of Mosaic faith or Jewish Poles, and might well have jumped at the chance to present the Jewish community as ethnically Polish, even if only nominally. This would have especially been the case in the immediate aftermath of the 1881 pogrom, which received a great deal of attention in Western and Central Europe.

The Jewish assimilationist weekly *Izraelita* [Israelite] throws more light on the affair. In the summer of 1881, members of the city census commission debated about the proper Jewish response to the question on ethnic identity. Zalewski and Natanson held that, "Local Jews do not have an ethnic identity; thus persons of the Mosaic faith who were born here and live here permanently have to be listed as Poles."[23] (Among their opponents was Jan Jeleński, a leading local anti-Semitic writer and editor.) The commission decided against this, and planned to allow Jews to respond as they pleased to the question.

Subsequent articles in *Izraelita* called for Jews who would be census takers in Jewish areas to encourage Jews to claim Polish ethnic identity:

> It should also be explained to the ignorant . . . that they are local inhabitants, that despite differences of faith and religious tradition . . . they belong to the people among which they live.[24]

Evidently, the *kehile* board had decided to follow up on Natanson's and Zalewski's wishes and the suggestion that census takers advised people to claim Polish ethnic identity is correct; perhaps they told Jews that the question referred to birthplace or residence in the Polish Kingdom rather than to ethnic identity as such.

It is very impressive that the board, which was distrusted by most traditionalist Jews, managed to get the results it wanted. *Izraelita's* tone in commenting on this was self-congratulatory, noting that almost all, "with the very small exception of non-permanent and transitory persons, entered themselves, or said that they should be entered for ethnic identity as local inhabitants."[25] (Due to stringent press censorship, *Izraelita* had to use *krajowcy* [local inhabitants] in place of *Polacy* [Poles]; in the published census, *Polacy* was used.) There have been no suggestions that wholesale falsification of the results took place when they were aggregated, but that must remain a possibility.

The 1897 data on native language (*rodnoi iazyk*, in Russian) are far more useful. The instructions to the census takers read: "Here should be written the name of the language which each person considers to be native for himself."[26] Native language evidently referred to first-learned or mother tongue.[27] Table 2-5 presents data for the entire present population (including the garrison), cross tabulated with those for faith.

Of all Catholics, 98.8 percent were Polish-speakers; of all Polish-speakers, 89.8 percent were Catholics, and 7.5 percent Jews. Of all Jews, 83.7 percent were Yiddish-speakers, and 13.7 percent Polish-speakers; of all Yiddish-speakers, 99.8 percent were Jews, the rest no doubt converts to Christianity. Most Orthodox were Russian- or Ukrainian-speakers, and the Protestants were split between Polish and German. The Russian-speakers were chiefly Orthodox with a significant Jewish minority, and German-speakers mostly Protestant with Catholic and Jewish minorities.

The data confirm that faith and native language for Warsaw's two largest groups roughly coincided; that is, the Polish language was closely associated with the Catholic element, and Yiddish with the Jews. The most important group for whom this was not the case consisted of the Polish-speaking Jews. Some members of this group saw themselves as assimilated Poles of Mosaic faith or Jewish Poles, but others were simply Polish-speaking Jews; the evidence does not allow us to draw firm conclusions about the relative sizes of these different groups nor of their political and ethnic allegiances.[28]

Patterns of Jewish Acculturation and Assimilation

As the city's Jewish community grew, it became increasingly diverse. In the first half of the nineteenth century, the *Misnagdim* (non-Hasidic orthodox) formed the "center" of the Jewish community; Hasidic elements were gaining ground; and there were small minorities of *Maskilim* and of Polonized or Germanized Jews. By the late 1890s, however, the *Misnagdim* "were slowly disappearing from view," as Nahum Sokolow wrote.[29] The *Hasidim* became far and away the largest orthodox element; indeed, by 1866 a visiting Jewish writer had noted that Warsaw appeared to be "an Hasidic city."[30]

By the turn of the century, the secularization of many aspects of Jewish life and the adoption by significant sections of the Jewish community of the culture of the surrounding gentile world was well under way. While the *Hasidim* continued to make up the greater part of the Jewish community, the movement had lost much of its creative and expansive impetus, and many young people were turning away to take less religious paths. Polish and Russian culture both were gaining influence in Jewish Warsaw; Germanization, however, had ceased to be an attractive option for Warsaw's Jews. Changing patterns of inmigration were also affecting the community by bringing in thousands of Jews from the Empire's Ukrainian, Belorussian, Lithuanian, and Russian provinces, not only from the Polish areas that had hitherto provided most of Warsaw's residents. This led to the rise of Warsaw's Litvak community, which became a major factor in local politics and polemics.

The diversity of the Jewish community is reflected only to a limited degree in the censuses. There are no data cross tabulating faith and birthplace (so we cannot estimate the number of Litvaks), nor on *Hasidim, Misnagdim,* or *Maskilim,* nor on how many Jews had moved away from traditional ways of life and belief. We can, however, use the 1897 data on native language as the basis for a discussion of Jewish acculturation and assimilation.

Language use and change in Warsaw was a crucial aspect of acculturation, as well as one of the most obvious. Acculturation in this context can be defined as the adoption by members of a particular group of the cultural patterns of another group.[31] In the Polish lands in the nineteenth century, change in language use was an important marker of acculturation, and the only one that turns up in the censuses, but there were others that were important to the people and governments of the time, such as the issue of traditional Jewish versus "European" clothing. Acculturation should not be equated with the concept of assimilation, which ought to be reserved for questions of ethnic self-identification.

Jewish acculturation in Warsaw was concerned with Jewish adoption of Polish (or Russian, or German) cultural patterns, among which language use was one of the most obvious and important. Assimilation occurred when Jews strongly identified themselves with Polish (or another) identity. The former phenomenon by no means necessarily led to the latter, but assimilation was unheard of without very significant acculturation. Assimilationists had believed since the first part of the nineteenth century that adoption of the Polish language by large numbers of Jews would be a crucial step on the road to the large scale assimilation which they felt would solve the "Jewish question" in Poland. But by the end of the century, even though use of Polish and other aspects of acculturation were becoming increasingly common, Jewish assimilationism as a movement to adopt Polish ethnic identity was approaching "bankruptcy."[32] This was due to the hardening of ethnic boundaries, rising Polish political anti–Semitism, and the appearance of new models of Jewish life for those Jews who did not wish to be tied to traditional Jewish ways of life and belief, but who also did not follow the model of the Poles of Mosaic faith, that of complete assimilation.

Any contact situation provides many facets and gradations of acculturation, and it is quite possible for a given group, or any elements within the group, to adopt others' cultural patterns while retaining a strong sense of itself as distinct. Acculturation should not be seen as a linear progression, or an "either/or" process; it can lead to novel, more–or–less stable, perhaps mixed affiliations and accommodations. Ethnic and cultural boundaries and the markers which differentiated Poles from Jews (and each from other groups) were shifting, but overall the boundaries remained very strong and the markers were clearly visible to the people of the day.

While language use and change was only one aspect of acculturation, its importance is shown by the intensity and range of the "language debates" which took place. In late nineteenth and early twentieth century Warsaw the Jewish "language question" was a five–dimensional one: Yiddish, Polish, Russian, German, and Hebrew.

Five–sixths of Warsaw's Jews were listed as native speakers of Yiddish in 1897. Yiddish was the first language of Jewish Warsaw in the entire period up to World War I, though patterns of language use were changing. The position of Yiddish was especially anomalous. Despised by many Poles and Jews alike as "jargon" or as "jabbering" (*szwargot*, in Polish), and regarded not as a real language but rather a distorted dialect of German, by the beginning of the twentieth century it was experiencing a literary flowering and gaining considerable strength as a language of cultural and political activity. But it was also facing challenges from advocates of Hebrew as the language of the Jewish future, and from the growing strength in Jewish Warsaw, and elsewhere in Congress Poland, of Polish and Russian.

Polish–speakers were the second largest group among Warsaw's Jews, almost one in seven; Jews made up one–thirteenth of all native speakers of Polish. Warsaw was far and away the largest center for Polish–speaking Jews in the Polish Kingdom, and the data reflect the city's role as a center for Jewish adoption of Polish cultural patterns. By the start of the twentieth century, however, it was becoming clear in Warsaw as elsewhere that use of Polish often had little to do with Jewish ethnic and political allegiances. Younger members of some thoroughly Polonized families had become active by 1905 in expressly Jewish political movements; examples included young Zionist leaders such as Jan Kirszrot and Apolinary Hartglas, and Bund leader Bronisław Grosser (all were born about 1880).[33] To use Polish terms, it was becoming obvious that *polszczyzna* (use of the Polish language) could not be equated with *polskość* (self–identification with "Polishness").[34] In interwar Poland, the use of Polish spread significantly among the Jewish community, in spite of the strength of expressly Jewish political and cultural movements, and harsh anti-Semitism. In 1914, Polish still ranked second to Yiddish as a Jewish native language in Warsaw, and many Jews would have known it as a second or third language, but we cannot say how much ground it may have gained or lost since 1897.[35] The evidence does not clearly differentiate between Jewish adoption of Polish as a native tongue, and use of it as a second or third language, or as a *"Umgangssprache"* (language of daily use), to borrow a term from the Austrian censuses. It is crucial as well not to confuse spoken use of Polish with written command of the language, which was a much slower development.[36]

Only 2.2 percent of Warsaw's Jews claimed Russian as a native tongue, but this was a reflection of the "Litvak invasion," which became a major issue in these decades.[37] While there had been an eastern Jewish presence in Warsaw for some time, from the 1880s on there was a growing influx from the lands of the former Lithuanian Grand Duchy and Russia proper to Congress Poland, where the legal and economic situation for Jews was somewhat better.

There is no way to tell how large this influx actually was; estimates have ranged as high as three hundred thousand for the whole Kingdom around the turn of the century, which is too high. The Russian–speaking Jews were presumably part of this group, but many Litvaks, perhaps most, were Yiddish–speakers. Also, "Litvak" was a loose popular notion, not a clearly defined category; it commonly appeared as a derisive term that Polish Jews used for Jews from the lands of the former Lithuanian Grand Duchy and Russia. Author and journalist Samuel Hirszhorn noted in 1906 that, "a true Warsaw chauvinist calls all Jews who do not live in Warsaw Litvaks, not excluding the inhabitants of the suburb of Praga."[38] Bernard Singer recalled that his mother's very pious Polish Jewish relatives saw his father, from Lublin in southeastern Poland, as a "Litvak with a concealed cross on his forehead."[39]

The Litvaks differed from the Polish Jews in many respects: their dialect of Yiddish was different; they were more likely to know Russian than Polish; and religious individuals were less likely to be Hasidic. They remained to some extent a distinct group in Jewish Warsaw. They were not a unified or completely isolated group, however; they were as diverse as the Polish Jews, with both religious and unreligious and political and unpolitical elements, using chiefly Russian and Yiddish but sometimes learning Polish. They faced a certain amount of antipathy from local Jews, due to cultural differences and economic and professional competition. They provided a focus for the anti-Jewish views of extreme Polish nationalists, who saw them not only as bearers of Russian culture and of Jewish political movements, but also as unwelcome immigrants bolstering Jewish numbers in the city and Kingdom. These eastern Jews played major roles in the rise of Jewish political movements in Warsaw, both of socialist and nationalist orientations, and in the rise of the Yiddish press after 1905. They were important as well in the increasing use of Russian and the influence of Russian culture in Jewish Warsaw, a trend which can be traced back to the 1870s–80s. Evidence of the growing influence of the Russian language includes private Jewish secondary schools with Russian as their primary language.[40] It is clear that a higher share of Warsaw's Jews were Russian-speakers in 1914 than in 1897, but the extent to which this was due to inmigrants, as opposed to local Jews learning Russian instead of (or along with) Polish, is unclear.

A very small share—0.4 percent, less than a thousand Jews—claimed German as a native tongue. A noteworthy migration of German Jews to Warsaw dated back to the days of Prussian rule. German survived as an important language among the city's Jewish educated and upper classes until Polonization gained impetus in the 1850s–60s; it was in the late 1850s, for example, that leaders of the "German synagogue" on Daniłowiczowska Street decided that Polish should be used in sermons. *Izraelita* claimed in 1882 that Polish had largely replaced German in the formerly German-speaking Jewish families.[41] In the same period the German Christian community in Warsaw began to be absorbed by the Polish Catholic majority.

German was also important in the cultural history of the Jewish community in Warsaw because the Haskalah (Jewish enlightment), in the late eighteenth and early nineteenth centuries, came to central Poland from Germany and Austria. German had considerable prestige as the "language of culture" for large parts of the Jewish community well into the nineteenth century.[42]

A final group which appears in the 1897 language data consists of Yiddish-speaking Christians, who were presumably all converts. Few Jews converted to Christianity in nineteenth century Warsaw. Conversion was commonly done for pragmatic reasons, to advance one's own career or to open up opportunities for one's children. It could also be a result of intense identification by some families with Polish culture and ethnic identity; of course, pragmatism and *polskość* could both be involved in particular cases. The 1897 census found 212

Catholics and 59 Protestants and Orthodox who were native speakers of Yiddish; this was not a complete count of converts, because some were native speakers of German, Polish, or Russian.[43] Among Warsaw's better known converts were entrepreneur Jan Bloch; the wealthy and thoroughly Polonized Kronenberg family, including Leopold Kronenberg, a great rival of Bloch's; Aleksander Kraushar, a participant in the 1863 Polish uprising and an historian; and publisher Salomon (Franciszek Salezy) Lewental, who converted after purchasing one of Warsaw's most popular Polish newspapers, *Kurjer Warszawski* [Warsaw Courier], reportedly so as not to hurt the paper among its Christian readership. Lewental had been active in local Jewish affairs until his conversion; Bloch kept an active interest in Jewish issues his whole life.[44]

Hebrew, as well as German, was promoted by the Haskalah. Hebrew was the traditional language of faith and learning, and now was promoted by the Zionist movement as the language of the Jewish future. It was no one's mother tongue, though in nineteenth century Eastern Europe and Russia it gained as a language of secular as well as religious debate and literature. But it faced severe challenges as the language of Jewish intellectual life from Yiddish and the regional vernaculars. Both the rise, and the weakness, of Hebrew outside of religious life were demonstrated in Warsaw by the Hebrew periodical press, which, despite greater freedom after 1905, could not compete with Yiddish titles. Knowledge of Hebrew was much more common among men than women, who rarely got religious educations.[45]

The 1897 native language data are very useful, but there are many things they do not and cannot tell us, and care must be used in interpreting them. They say nothing about second language (or third), or language of daily use, a serious drawback in a community as multilingual as Warsaw. The 1897 data represent a still life or snapshot made in the middle of a period of intensive change, and remain unique; the next census touching on languages in Warsaw was not taken until 1931.

It is very difficult to gauge how much we are seeing language shift—more Jews with Polish or Russian as a preferred tongue—and how much the spread of multilingualism. Polish and Russian were becoming more common in Jewish Warsaw, but their respective shares by 1914 are unknown. Yiddish was expanding its range of use, but it may also have been losing recruits as a result of Jewish acculturation to the surrounding Polish and Russian worlds. Hebrew remained the chief Jewish religious language, but despite its progress as a language of literary and intellectual usage, it could not compete successfully with its rivals in the secular sphere. German, long the "language of culture" among significant parts of the Polish Jewish community, was gradually declining.

Some of the fluidity of the Jewish language situation in turn of the century Warsaw is clear from the memoirs of Bernard Singer. He recalls the speech of sabbath strollers from the Jewish community as they walked into the city center.

On Muranowska, Miła, Nalewki the couples spoke exclusively in Yiddish. On Bielańska these same strollers mixed Polish with Yiddish, and in the Saxon Gardens and on Marszałkowska they spoke exclusively Polish. Towards evening they returned to their quarter. And again on Bielańska Polish was mixed with Yiddish, and on Nalewki Yiddish ruled.

But he also notes that, by the eve of World War I, these strollers were "loudly discussing everything, in Polish, Yiddish, Russian."[46]

The different categories that emerge from the 1897 native language data can be seen as representative to some degree of important trends within Warsaw's Jewish community. Many people were actively exploring new options, including patterns of language use, and adopting Polish, Russian, or German cultural patterns to greater or lesser degrees, while still remaining Jewish; small numbers went further, and left Judaism behind by conversion. But using the data on languages to represent larger cultural patterns must not be pushed too far. Language use and change for many people was only a practical matter, one divorced from ethno–political, nationalist, or religious concerns, and Warsaw's Jewish community was highly multilingual. Language use was only one aspect of acculturation. It was a very important factor, but cannot be used to represent directly other developments such as assimilation to Polish identity, the rise of expressly Jewish political movements, the secularization of parts of Jewish life and the Jewish community, or changes in the lives of the majority of the Jewish community that nonetheless remained traditionally religious.[47]

While the Catholic and Jewish shares of the city population changed little in the last decades of Russian rule, over the entire partitions era the growth of the Jewish community was remarkable. Further, it became increasingly diverse, thanks to changing patterns of in–migration and processes of acculturation and assimilation. The size of and changes in the Jewish community became a particularly important issue when open and organized political life revived in Warsaw in 1905–14. Polish leaders had long felt deeply threatened by Russian rule and Russification; and now ever more detailed and consistent official statistics were making it clear that Poles had only a small majority in their own historic capital. Polish scholars, publicists, and political leaders discussed the evident rapid growth of the Jewish population of Congress Poland and of Warsaw in particular; some saw a deliberate Russian policy of using the region as a "dumping ground" for Jews pushed out of other parts of the Empire, for example during the expulsion of the Jews from Moscow in 1891.[48] References to an "invasion," to fears of the "Judaization" of Warsaw and of Congress Poland, became commonplace; and so, too, even as Jewish use of Polish and Russian and other aspects of acculturation became increasingly widespread, did statements from Poles and Jews alike that mass assimilation could not or should not take place.

There are a great many published examples of Polish fears about the "Jewish danger." But in 1911 an anonymous editorial writer in the moderate and cautious Polish daily *Kurjer Warszawski*, responding to an article by Zionist leader Isaac Grünbaum in *Der Fraynd* [The Friend] about growing anti–Semitism, summarized these fears well. The writer showed the connections between Jewish numbers, in–migration, and Polish perceptions of a new, hostile Jewish community. He referred to,

"the new type of Jewry," which appeared during the revolutionary years. . . . This type is the Jewish multitudes pouring into the Kingdom from Russia every day, which already are dangerous for Polish society because of their numbers. But not only because of their numbers. Because of all their character, all their separatism, all their provocative arrogance, they are a corrosive acid in the festering wounds of our relationship. In the revolutionary years, the opposition of the Jews to the interests of the Polish nation began, and today this process continues to develop further, constantly and consistently, albeit in less flagrant forms. We feel inundated not only by a foreign, but simply by a hostile wave—and this is that "new type of Jewry," which has had to evoke an anti–Semitic reaction. We are not fighting the Jews, but Jewish enemies of our nation.[49]

Considering the strident anti–Semitism which *Kurjer Warszawski* and other Polish serials sometimes took up in the last years before the war (as we will see in Chapter 6) the last sentence was, at least, disingenuous.

The next chapter discusses the face of the city, including other aspects of the ethnic factor in Warsaw's society, by examining the dissimilar distributions of the Poles and Jews about the different parts of the city.

Chapter 3

The Faces of the City

On a spring evening in 1876, Fritz Wernick, a German travel writer, arrived in Warsaw. His first impressions included:

> the gloomy light of a few gas lamps stood out in wide, deep and grimy pools; only rarely did a more imposing building interrupt the long ranks of poor, one-story homes standing on both sides of the extremely wide streets. . . . Warsaw still does not feel any lack of room, it does not have to restrict itself and to grow upwards with the help of multi-story, barracks-like tenements.[1]

Wernick admired Warsaw's greenery and spaciousness, and noted how quiet the streets were. He found little of architectural or historic interest, however, pointing out that the oldest surviving sections of the city dated chiefly from the late sixteenth and seventeenth centuries.

About 1910, the young Isaac Bashevis Singer came with his family from a small town to live in Warsaw.

> A broad river with the sky in it stretched beneath us. Ships floated by. Over the bridge, which had intricate ironwork columns, trolleys and omnibuses raced. We came upon tall buildings, crooked roofs, ironwork balconies. It looked as if there was always a fire raging in Warsaw, because people were always running and shouting. It seemed like an endless holiday. I saw a tremendous pillar, and on it a figure with a sword in his hand. This was the monument of King Zygmunt. Beneath him, four stone maidens drank from large beakers. . . . After passing the better neighborhoods, we arrived at Krochmalna Street. Stopping before one of the houses, the [droshky] driver said, "This is it."[2]

The contrasting impressions of two new arrivals, a middle-aged German journalist and a young Jewish boy, bring out two basic facts. First, Warsaw was the scene of sharp contrasts and presented many different faces to the world. Second, in these decades, the city changed radically; as the population more than doubled, new areas were built up, stone and brick replaced wooden structures, and much larger tenements appeared. Later writers also found a noisier, more crowded city.

Warsaw's neighborhoods varied greatly in their ethnic and socioeconomic characters and experienced substantial change in the period under discussion. This chapter presents a portrait of Warsaw by drawing on travel literature, memoirs, and other writings. It expands on the picture of the population already presented, by tracing the distribution of the major religious groups throughout the city, including the issue of residential segregation.

It is impossible to obtain completely comparable territorial subunits for the city which cover the entire period. Boundaries of precincts changed, and sizable suburban areas were annexed. However, by combining individual precincts into larger units, we can indicate the general course of changes and population growth. Table 3-1 presents data on the growth of the city's precincts and on the distribution of Catholics and Jews, in 1882, 1897, and 1910, a period in which the city's population doubled and the city's area increased by one-fifth. In the table and in this chapter the city is divided, for convenience, into five large sections: the central, southern, southwestern, and northwestern areas on the west bank of the Vistula, and Praga, across the river.

Central Warsaw

The central precincts (I/XI and II/III in 1882, I and II in 1897, and I, II, and XII in 1910) grew by only 50.6 percent in 1882-1910, less than any other section. The north-central area included the oldest parts of Warsaw, the Old City and its northern extension, the New City. The Market Square of the Old City had been the heart of Warsaw all the way through the eighteenth century. In the nineteenth, the area largely degenerated into slums. Government offices, fine residences, and the city's finest shops moved southwards, to the sections around Senatorska Street, the Saxon Gardens, Krakowskie Przedmieście, Nowy Świat, and Marszałkowska Street, and the Old and New Cities were increasingly inhabited by the poor. Wernick was unimpressed by the narrow streets, crowding, poverty, and isolation of this oldest part of the city, describing it as "old and gloomy."[3] A generation later, a Polish source described it as, "a network of winding and dirty streets, with buildings of several stories, which were once the adobe of the wealthy citizenry, today populated chiefly by the Jewish population, as well as artisans, workers and peddlers."[4]

After the turn of the century, regeneration of this section began. It lay near the center of the city, and had many of its oldest churches and historic sites, such as the Royal Palace, now used by the Russian governor-general, and the Cathedral of St. John, one of the largest and most popular churches in Warsaw. Preservationists began to take an interest in its old buildings and crooked streets. An important step in the preservation and restoration of the area was taken on the eve of World War I, when the active market was removed from the Old City's Market Square.

Restoration was a slow process, and much of the Old and New Cities remained slums. The recollections of poet Antoni Słonimski concerning the interwar period also apply to the years before World War I.

The Old City was already, in the period between the wars, restored and covered by painting filled with gilt; but it should not be forgotten that these richly decorated facades on small tenements covered interiors full of dirt and foul air, where in a two room bug-infested apartment, without a bath and often without running water, more than a dozen people made their home.[5]

Below the Old City lay the northern part of the central city. Krakowskie Przedmieście, which ran south from the area of the Old City, marked the beginning of "Warsaw's busiest and most important artery. . . . Here scholarly life, public institutions, churches, and aristocratic residences are chiefly concentrated."[6] The area included both major institutional buildings and housing for the city's wealthy. Wernick commented, "What Corso is for Rome, Ringstrasse for Vienna, Jungfernistieg for Hamburg, Alee unter den Linden for Berlin, so is Krakowskie Przedmieście for Warsaw."[7]

A little to the west lay the Saxon Gardens, the favorite park of the city center, "one of Warsaw's most pleasant ornaments, a true oasis of fresh air and greenery among the foul air and dust of the neighboring streets."[8] Not all the residents could enjoy it, however. The poor, and Jews in traditional garb, were kept out by guards. The Gardens were ringed by squares and open spaces. Iron Gate Square had one of the city's largest markets; on Saxon Place, just to the east of the Gardens, a Byzantine-style Russian Orthodox cathedral was built. Many local people saw it as an offensive symbol of foreign rule and, moreover, as discordant with local architecture.

While the composition of the central precincts remained largely Catholic, the Jewish share increased from 21.1 percent in 1882 to 28.7 percent in 1910. The Jewish population was especially heavy to the north, in the area of the Old and New Cities. The section centered on Krakowskie Przedmieście had one of the highest Catholic percentages in the city.

Southern Warsaw

The population of the southern precincts (IX and X in 1882 and 1897, and IX, X, and XIII in 1910) grew by 69.7 percent in this period. The western part of precinct X included a major part of the central city, in particular the quadrant bounded on the west by Marszałkowska Street, on the south by Jerozolimskie Avenue, on the east by Krakowskie Przedmieście and Nowy Świat, and on the north by the Saxon Gardens; an area in which "the most beautiful section of Warsaw is to be found."[9]

Nowy Świat continued Krakowskie Przedmieście southwards:

Krakowskie Przedmieście, then Nowy Świat, down to Ujazdowskie Avenue—this is the elegant world, the world of wealthy people. There are the palaces of the mighty and the homes of the rich, the seats of learning and art, monuments of love and praise, the temples of the refined world, such as the Church of the Visitation, or the Church of the Holy Cross with the inscription "Sursum corda!" which is constantly filled with people.[10]

(The Church of the Holy Cross was also the site of the panic and disaster which set off the 1881 pogrom.)

This route continued past the Square of the Three Crosses down Ujazdowskie Avenue, "decorated with beautiful homes and splendid villas, the favorite place of Warsaw's residents for walking."[11] Several of the city's loveliest parks, Łazienki, Ujazdowski, and the Botanical Gardens, lay along it; by the early years of the twentieth century these parks had surpassed the Saxon Gardens in popularity among the city's upper classes. Polish novelist Stefan Żeromski wrote in the late 1880s: "After dinner, like a respectable citizen of Warsaw, I walked in the Avenue. A multitude of carriages and coaches, a procession of ladies in their finest, laughter, gaiety, and happiness."[12]

Ujazdowskie and its neighboring streets were developed mostly in the late nineteenth and early twentieth centuries.

The district around the Avenue is completely new; the streets which intersect Marszałkowska, such as Nowogrodzka, Żórawia, Wspólna, Hoża, Sadowa, Wilcza, Piękna, and Koszykowa, are the favorite abode of Warsaw's official world, whose offices are distributed chiefly among old districts, but that lives here most willingly.[13]

Eastwards of Krakowskie Przedmieście, Nowy Świat, and Ujazdowskie Avenue (beyond the parks) lay Powiśle, one of the city's most decayed and impoverished districts. This was still an important industrial area; many local people worked in its metalworking plants, in the gas works, or on the river.

In his novel *The Doll (Lalka)*, published in the 1880s, Bolesław Prus described a walk through this quarter by the novel's hero, Wokulski.

> He stopped half-way along the road and looked at the district between Nowy Zjazd and Tamka Street, stretching out at his feet. . . . And he thought bitterly that this area of riverside earth, strewn with the refuse of the whole city, had given birth to nothing but two–storey houses colored chocolate and bright yellow, dark green and orange. To nothing but black and white fences surrounding empty spaces, in which a several–storey apartment house rose here and there like a pine tree spared in a forest laid waste by the axe and uneasy at its own solitude.
>
> "Nothing, nothing . . . ," he repeated, wandering through the alleys with their shacks sunk below street level, roofs overgrown with moss, buildings and shutters and doors nailed shut, with tumbledown walls, windows patched with paper or stuffed with rags. He walked along looking through dirty window–panes into dwellings, and absorbed the sight of cupboards without doors, chairs with only three legs, sofas with torn seats, clocks with one hand and cracked faces. He walked along and smiled to himself to see laborers interminably waiting for work, craftsmen employed only at mending old clothes, women whose entire property was a basket of stale cakes—and to see ragged men, starving children, and unusually dirty women.[14]

After the turn of the century, publicist Adolf Suligowski wrote that Powiśle and the main part of the city were "two separate worlds . . . strange and unknown to each other," and that in Powiśle "everything is different, meaner, poorer, and worse."[15]

The whole southern quarter—both the wealthy uplands and the impoverished river valley—had the highest Catholic and lowest Jewish pecentages in the city. However, the Jewish share increased in 1882–1910 from 9.5 percent to 17.3 percent.

Southwestern Warsaw

The population of the city's southwestern quarter (precincts VII and VIII in 1882, and VI, VII, VIII, and XI thenceforth) grew the fastest of any of the west bank areas: 124.2 percent in 1882–1910. A major factor was the substantial extension of the city's boundaries to the south and southwest, especially into the industrial Wola section of the commune of Czyste. Also, precinct VII was extended northwards, into the heavily populated area between Grzybowska and Leszno Streets. The area south of Jerozolimskie Avenue and west of Marszałkowska Street was developed in this period. Ludwik Krzywicki recalled that when he came to Warsaw as a student in 1878, a number of streets "existed only in the part from Marszałkowska [eastwards] to Ujazdowski Avenue.. On the other side, towards [the suburb of] Ochota, stretched gardens and orchards, and in them little wooden houses."[16]

The quarter included the city's most important industrial section. It was roughly bounded on the south by Jerozolimskie Avenue, on the east by Żelazna Street; it reached well into the suburbs, particularly Wola, on the west, and also into the city's northwest section. The Warsaw–Vienna railway station, built in the 1840s at the intersection of Jerozolimskie and Marszałkowska, was a major spur to the development of the southwestern precincts. The railway line to the west ran parallel to Jerozolimskie, which became the city's main east–west artery. Marszałkowska Street, meanwhile, by the early twentieth century had become the city's most important commercial thoroughfare.[17]

The Catholic population of this quarter rose from 56.7 percent to 62.2 percent in 1882–1910. This resulted partly from the annexation of largely Polish suburban areas. Also, most of the people moving into the rapidly developing area below Jerozolimskie were Poles. In both 1897 and 1910, precinct XI, to the south of Jerozolimskie and largely to the west of Marszałkowska, had among the city's highest Catholic and lowest Jewish percentages. The sizable Jewish concentration in the southwestern quarter was above Jerozolimskie and in towards the center of the city, in precincts VII and VIII (1897 and 1910 boundaries). Krochmalna Street, which lay just north of Grzybowska, was where Isaac Bashevis Singer's family made their home. The section centered on Grzybów Place became one of Warsaw's most important Jewish districts. Singer recalled his family's apartment building:

> No. 12 [Krochmalna Street] was like a city. The dark entrance always smelled of freshly baked bread, rolls and bagels, caraway seed and smoke. Koppel the baker's yeasty breads were always outside, rising on boards. In No. 12 there were two Hasidic study houses, the Radzymin and the Minsk, as well as a synagogue for those who opposed Ha-

sidism. There was also a stall where cows were kept chained to the wall year round. In some cellars, fruit had been stored by dealers from Mirowski Place; in others, eggs were preserved in lime. Wagons arrived there from the provinces. No. 12 swarmed with Torah, prayer, commerce, and toil.[18]

Northwestern Warsaw

The population of the city's northwest side increased by 105.3 percent in 1882–1910. The greater part of this growth was in the west, in the area covered by precinct V/VI in 1882 and by III and V in 1897–1910. North of these precincts stood the Russian Citadel, and to the west were the city's largest cemeteries.

The northwest quarter had the largest Jewish concentration in Warsaw, and this in all Europe. It formed the heart of what Bernard Singer called "the unknown Warsaw."

> The Jewish quarter in Warsaw occupied one-fifth of the city[h]. It had 250,000 people, and thus one-third of the population. There were no drawbridges or guards on its borders; the ghetto had been abolished long before, but nevertheless there still existed an invisible wall which separated the quarter from the rest of the city. Many Polish children spoke about it with fear, and their elders often treated it with contempt.[19]

The development of this area as the main Jewish section began in the early nineteenth century, when most of the city's centrally located and desirable streets were "exempted" from Jewish residence. By the 1860s, when these restrictions were abolished, the northwest side had become the main site for Jewish residence.

While much of this quarter was a region of abject poverty, densely populated by petty traders, artisans, and the unemployed, it was also the home for much of the city's Jewish upper and middle classes, and a major commercial and industrial area. Of Nalewki Street, the main north–south street of the ghetto, Isaac Bashevis Singer wrote:

> The Nalevki [sic] was lined with 4- and 5-story buildings with wide entrances, plastered with signs in Russian, Polish, and Yiddish. A world of trade: shirts and canes, cotton and buttons, umbrellas and silk, chocolate and plush, hats and threads, jewelry and prayer shawls. Wooden platforms were piled high with wares. Draymen unloaded crates and yellowed out in hoarse voices. Crowds went in and out of buildings. At the entrance to a store a revolving door spun

around, swallowing up and disgorging people as though they were caught in some sort of mad dance.[20]

"The secrets of Nalewki" (*tajemnice Nalewek*) became a popular theme for Polish fiction.[21] The notion of the Jewish quarter as dark, mysterious, and threatening, but also vibrant and exciting, occurs often in contemporary comments.

The diversity of the northwest side is clearly described by Bernard Singer.

> The beginning of Miła Street had a reputation for wealth. In the front rooms lived the owners of shops on Nalewki. Its extension, called Nowomiła, , was an area of poverty. Artisans, tradesmen, vendors, persons of undetermined and extremely suspicious occupations, the unemployed, filled this street.
>
> Gęsia at Nalewki was a shopping street; farther beyond Dzika up to Okopowa the poor found shelter. The only works of art there were the monuments done for the Jewish cemetery, free entertainment—funerals.
>
> In the houses with low numbers on Dzielna and Pawlia lived more or less respectable merchants, but farther beyond "Pawiak" the streets did not differ in the least from Nowomiła.[22]

Precinct IV was overwhelmingly Jewish: 87.5 percent in 1882, 92.6 percent in 1910. In the rest of the northwest side, the Jewish percentages rose from 44.4 percent to 66.5 percent while the Catholic dropped from 48.8 percent to 30.7 percent.

Praga

Praga grew the fastest of any of the major parts of the city. This section included precinct XII in 1882 and 1897, and XIV and XV in 1910; its population rose 376.3 percent in this period. Much of this increase resulted from the 1889 annexation of large suburban areas (Nowa Praga, Kamionek, and Szmulowizna), which doubled Praga's area, but even in 1897–1910, when no major new annexations took place, Praga's population still grew more than did that of the west bank.

Up until the second half of the nineteenth century, Praga was little more than an overgrown country town, noted as a center for trade in agricultural products and livestock. Wernick wrote of Praga that it was, "A small hamlet, hidden among greenery, made up of wooden cottages, scattered widely across the plain. . . Life there differs significantly from the life which takes place on the streets of Warsaw."[23] It resembled more a sleepy Polish provincial town than a section of the greatest of Polish cities.

Major factors in Praga's development were railroad construction and the building of Warsaw's first permanent bridges over the Vistula in the 1860s-70s. Praga soon had three major railroad stations—for the St. Petersburg, Terespol (in the Ukraine), and Vistula lines—and became the focal point for communications between Warsaw's factories and the huge market which the Empire represented for them. Praga also became an important industrial district in its own right. But it remained a backward area in such sectors as housing, streets, and all possible public works.

Two large churches came to dominate Praga's skyline. One was the new Russian Orthodox cathedral, which Wernick saw as a symbol of Russian dominance, a "standard of Orthodoxy;" the other was the Catholic church of St. Florian, which, in the view of a Polish author, dominated all Praga "by the height of its two Gothic towers."[24] Alexander Park became very popular, with theatrical and other amusements. It became the site, around the turn of the century, for officially sanctioned, mass outings which were aimed at providing the population with an alternative form of entertainment to heavy consumption of alcohol.[25] Saska Kępa, south of Praga, was a suburban village which also became a popular holiday spot in the late nineteenth century.[26]

Praga's Jewish and Catholic percentages were roughly equal in 1882: 44.9 percent and 48 percent, respectively. By 1897, however, the number of Catholics had grown four-fold while that of Jews had only doubled, showing that the 1889 annexation had brought in largely Catholic areas. In 1910, Praga was 60.8 percent Catholic and 28.9 percent Jewish.

The Suburbs

Warsaw's suburbs experienced considerable growth. Industrialization was a primary factor in this, as new plants were established there or existing ones moved from other areas, such as Powiśle. The conditions of life in the suburbs were more primitive than in the city proper. At the time of the "great incorporation" of the suburbs in 1916, when the city's territory tripled, one writer noted that the suburbs were "neglected in every respect; largely deprived of sewers, pavement, and suitable lighting, they are in deplorable sanitary condition."[27] The circumstances of some suburban areas more resembled life in villages than in the outskirts of a great city.

Travel writers and journalists rarely visited the industrial suburbs. Indeed, police and writers agreed in seeing these areas as refuges for criminals, as fearful lawless sections which the wise avoided. To the west of the city lay "Bloody Wola . . . known until now only for its cutthroats, audacious murders, bold robberies, and daily crimes;"[28] and also Czarny Dwór (the name means, ominously, the Black Manor), which one writer called, "the most dangerous suburb of our city. . . . As an abode of the meanest prostitution, it is a sink of vice and crime."[29]

Wola was also the site of the chief attempt to provide better housing for the poor. Around the turn of the century Jewish businessman and philanthropist Hipolit Wawelberg built new tenements with several hundred small apartments at reduced rents. The "Wawelberg homes," on Górczewska Street, were meant to help ease ethnic tensions as well as to provide inexpensive, clean housing; one of Wawelberg's hopeful beliefs was that if poor Poles and Jews could live together, bigotry among them would disappear.[30]

The suburbs were more Catholic and less Jewish in composition than was the city proper. The 1897 census noted that of 59,503 persons in selected parts of the inner suburbs, 65.3 percent were Catholics, 16 percent Orthodox, 14.5 percent Jews, and 3.8 percent Protestants. As concerns native language, 66 percent were native speakers of Polish, 14.3 percent Yiddish, and 12.8 percent Russian.[31] (The high Russian and Orthodox shares resulted from the fact that almost one-sixth of the sample consisted of military personnel.) Table 3-2 shows the respective sizes of the Catholic and Jewish communities in 1893 and 1909 in the four suburban communes most affected by urbanization: Czyste, Młociny, and Mokotów west of the Vistula, and Bródno outside Praga.

Segregation

On the Vistula's west bank the Jewish population was heaviest to the north, and the Catholics dominated in the southern and central parts of the city as well as in the suburbs. A significant question is the extent to which the Jewish and Catholic populations lived separately, and the degree to which the Jewish minority was concentrated in certain parts of the city. It is clear that there was a main Jewish area, north and west of the central city, but, as a contemporary writer noted, "The Jews are scattered around all of Warsaw, living both in the most magnificent homes of Ujazdowskie Avenue and in the desperately poor corners of Powiśle or the alleys around Okopy."[32]

Precinct maps show the expansion of the Jewish population. In 1882, the Jews were a majority only in precinct IV, and made up

The Faces of the City   49

at least 40 percent only in the neighboring precinct, V/VI, and in Praga. The northwest side had 45 percent of the Jewish total. In 1910, they were a majority in all three northwestern precincts (III, IV, V), and made up a plurality in one southwestern precinct (VIII). The northwest side had 49 percent of the Jewish total. The only precincts which were less than one-fifth Jewish lay along the river or below Jerozolimskie Avenue (I, IX, X, XI). After legal restrictions on Jewish residence and property ownership were lifted in the 1860s, many Jews began to buy property and build homes outside the old ghetto.[33] The expansion of the Jewish neighborhoods was so marked that writers have described it in terms appropriate to a military campaign. Ludwik Krzywicki recalled the changes he had seen after his arrival in Warsaw in the 1870s.

> Movement out beyond a straight line shielded by a row of tenements, in the direction of the Citadel and Marymont . . . was impossible. Thus the people of the Old Testament [the Jews], who had settled on Nalewki, Gęsia, Franciszkańska, and Świętojerska . . . from necessity had to press towards the south. . . . They occupied Pawia Street, from there pushed through Karmelicka, occupying the neighboring parts of Nowolipia and Nowolipki, did not become very acclimated on Leszno, through Żabia reached to Grzybów . . . and moved to Twarda Street, occupying Grzybowska, Pańska, and Śliska. On the other side, the native [Polish] population slowly withdrew from these districts. The wealthier population lived between Jerozolimskie Avenue and Mokotów, bringing to life that whole section of the city which lies today between Marszałkowska and Ochota. The poorer people settled outside the city limits towards Wola, Czyste, Ochota, and Wierzbno.[34]

The heart of Jewish Warsaw remained the northwest side. It became more and more densely populated, absorbing most of the rapidly growing Jewish population. As Krzywicki and other writers noted, and as the statistical data indicate, the area covered by Jewish Warsaw expanded somewhat in this period. Also, many Jews lived in largely Polish neighborhoods, and Poles in Jewish sections. Each group nonetheless retained its own large and distinctive areas—particularly the Jewish northwest side and the Catholic south, center, and suburbs. Residence remained a sphere of life which supported and encouraged ethnic separation, in spite of the elimination of legal restrictions on Jewish residence in the 1860s.[35]

The next factor to be considered is employment. As was the

case with residence, this was an area in which Polish-Jewish separation was the norm. Moreover, Polish nationalists saw the Jewish concentration in certain fields, especially commerce, and apparent advances in industry and in some professions as a threat, creating dangerous possibilities of "foreign" domination of the economy, and of prevention of economic "nationalization" (*unarodowienie*) and Polish advance.

Chapter 4

Patterns of Employment

Polish Catholics in central Poland had traditionally made up the upper and lower reaches of society, the gentry, the nobility, and the peasantry. Jews were concentrated in commerce at all levels, in certain crafts and industries, and in such areas as innkeeping, banking, and carting. In Warsaw, where Jewish settlement had long been restricted, Poles had made up an important part of the bourgeoisie and artisanry as well as the resident nobility and the serving and laboring classes. The city's relatively small German community in the eighteenth and nineteenth centuries played a major role in commerce and industry. Russians began to come to Warsaw in substantial numbers only in the late nineteenth century, chiefly because of official or military service.

This chapter analyzes the employment data from the 1882 and 1897 censuses. Following a discussion of the general pictures presented by these sources, we will study in greater depth the government service and professional employment categories—areas in which most members of the intelligentsia sought to make their careers. Because the next census took place only in 1921, this discussion does not attempt to cover the post-1897 period in any depth.

Warsaw was a major industrial city, but it was neither a factory town, like Łódź, nor a leader in technological innovation or the manufacturing of new products, like Riga, in the Empire's Baltic provinces. Warsaw had a very broad range of economic activities, from manufacturing, to trade, to transport, to creative activities and crime, and on to practically any other means that city people could use to earn a living.

Manufacturing was a very important sector. The number of factory workers rose from 14,000 in 1879 to 80,000 in 1914. The value of factory production increased from 27,000,000 to 193,000,000 rubles. The most important areas were metalworking, chemicals, textiles, comestibles, and clothing. By 1913, the metalworking factories of Warsaw, led by three giant firms—Rudzki, Borman and Szwede, and Lilpop, Rau, and Loewenstein—employed 31,000 people and produced goods with a value of 58,000,000 rubles.[1] These large firms made iron and steel products for the Russian market, especially rails, bridge materials, railroad wagons, industrial and farm machinery, and goods for the Russian military. Many smaller plants concentrated on supplying local needs, including machinery for the larger firms.

Small scale craft industry remained a major employment sector. In 1866, according to official statistics, 11,000 artisans produced 6,000,000 rubles worth of goods; in 1894 there were 62,000 artisans producing 57,000,000 rubles worth.[2]

In the next two decades the number of artisans certainly increased, thanks in part to the heavy Jewish influx to the city; craft industry was an area in which the Polish Jews were heavily concentrated (the data after the mid-1890s are not comparable with the earlier figures, due to changes in official statistics). Warsaw's artisans worked in a great range of circumstances, from cramped apartments to sizable workshops, but most were quite poor. They produced an enormous variety of goods, although such areas as clothing, comestibles, and construction were among the most important.

Warsaw's west side, beyond the Warsaw–Vienna railway station, became its most important industrial district. The western suburbs, especially Wola, also became the site of many factories, as the older industrial districts, particularly Powiśle, declined. The Jewish northwest side was important for both craft and factory industry.

Commerce also assumed many forms in Warsaw. In the retail trades, the fancier shops, whether owned by Jews, Poles, Germans, or Russians, were near the city center, often along Nowy Świat or Marszałkowska Street. The city swarmed with peddlers and hawkers; huge open-air markets and "commercial halls" were distributed about the city, for example in the Market Square of the Old City, in Iron Gate Square, or Mirowski Place;[3] and there were tiny shops of all kinds. Such shops proliferated on the northwest side. Bernard Singer recalled: "Nalewki [Street] sold lace, haberdasher's goods, and hosiery. Gęsia traded in products from Moscow and Łódź. Franciszkańska had hides from Radom. Grzybów [Place] traded in iron."[4] A Polish observer stated,

> The huge wholesale goods shops in the extensive courtyards of Nalewki are very interesting. From the deep basements all the way to the stifling rooms on the fourth floors, all dwellings are filled with materials for trade. Here is the heart of trade of Warsaw and of the Congress Kingdom.[5]

Other employment sectors provided work for the rest of the population. Many recent Polish in-migrants worked as servants (especially young peasant women), or as day laborers. Warsaw's role as a major cultural and administrative center drew many people to work in the professions (education, law, medicine, journalism, etc.) or the government bureaucracy. The official presence, both civil and military, was very strong. A large part of the population lived from "undetermined and extremely suspicious occupations," to quote Bernard Singer; these included Polish day laborers and Jewish *luftmentshn*, as well as professional criminals and a great many prostitutes.

The 1882 Census

The two censuses provide the earliest detailed and comprehensive information on the employment structure of Warsaw's population.[6] However, the two sets of data can be meaningfully compared only on a general level. The two censuses do not use identical employment categories; moreover, it is often difficult to ascertain exactly which jobs and professions a given category included. Further, the 1882 census presents employment data on the resident population broken down by faith, while the 1897 data on the present population are analyzed by native language. The censuses present two discrete portraits, fifteen years apart, of employment in Warsaw.

There is little information on the 1882 census. The 1897 census asked for a person's main "occupation, craft, trade, post, service." The unemployed were to state their last or usual occupation. Members of a family who assisted the head of the family were not listed as actively employed; this particularly affected such groups as artisans, shopkeepers, and street vendors.[7]

There are two primary approaches to distinguishing types of employment:

> the *occupation* of each individual (the actual type of work performed—farmer, bricklayer, lathe operator, or typist), or the *industry* where the person is employed (agriculture, construction, machine shop, or banking institution).[8]

The two censuses generally tried to follow the latter principle, but did not do so consistently. For example, they normally listed administrative personnel in private enterprises as a particular group, separate from the institutions or industries in which they worked.

The 1882 census presents its data on faith and employment in 38 major employment categories, further divided into 199. There are five religious groups listed: Roman Catholics, Jews, Orthodox, Protestants (apparently Lutheran, Reformed, and Anglicans), and Others.[9] The data are presented in Table 4–1, rearranged into ten employment

categories, and three religious groups—Roman Catholics, Jews, and Others—along with the percentages within each religious group. In order of size, the employment categories are:
1. Industry: factory and craft industry of many sorts, mining, and construction. Owners of private business are apparently counted along with workers, but administrative personnel are not.[10]
2. Trade: trade in many sorts of goods, banking, letting of rooms, street peddling, insurance, restaurants, brokerage, and hotels. Owners of businesses, again, seem to be included with workers, but most administrative personnel are not.
3. Servants.
4. Government service and the professions: government service at all ranks, including the police; legal practice, and persons employed by religious bodies and in the areas of health, education, the arts, literature, and the press; and private officials. This sizable last group evidently consists of administrative personnel in private enterprises and institutions, and perhaps also high-ranking servants, such as private secretaries and stewards.
5. Unskilled laborers: *wyrobnicy bez specjalnego zajęcia* (workers without special occupations) in Polish, *chernorabochie* (black laborers) in Russian, probably also including many unemployed and occasionally employed persons. Many of these laborers actually worked in industry, construction, trade, or transport, but on an irregular or day-to-day basis.
6. Property owners and capitalists: persons living on the income from property or capital.
7. Transport and communications: those in the postal, telegraph, and telephone systems, and in railroads, carting, water transport, and messengers. Owners of private firms appear to be included, but not most administrative staff.
8. Pensioners: persons receiving pensions for governmental or military service.
9. Agriculture: with gardening, forestry, and fishing as well.
10. Others and unknown: including persons living on charity, prostitutes, beggars, young people studying away from their families, persons of undetermined occupations, and those under detention.

The separate military category in Table 4–1 includes residents only, not the larger garrison.

Table 4–2 presents the percentual breakdown by religious group of each employment category. The actively employed and their dependents appear together.

Catholics were widely dispersed through the employment structure. Their largest single category was industry, which supported 36.5 percent of Warsaw's Catholics; servants and their dependents made up another 18.2 percent. Groups in which Catholics were over 75 percent consisted of agriculture, service, and pensioners. The only categories in which they were substantially underrepresented relative to their share of the total population (58.3 percent) were trade (17.3 percent Catholic) and the military (26.3 percent).

Major branches of industry in which Catholics made up at least two-thirds of the employed and their dependents were metalworking (71.1 percent of 19,749 people), woodworking (69.9 percent of 16,176), shoemaking (76.9 percent of 20,809), "women's occupations" (seamstresses, milliners, and women's tailors—76.8 percent of 6,598), and construction (78.8 percent of 7,735). Among other major categories, they were a minority only in textiles (20.6 percent of 3,377), and clothing (37.6 percent of 14,776). Polish Catholics made up the great majority among factory workers; while they were strong in many areas of craft industry, they did not numerically dominate it to the extent that they did factory work.[11]

Service and unskilled labor supported 29 percent of all Catholics, and they made up three out of every four people in these categories, which included many of the city's poorest people. Many of Warsaw's wealthier Catholics fell into the property owners' and capitalists' group, which was 65.6 percent Catholic and included 5.5 percent of all Catholics.

Fully 67.9 percent of the Jews were found in industry and trade. They numerically dominated only a few branches of industry, specifically clothing, textiles, and tobacco processing, in which they made up 59.5 percent, 68 percent, and 79.2 percent, respectively.

In nineteenth and early twentieth century Eastern Europe and Russia, few Jews worked in the largest and most modern factories. A commonly cited reason for this was the refusal of many Jews to work on Saturdays. Also, in Warsaw, assimilationist Jewish businessmen were sensitive to Polish charges that the Jewish role in the local economy was too strong and they therefore rarely hired Jewish workers. Further, it was commonly felt that Jewish workers were more radical and likely to participate in unions than Polish ones.[12] One result was that home labor—managed by " 'factory owners' without factories"—was very common in Jewish Warsaw.[13]

But Hilary Nussbaum stated succinctly that the essential reason that few Jews worked in large factories was, "Christians don't want to have Jews in their factories, and the progressive Jews reject them only because they are brothers of the same faith."[14]

It was reported in the mid-1880s that of 146 plants in the city with 25 or more workers, 33 were Jewish-owned; in the latter, half of the technical and supervisory personnel were Jews, but only 11 percent of the workers were. Christian-owned factories had even fewer Jewish workers; the 33 Jewish-owned plants had 82 percent of the Jewish factory workers in this sample.[15]

Another factor was hostility between Polish and Jewish workers. Bundist Vladimir Medem recalled that in 1911, Polish shoeworkers expelled

> Jews from the factories. It somehow became a kind of unwritten law among them: Jews must not be permitted to work in mechanized shops! They were transgressing upon the rightful claims of the Christians![16]

One example, however, of a large plant that employed chiefly Jews was the Poliakevitch tobacco processing factory on Bonifraterska Street, which had nearly eight hundred workers in the mid-1880s. It became the subject of a workers' song: "The wheels spin fast, the machines bang / [In] the factory on Bonifraterska Street / Your head whirls, your eyes grow dark / Dark from labor and sweat."[17]

Jews in manufacturing thus worked chiefly in small, unmechanized, Jewish-owned workshops and plants, or in their own dwellings, typically in the clothing, textile, tobacco, leather, and comestible (such as special Jewish bakeries) industries. Writing in 1920, socialist Julian Marchlewski stated that:

> . . . in the big tenements on Nalewki, Nowolipia, and Muranów exist hundreds of workshops, processing textiles, ribbons, belts, buttons, tinware, pewterware, brassware, artificial flowers, and many other things, and employing exclusively Jewish workers.[18]

Commerce and trade of all sorts was, however, the primary traditional Jewish economic role in the Polish lands. The stereotype of the impoverished Warsaw Jew included street peddlers as well as tailors, cigar-rollers, and the like; of 4,145 people supported by peddling, 86.2 percent were Jews. In the large category of trade in various sorts of goods (40,152 people), 80.4 percent were Jews; in brokerage, 96.6 percent were. There was a veritable "army" of Jewish shop clerks,[19] in the many small, Jewish-owned stores on Warsaw's northwest side. In all, Jews made up 79.3 percent of people in trade.

Jews were prominent in the "heights" of commerce as well. The image of the wealthy Jew was that of the great assimilationist entrepreneurial families, such as the Kronenberg, Natanson, Wawelberg, and Epstein families, and Jan Bloch.[20] These families often had built their fortunes in banking and commerce in the early nineteenth century and subsequently branched out into other fields, including industry and the professions. They included some of the city's most prominent converts, for example the Kronenbergs and Bloch. The Jewish upper classes were by no means exclusively assimilationist; there were many examples of wealthy Misnagdic or Hasidic families.

Among the city's smaller religious groups, 42.8 percent of all Protestants were in industry, reflecting the significant role played by Germans in nineteenth century industrial development. Of the Orthodox, 43.8 percent were in government service and the professions (chiefly the former), making up 9.3 percent of this category. Further, 64.1 percent of the resident military group were Orthodox, and most of the larger garrison was as well.

The 1897 Census

The data on employment and native language from the 1897 census are presented in sixty-five categories, rearranged here into eight large groups.

1. Industry: factory and craft industry, construction, and mining. Owners of factories are apparently included with workers, but administrative personnel are not.[21]
2. Private service and day labor: chiefly servants (68 percent of this category's 72,776 employed), and day laborers (23.6 percent). The rest of the employed (8.4 percent) consist of administrative personnel in private institutions and such high-ranking servants as secretaries and stewards.
3. Trade: trade in various goods, banking, credit, brokerage, inns, hotels, restaurants, and street peddling. Owners of businesses appear to be included, but not most administrative staff.
4. Government service and the professions: government service at all levels, public and class service, private law practice, religious bodies and charitable institutions, and people in the fields of education, scholarship, the arts, and health.
5. Transport and communications: water and land transport in general, carting, and the postal, telegraph, and telephone systems. Owners of private companies are listed here, as are some administrative staff, as well as workers.
6. Property owners and pensioners: persons living on the income from real estate, capital, pensions, or on income from relatives.
7. Agriculture: with fishing, hunting, apiculture, sericulture, livestock raising, and forestry.

8. Others and unknown: including prisoners, prostitutes, people supported by charity, those employed in the fields of cleanliness and bodily hygiene, and those of unknown occupations.

The military—the army, the navy, and border guards—is listed separately in tables 4-3 and 4-4. Besides the entire garrison and other military personnel, civilians in the military ministries are included.

Table 4-3 presents the data on employment and native language in 1897; the employed, and the employed plus their dependents, are listed separately. Also included is the percentual breakdown by employment category of the major language groups. Table 4-4 provides the percentual breakdown by language group of each employment category.

The ratio of employed persons to dependents is very different for the Polish- and Yiddish-speaking categories. For the entire population, there were 88 employed per 100 dependents; for Polish-speakers, 90; and for Yiddish-speakers, 57. This reflects the larger families and in particular the greater number of children in the Jewish community. Members of families who worked assisting the head of the family were counted as dependents; they were especially common in craft industry and trade, areas in which many Jews worked.

Polish-speakers were widely dispersed through the employment structure. The largest single groups, 38.1 percent and 25.9 percent, were supported by industry, and by private service and day labor. Polish-speakers made up the great majority in transport and communications, private service and day labor, property owners and pensioners, and agriculture. The only groups in which they were notably underrepresented were trade and the military (33.5 percent and 3.5 percent).

In major industrial categories, Polish-speakers were very numerous: of 24,387 people supported by woodworking, 74.9 percent were Polish-speakers; of 32,506 in metalworking, 80.2 percent; and of 21,426 in construction, 82.1 percent. Polish-speakers also made up 83.6 percent of the 16,077 people in the railroads category.

Fully 75.8 percent of the Yiddish-speakers were supported by trade or industry; they made up 62.2 percent of all people in trade. They were a majority in only three industrial categories: tobacco products (69.2 percent of 1,255 people); production of drinks other than beer, wine, or mead (59.2 percent of 773); and textiles (53.7 percent of 6,896). The largest single group of Yiddish-speakers supported by industry, 27,650, was in the clothing industry. They were underrepresented in agriculture, government service and the professions, private service and day labor, among property owners and pensioners, and in the military. This was partly due to the traditional exclusion of Jews from government service and agriculture, and also to the fact that many Warsaw Jews in the professions, outside of the clergy and religion teachers, were primarily Polish-speakers. Jews were relatively few in private service because while it was common for prosperous Jewish families to have Christian servants, the reverse was very rare. While Jews were weak overall in transport and communication, they made up one-third of the land transport category (outside of the railroads); many Jews worked as carters or cabbies.

The census does not identify the categories that Polish-speaking Jews were chiefly employed in. It is probable that many were in the secular professions, and the city's entrepreneurial upper and middle classes.

Yiddish-speakers dominated almost all branches of trade. The place of Jews in the economy became a major issue in the second half of the nineteenth century, as Polish writers began to call for the "dejudaization" (*odżydzanie*) or "nationalization" (*unarodowienie*) of commerce and industry. Jews should be pushed out of the economy of Poland, many felt, and ethnic Poles supported; the idea of boycotts of Jewish-owned stores, markets, and commercial efforts in general became increasingly widespread after the turn of the century. The issue of the rise of Polish rural cooperatives from the 1890s on is instructive. On the one hand, Poles pointed to them as helping Polish peasants and villagers gain some degree of economic independence; but Jews responded that they were, essentially, anti-Jewish undertakings, with the elimination of Jewish traders in farm products as a basic goal.[22]

By the time of World War I,

> one of the fundamental axioms of Polish nationalist thought of all ideological shadings [was]: the notion that a necessary prerequisite to the reconstitution of an independent Poland was the conquest of commerce and manufacturing by a native Polish commercial and industrial middle class and urban proletariat. The Polonization of commerce and industry was for Polish nationalists of virtually every stripe not only a matter of the Polish community's social and economic wellbeing but also an essential component of the movement for national rebirth.[23]

Jewish economists saw a declining Jewish role in commerce and a shift to manufacturing, combined with the advance of ethnic Poles in commerce.[24] This shift to manufacturing was more in small scale craft industry than in areas which might lead the Jewish urban poor out of poverty, which indeed deepened in interwar Poland.

The Russian role in the city is clear from the place of Russian-speakers in the employment structure: 17.6 percent of people in government service and the professions, and 61.8 percent in the military (much of the rest of the military was Ukrainian–speaking). German-speakers, like the Protestants in 1882, were relatively strongest in industry.

Government Service and the Professions

One particularly important employment category was government service and the professions, which made up the greater part of the city's intelligentsia. The government sector's importance came from the fact that it provided local administrative control, while the professions included much of the city's cultural and political leadership.

The term "intelligentsia" came into general use in the late nineteenth century, at the same time that it was developed as a self-conscious social class in Poland and elsewhere in Russia and Eastern Europe.[25] It usually covered members of the free professions, such as writers, journalists, doctors, lawyers, scholars, teachers, and engineers. There was a strong connotation of independent work in the term, and of some degree of opposition to the existing social and political system. The intelligentsia in late nineteenth and early twentieth century Poland developed into a distinct group which saw itself as the nation's cultural and political elite, providing leadership for the larger community; this was true for the Jews as well as the Poles. In the case of the Poles, members of the intelligentsia after the January Insurrection regarded themselves as the heirs of the Polish "political nation," the gentry (*szlachta*) patriotic leadership, which had suffered enormously as a result of the failed insurrections and Russification. In the oppressive circumstances of Russian Poland, the intelligentsia's leadership role was limited, but it was still an influential group.

The censuses included in these categories low-ranking employees who could not be seen as members of the intelligentsia, such as policemen and servants in hospitals or educational institutions, and leaves out many white collar employees in 1897, which distorts the overall picture.

Many members of Warsaw's intelligentsia earned their livings outside of their areas of creative endeavor. Non-Russian scholars, due to the Russification of the educational system, had great difficulty finding academic positions. They tried to find office jobs which left them time and energy to pursue their studies. Ludwik Krzywicki recalled that the offices of the Warsaw-Vienna railway were an "asylum for Polish learning" for this reason.[26] The Discount Bank was sometimes called the "Polish Academy of Sciences," and the Commercial Bank, the "Polish Literary Club" (both were Jewish assimilationist-owned).[27] Jewish intellectuals followed similar strategies in seeking office work or wealthy patrons; for instance, author Isaac Leib Peretz, one of the great figures in the rise of Yiddish belles–lettres, worked as an official of the Warsaw *kehile*. Jewish intellectuals as a group had a more difficult time than Poles; they could get little support from wealthy assimilationist families (and certainly not from wealthy Poles), and hardly any could work in any quasi–governmental posts such as the railroads. The press became an important source of income for both Polish and Jewish intellectuals.

The data in Table 4–5 concern the government service and professional employment categories in 1882. Catholics made up the greater part of this category in 1882. They dominated numerically literature and the press, private law practice, government service, and the arts and entertainment (70–80 percent in each). In government service and the schools, however, they were concentrated in lower ranks. Not only were the highest official posts, such as governor–general, city president, *oberpolitseimeister*, and curator of the Warsaw Educational District reserved for Russians, but so were many middle rank positions, such as school administrators. Particularly after the 1870s, the government pushed Poles out of teaching positions in the Imperial University and other state educational institutions. In the courts, also, Poles were chiefly found in the lower ranks.[28] One side effect of Russification was that many qualified Poles left the Kingdom. To take an example from the area of government service, in 1897 in the city of Riga and its suburbs, 20.9 percent of the people employed in the administration, courts, and police category were native Polish-speakers, even though this language group made up only 4.8 percent of the local population.[29]

Catholics in 1882 were numerically weakest in the areas in which the Jews were strongest: religion, education, and private administration. Jews were a majority only in education, a result of the fact that there were many *khadorim* scattered about the city. Teachers in these schools were high in number but low in professional status. The Jewish plurality in the private administration category indicates that many Jews had clerical or administrative positions in private businesses. Jews were, of course, largely excluded from government service, including state schools.

Warsaw, as the leading Polish cultural center, drew intellectuals from all the partitioned Polish lands, although most came from the Russian Empire. The feelings of historian Janusz Iwaszkiewicz were representative of the feelings of many young men and women who came to the city.

Warsaw, which I had known fleetingly, having been there for several days in 1896, seemed to me to be some sort of Mecca of Polishness. I had no illusions as to the scholarly qualities of the University . . . but I expected that I would make up for that through contact with the Polish intellectual and scholarly elite concentrated in Warsaw. That had been my dream for many years.[30]

A sizable part of the Polish intelligentsia in Warsaw consisted of scions of impoverished gentry families who had been "thrown out of the saddle," as the saying went, after the 1863 uprising. Many others were children of the local bourgeoisie and, by the end of the period, of parents who were themselves members of the intelligentsia.

Warsaw had a great attraction for young Jews as well as Poles. Isaac Leib Peretz came to Warsaw from Zamość, in southeastern Poland; Nahum Sokolow came from the nearby Płock area. Many Russian Jewish intellectuals also came to the city. In the field of Yiddish journalism, outstanding examples were Samuel Jackan (Yatskan) and Zevi Prylucki, both of whom arrived in Warsaw after the turn of the century, and founded two great rival newspapers: *Haynt* [Today], founded in 1908, and *Der Moment* [The Moment], 1910.

The data in Table 4–6 concern the native language of people in the government service and professions categories in 1897. An important difference between the elements covered by these data and those from 1882 is that the private administration group, which made up a sizable part of Warsaw's white collar workers, does not appear because it was counted in 1897 as part of the larger private service and day labor category. It is likely that this reduces the presence of the Yiddish-speaking group in this table.

The Polish-speakers, Jews as well as Christians, dominate Table 4–6; of eight categories, they make up the majority in six. They were especially strong in private legal practice, public and class service, service in charitable institutions, and in scholarship, literature, and the arts (over 80 percent of the employed plus their dependents). While they were a majority in government service, they were, if anything, even more confined to the lower ranks than the Catholics had been in 1882; the pressures of Russification had intensified since the early 1880s.

Russian participation was greatest in official service and education. The Yiddish-speaking group was strong only in religion and education. A large part of the Jewish intelligentsia by this time was primarily Polish-speaking. Many went into such fields as law, medicine, dentistry, and journalism.[31] One particularly active and influential assimilationist family consisted of the children and grandchildren of Wolf Zelig Natanson. Eleven of them appear in the authoritative *Polski słownik biograficzny*. Natanson (1795–1879) made the family's fortune in trade, manufacturing, and banking. Among his sons, the most outstanding was Ludwik (1822–96). He was a doctor, the founder of the prestigious journal *Tygodnik Lekarski*, and from 1871 to his death the president of the Jewish communal board. His older brother Henryk (1820–95), a banker and publisher, has five sons in the *Słownik*: Kazimierz, a lawyer and banker; Józef Eryk, a naturalist, editor, and banker; Antoni, a doctor; Bronisław, a lawyer; and Stefan, an engineer and music critic. All were evidently strong assimilationists and were involved in Polish patriotic political efforts, scholarly or publicistic writing, and social welfare.

Of course, the Natanson family was untypical, both in its wealth and consistent success, and in its strong assimilationism. Many more intellectuals won a hard and scanty living through tutoring, writing for the Jewish press, or working in offices. Warsaw's Jewish secular intelligentsia was as diverse as the larger Jewish community. It included dedicated assimilationists; younger people who turned to Jewish nationalist and autonomist parties, after growing up in assimilationist families, such as Jan Kirszrot or Bronisław Grosser; leaders of the Polish socialist movements, including Stanisław Mendelsohn; Litvaks, such as the early Zionist leader and Hebrew writer S.P. Rabinowitz; and many more who had experienced considerable acculturation without assimilation, for example Peretz and Sokolow.

Polish and Jewish intellectuals in Warsaw found themselves in a difficult position. It was hard to find rewarding careers, to gain suitable recognition for their achievements, or often even to make ends meet. They had limited political influence, yet at the same time were coming to see themselves as the natural leaders of their respective peoples. The Polish intelligentsia felt itself to be the successor to the older Polish gentry leadership; and the new, secularist Jewish intelligentsia worked to find ways to mobilize the Jewish community politically, in one of several main orientations—assimilationist, nationalist, socialist, or some combination thereof.

The respective Polish and Jewish roles in Warsaw's employment structure and economic life became a key polemical issue in the late nineteenth century. To Polish nationalist writers, it was a commonplace that commerce and industry were dangerously near to being Jewish monopolies. There were many calls for boycotts, for the "dejudaization" and "Polonization" of the local economy by the eve of World War I. Jewish authors, meanwhile, pointed to the narrow restrictions on Jewish employment which had been the cause of keeping Jews in, particularly, commerce, and to the profound poverty of much of the Jewish population. They also suggested that a "process of productivization" had begun, whereby Jews were leaving commerce and entering the supposedly more "productive" field of manufacturing, at the same time that Poles were gaining strength in traditionally Jewish commercial activities. Writers and scholars on both sides made use of the detailed new statistical data that were appearing for the first time, in the censuses and in other official publications. However, the data were (and remain today) only detailed and reliable enough for general portraits, isolated still lifes; there were no useful time series of employment figures. It is clear that many of the debaters were engaged in propaganda, not in making use of the data to develop rational, thoughtful studies of the present state and future course of the economy of Poland. It seems, further, that Polish nationalist writers implicitly defined the Polish economy that they wished to see developed only as that part associated with or controlled directly by ethnic Poles. In the economic equations developed by these Polish writers, the data on the Jews were seen as strictly negatives, or were left out entirely. These equations were profoundly unbalanced as a result.

The information which has been presented in the preceding three chapters on population, residence, and employment shows that Warsaw had a mixed Polish and Jewish population. Due to this and to the separate development of the two groups, in important respects Warsaw was a bi-ethnic city, a *Zweivölkerstadt*, to borrow a German term. The pressures of intensive socioeconomic change did not encourage either mass assimilation or even the recognition of shared interests. The essential isolation of the two groups from one another continued.

The demographic and social issues discussed so far were crucial to the development of Polish approaches to the "Jewish question:" the rapid growth of the Jewish community; radical changes in its character, due to acculturation, assimilation, and the "Litvak invasion;" the huge and separate Jewish quarter, exotic and alien to Polish observers—which moreover was growing, pushing Polish neighborhoods to the south and west; and the persistence of separate patterns of employment, including such issues as the traditional Jewish domination of commerce and real or potential advances in other sectors, especially industry and the professions.

The periodical press was the first means of mass communications, and provided the main forum for developing and spreading the views of the Polish and Jewish political and cultural leaderships; the issues surrounding the "Jewish question" in Polish politics came to a head during the elections to the Russian State Dumas in 1906-12. It is to these topics—the rise of the press, and the elections—that we now turn.

Chapter 5
The Periodical Press

In the late nineteenth and early twentieth centuries, the periodical press developed into the first effective means of mass communications in Russia and Eastern Europe. In Warsaw the press became a system with two major, partly overlapping subsets, one Polish in orientation, the other Jewish. The former remained much the stronger until after the 1905 revolution, when the latter also began to grow rapidly. Warsaw thus served as a leading center for the production and dissemination of information for both Poles and Jews. This chapter will compare and contrast the developments of the Polish and Jewish periodical presses in Warsaw.

The use of the terms "Polish" and "Jewish" in speaking of the press in Warsaw requires clarification. The Polish press consisted of those titles which were oriented towards a largely ethnically Polish readership, and the Jewish press those which were directed towards Jewish readers. Language of publication is not in itself always a sufficient criterion for distinguishing between the two presses. Hebrew and Yiddish titles fell under the Jewish rubric, but there were also journals in Polish which were expressly aimed at Jewish readers, such as the assimilationist weekly *Izraelita* and the Zionist *Głos Żydowski* [Jewish Voice] and *Życie Żydowskie* [Jewish Life].

In almost all cases an ethnic orientation was clearly visible, but the line between the Polish and Jewish presses was not in all respects hard and fast.[1] Many Jews read Polish titles, and Jews worked in the Polish press, such as Aleksander Kraushar, publisher Salomon Lewental (one of several Jewish converts who were prominent Polish publishers), and liberal editor and publisher Stanisław Kempner. The reverse did not hold true; non-Jews rarely read or worked for Jewish titles.[2] Both Jews and Poles read periodicals that were neither Jewish nor Polish in orientation, including Russian or German ones, and also read non-local titles.

Until 1905, government policies and censorship severely handicapped the growth of the press in Warsaw. From 1905 to the war, a period in which censorship was less repressive and there was considerable press growth, the press not only reflected the new types and levels of political and cultural activity which were then taking place, but also played an active role in the political mobilization of the population.

The rise of the press was an important marker in the development of the peoples of Russia and Eastern Europe in this period. The appearance of a periodical press oriented expressly towards a given people was usually a major step in the political mobilization of the people and in the development of a nationalist or autonomist movement. In the case of the Poles, the Polish nationalist movement was a powerful force in the partitions era, and there was always some sort of recognition—generally hostile and repressive—of this fact by the partitioning states. The rise of the mass circulation Polish press in the late nineteenth century reflected and promoted the widening of the concept of Polish political nationality to include many ethnic Poles whom nationalist leaders had previously ignored or slighted, especially the peasantry and urban working classes. Warsaw was the single most important center for the Polish press in all the partitioned Polish lands. L'vov and Kraków, in the more liberal environment of Austrian Galicia, were also significant, but their titles normally had much smaller circulations than Warsaw's leading titles.

For the Jews, the rise of an active and widely read periodical press in Yiddish, the daily language of most of the Jewish population, was closely connected to the emergence of expressly Jewish political movements around the turn of the century. Earlier Jewish titles in other languages had not reached a large audience. The rise of the Yiddish press (the "jargon press," *prasa żargonowa*) was a special sore point to Polish nationalists and Jewish assimilationists alike in Warsaw. They rightly saw it as a sign of the growing strength of Jewish political movements, and they viewed its rapid development in the unofficial capital of Poland as a particular provocation; the existence and explosive growth of the Yiddish press became an additional factor in the "Jewish question" in Polish politics. Bolesław Prus commented in 1909 that the Yiddish press had "multiplied like yeast bacteria," to cite one hostile example.[3] Up until the rise of the Yiddish press, which began in 1905, the Jewish press in Warsaw was on a small scale, as it was elsewhere in the Empire. Warsaw became one of several major centers for the Jewish press in the Empire, along with Odessa, Vilnius, and St. Petersburg. While Warsaw did not lead the Jewish press to the extent that it did the Polish, it nevertheless had the largest concentration of high-circulation Yiddish titles in the Empire. Warsaw periodicals, both Polish and Jewish, were read all over partitioned Poland and in many parts of the Russian Empire. By its very structure, thus, each press system was integrative *within* its ethnic group, as newspapers tried to reach and to speak for as many of "their own" people as they could; and divisive *between* ethnic groups, in that all but a very few titles aimed just at the Poles, or at the Jews.

Especially after 1905, the structure of the press served to emphasize ethnic separatism and encourage divisiveness, at a time when Polish–Jewish tensions were rising. In addition, sizable parts of both presses actively worked to encourage at least mutual suspicion, and sometimes outright hostility. Much of the Polish press became more or less openly anti–Jewish; most of the Jewish press strongly supported expressly Jewish political movements, and opposed any manifestations of assimilationism or anti–Semitism. The open hostility which sometimes reigned in the last years before World War I between the Polish nationalist and Jewish presses exacerbated an already difficult ethnic situation.

The Polish Press

From the 1870s to World War I, major changes and substantial growth occurred in Warsaw's Polish press. The number of titles and their circulations increased enormously, as did the range in types of periodicals. Journalism developed from a larger amateur (or semiprofessional), part–time undertaking into a profession engaging hundreds of writers, editors, artists, printers, and others. New methods of organizing and financing publishing enterprises and many technological advances were introduced.[4]

The growth of the press is clearly illustrated by the increases in the number of titles and in the sizes of their average print runs. From 1884 to 1914, the number of Polish–language dailes in Warsaw rose from nine to fourteen, and of weeklies from thirty–three to sixty–one.[5] The city's five leading Polish dailies in 1870 printed from 800 to 4,000 copies; they had a combined run of 13,600 copies, an average of 2,720 each. In 1909, the five largest Polish dailies printed from 20,000 to 33,000, and had a combined run of 123,000, to average 24,600 each. In 1870, the five largest Polish weeklies had a combined run of 10,920, averaging 2,184 apiece, while in 1909, these figures were 78,700 and 15,740.[6]

Thus, in a period in which Warsaw's population trebled from about a quarter of a million to nearly eight hundred thousand, the average printings of the leading Polish dailies increased nine–fold, and of the weeklies seven–fold.

Among the leading dailies of the time were *Kurjer Warszawski* [Warsaw Courier], founded in 1821; *Kurjer Poranny* [Morning Courier], from 1877; *Gazeta Warszawska* [Warsaw Gazette], since 1774; *Kurjer Codzienny* [Daily Courier], 1865–1905; *Słowo* [Word], from 1882; and the very popular *Goniec* [Messenger], from 1903. Several illustrated weeklies, the most popular and successful of which was the appropriately named *Tygodnik Illustrowany* [Illustrated Weekly], from 1859, competed furiously for readers. Important social and political reviews included two positivist titles, *Przegląd Tygodniowy* [Weekly Review], 1866–1905, and *Prawda* [Truth], founded 1881, and the strongly nationalist *Głos* [Voice], 1886–1905. Jan Jeleński's *Rola* [Field], 1883–1912, was a leading anti-Semitic forum.

The greatest obstacle to the development of the press was harsh prior censorship.[7] Up to 1905, the contents of each issue had to be submitted to the censors before publication. The censors were quick to eliminate criticisms of the government and evidence of Polish nationalist sentiment. Also, persons or groups who wished to establish a periodical had to submit a detailed program of the types of materials which the proposed title would include; permission was quite difficult to obtain in many cases. They also had to get approval for major changes. The editors and publishers had to be approved by the government as politically reliable; failure to do this could easily lead to the title's suspension, as happened to *Kurjer Warszawski* in the early 1870s. Because a number of leading journalists had histories of Polish nationalist activity, using figurehead editors and publishers became a common practice.

Despite the government's heavy hand, the Warsaw press played an extremely important role in Polish cultural and political life. Because it had many readers outside the city, it helped to link different Polish areas together. Polish periodicals could not be published in the lands of the former Lithuanian Grand Duchy, comprising modern day eastern Latvia, Lithuania, Belorussia, and central Ukraine, in which a significant Polish minority lived. The press became a major source of employment for the Polish intelligentsia, and one of the few sectors of public life in the Empire where Polish could be used and Polish issues discussed (if cautiously). The press was also important for Polish literature. In the 1880s, for example, Bolesław Prus's novel *The Doll* and Henryk Sienkiewicz's historical trilogy (*With Fire and Sword, The Deluge,* and *Pan Michael*) were published in Warsaw daily newspapers. A generation later, *Tygodnik Illustrowany* serialized three of the greatest Polish novels of the turn of the century: Sienkiewicz's *Crusaders,* Władysław Reymont's *Peasants,* and Stefan Żeromski's *Ashes.* Many Polish writers earned both their literary spurs and their daily bread in the Warsaw press.

At the same time as the number of titles and their circulations grew, the range of types of periodicals and of readers grew as well. Prior to the late nineteenth century, only a relatively small group–largely adult members of the upper and middle classes and intelligentsia—read the press. But in these decades, readership expanded to include members of the working classes, peasants, and even children. Many titles appeared which were directed expressly towards these new audiences. *Gazeta Świąteczna* [Holiday Gazette] had a large following among Polish villagers and reportedly had a circulation of thirty-two thousand by the eve of World War I. *Przyjaciel Dzieci* [Children's Friend] was an important children's title. Serials for women also appeared, such as the popular *Tygodnik Mód i Powieści* [Weekly of Fashions and Stories] and *Bluszcz* [Ivy].

Specialized, professional journals developed as well. The medical press was a good example; there were ten titles in the city by 1900. Among these the most important were the *Pamiętnik Towarzystwa Lekarskiego Warszawskiego* [Journal of the Warsaw Medical Society], 1837–1938; and the weeklies *Tygodnik Lekarski* [Medical Weekly], founded in 1847 by Ludwik Natanson, and *Gazeta Lekarska* [Medical Gazette], founded 1866. The public health journal *Zdrowie* [Health], which began in 1885 and is still appearing today as *Zdrowie Publiczne* [Public Health], aimed to educate not only doctors and health professionals, but all those whose work brought them into contact with public health issues, including engineers, builders, officials, and indeed the entire educated and concerned public.[8]

Until 1905, most Polish periodicals in the Empire were published in Warsaw. This was partly a result of the concentration of journalistic talent, printing equipment, and capital in the city, and partly of the government's refusal to allow Polish titles to be published elsewhere in any quantity. From 1905 to the war, Warsaw became less of a dominant center, primarily because of government concessions. Not only did it become easier to publish a journal anywhere in the Empire, but the specific ban on Polish titles in the lands of the former Lithuanian Grand Duchy was lifted. In 1904, 85 percent of the Empire's Polish periodicals were published in Warsaw. In 1908, this share was down to 73 percent; the next most important centers were Łódź, Lublin, and Vilnius, although none came near to threatening Warsaw's leading position in numbers or in quality of titles.[9]

A sizable part of the readership of the Warsaw press lay outside the city. For example, 17.6 percent of *Kurjer Warszawski's* eight thousand subscribers in 1875 were outside the city, and 26.5 percent of the twenty-five thousand in 1896; 28.5 percent of *Tygodnik Illus-*

trowany's five thousand subscribers were outside the city in 1875, and 31.1 percent of the eleven thousand in 1896.[10] These data suggest that a major factor in the growth of the circulation of Warsaw's Polish press in the late nineteenth century was increased readership outside the city. Because so few Polish titles appeared in the Empire outside Warsaw, many readers in the provinces of Congress Poland or farther to the east turned to Warsaw titles, which were also, in any case, of higher quality than most provincial ones.

The 1905 revolution proved a turning point in the history of the Warsaw press. Government control weakened considerably. Prior censorship ended, and it became much easier to obtain permission to start new periodicals. A particularly important consequence of 1905 was the politicization of the press. It took an active part in the mobilization of Warsaw's population to political concern and actions. Every significant political group tried to publish its own periodicals or at least to influence existing ones. Government repression of the press did not again become as severe as it had been before 1905, although the censors became increasingly active as the government regained strength and confidence in 1906–07. While prior censorship was a thing of the past, issues were still confiscated, journals and newspaper were suspended (often immediately reappearing under new titles), and editors and publishers arrested and fined. Particularly sensitive topics included the criticism of public officials, excessive enthusiasm on patriotic Polish holidays, and calls by leftist titles to support class struggle. Nonetheless, the press was able to participate energetically in the discussions of the key issues of the day.

A brief survey of the major dailies after 1905 will illuminate the political alignments of the press. The National Democratic Party had a particularly well–developed press system. Led by Roman Dmowski, this party represented the right wing of the Polish nationalist movement, and became the strongest Polish party in the Kingdom. It had in Warsaw a range of newspapers, aimed at all levels of the Polish population.[11] *Gazeta Polska* [Polish Gazette], controlled by the party in 1906–07, and its successors *Gazeta Codzienna* [Daily Gazette], 1907–08, *Głos Warszawski* [Warsaw Voice], 1908–09, and finally *Gazeta Warszawska* (revived in 1909) served as high–quality, low–circulation dailies, aimed at the intelligentsia. These complemented the party's "thick journals," such as *Przegląd Narodowy* [National Review], from 1909. *Goniec* (controlled by the party in 1905–08, then lost to a splinter group) had a much higher circulation; it was aimed at the city's middle classes, and was much more aggressive and sensationalist than the various "gazettes." Party dailies aimed at the city's Polish working and lower middle classes included *Naród*

[Nation], 1906–07, then *Wiadomości Codzienne* [Daily News], and finally, from 1912, the spectacularly successful *Gazeta Poranna 2 grosze* [Morning Gazette 2 groschen], the so-called "Dwugroszówka," which aggressively promoted anti–Semitism and became a symbol of Polish–Jewish discord. Dmowski himself was very active in the local press; Antoni Sadzewicz and Stanisław Kozicki were among the party's corps of editors and writers, as was Zygmunt Balicki, one of the movement's leading ideologists.

But the National Democrats faced a great deal of competition. Other Polish groups and parties had their own titles as well. The very popular *Kurjer Warszawski* tried to provide a middle of the road, non–party, but still nationalist voice. The conservative and aristocratic Realist Party for a time controlled both the low–circulation *Słowo* and the popular *Kurjer Polski*. The liberal Progressive Democrats expressed their views in 1906–07 in Stanisław Kempner's *Nowa Gazeta* and *Ludzkość* [New Gazette, Humanity]. Kempner and the Progressive Democrats subsequently moved apart, but his paper remained an articulate, widely–read voice of liberalism and of Polish–Jewish conciliation. *Kurjer Poranny* was a popular daily with ties to the progressives and a dislike for Dmowski; but like most of the "couriers," its chief interest was selling newspapers, not promulgating a consistent political or ideological program. A Roman Catholic press appeared as well, generally leaning towards the political right and anti–Semitism.[12] Its representatives in Warsaw included *Dziennik Powszechny* [Universal Daily] and the aptly named *Polak Katolik* [Polish Catholic].

Socialist groups, including the Polish Socialist Party and the Social Democratic Party of the Kingdom of Poland and Lithuania, published legal as well as underground titles, but these were generally short–lived with small circulations and constantly ran afoul of the government.[13] The Social Democrats moved their *Czerwony Sztandar* [Red Flag] in December 1905 from Kraków to Warsaw, where it briefly survived as a daily. It published ninety–three issues in 1906, twenty–three in 1907, and very few thenceforth. *Kurjer Codzienny* was a legal daily controlled by the Polish Socialists for part of 1905, but the authorities shut it down at the end of the year, and squelched later attempts by party factions to publish legal titles in the city. The period after 1905 was not a good one for leftists in the Kingdom—Poles and Jews alike—due to factionalism, popular apathy and exhaustion after the turmoil of 1905, and increasingly effective official repression. The various socialist parties and factions generally had to settle for publishing journals abroad or covertly.

The Jewish Press

The development of the Jewish press in nineteenth century Warsaw was slow compared to the Polish press. This was a result of the refusal of the government to allow periodicals in Yiddish, the only language which could draw a large readership in the Jewish community. From 1905 the Jewish press grew very rapidly, however.[14]

Only a few Jewish periodicals were published in Warsaw before 1905. The most important of these were the Hebrew *Ha-Zefirah* [usually translated as The Dawn] and the Polish *Izraelita*. Hebrew titles never attracted many readers; evidently much of the Jewish community found the Hebrew used by the press either inaccessible, or an unacceptable use of a sacred language.[15] While many Jews read Polish newspapers, there was little support as yet for separate Jewish titles in Polish.

At the end of the nineteenth century, Yiddish experienced a literary flowering. Major writers, all of whom published in Warsaw periodicals, included Mendele Mokher Sefarim, Sholem Aleichem, and Isaac Leib Peretz. Yiddish was also becoming a language of politics and scholarship; its expansion into all these spheres became important when the Yiddish press began to grow rapidly after 1905.

The year 1905 had an even more liberating effect on the Jewish than on the Polish press. It became possible to obtain permission to publish Yiddish serials in Warsaw and in many other cities. Thenceforth, the rise of Jewish political movements and of Yiddish literature gave impetus to the growth of the Yiddish press; and conversely, the Yiddish press became a major factor in Jewish political and cultural efforts. The Polish and Hebrew sections of Warsaw's Jewish press were much less significant than the Yiddish press after 1905.

The first Jewish journal was the bilingual weekly (Polish, and German in Hebrew letters) *Dostrzegacz Nadwiślański – Der Beobachter an der Weichsel* [Vistula Observer], which appeared in 1823-24.[16] Its publisher was the early assimilationist leader Antoni Eisenbaum, later director of the Warsaw Rabbinical Academy. The next Jewish title was the short-lived (and now lost) *Izraelita Polski* [Polish Israelite], a Polish-language weekly which appeared briefly during the 1830-31 uprising.[17] Three decades later another Polish-language weekly appeared, *Jutrzenka* [Dawn or Morning Star], in 1861-63.[18] It was an assimilationist title which supported the drive for legal emancipation of the Jews. The government closed it down in late 1863 and exiled its editor, Daniel Neufeld. None of these titles achieved a large readership, having at most several hundred subscribers.

The most important Hebrew title was *Ha-Zefirah*. It first appeared in 1862, then in 1874–1906; it was published intermittently in later years. Its founder was Hayyim Selig Slonimski, a noted scholar. The weekly's prospectus noted that its goal would be "to show the importance of the positive sciences and to be useful to people in trade, industry, and new inventions," which illustrates Slonimski's own technical and scientific interests. Its program also included publication of government regulations on the Jews, relevant news, and "Articles with moral and religious content, or belle–lettristic writings with scholarly and moral orientations."[19]

By the 1880s *Ha-Zefirah* began to pay more attention to current events. In this same period the young Nahum Sokolow began his association with the paper. A very prolific writer in several languages, he became one of the most popular and influential Jewish journalists of the day. His role in *Ha-Zefirah* steadily increased, and by 1886 he was part–owner. He turned *Ha-Zefirah* into a daily, following the examples of *Ha-Yom* and *Ha-Meliz* in St. Petersburg.[20] In the 1890s he became sole editor and publisher.

Towards the end of the century *Ha-Zefirah* reached the peak of its influence and popularity. With only two thousand subscribers in 1886, it was printing about five thousand copies per issue ten years later.[1] After the 1897 Zionist congress in Basel, Sokolow became an energetic supporter of the Zionist movement. (In the 1930s he was president of the World Zionist Organization.)

The second long-running Jewish title was *Izraelita*. Founded in 1866, it lasted, with breaks, to 1913.[22] Its founder and guiding spirit was Samuel Peltin (or Peltyn) who died in 1896. It was a strongly assimilationist title, and claimed to speak for Poles of Mosaic faith and Jewish Poles. It never found readers outside narrow assimilationist circles, and could not compete with *Ha-Zefirah* or with the later Yiddish titles (or indeed, with the general Polish press) in the broader Jewish community. Printing editions of only 330 copies in 1868, it reached its peak in 1901, with 1,300.[23]

Its main goal was the integration of Poland's Jews into Polish culture and society. Its ideal was a Poland in which Christian and Jewish Poles would be equal citizens, where Polish language, culture, and patriotism would win over the Jewish community; it did not advocate conversion or disappearance of the Jewish community. The weekly opposed both Polish anti–Semitism and Jewish nationalism. Around the turn of the century, when Sokolow was its literary editor, it expressed views favorable to Zionism, however.[24] By its last years, 1912–13, when Józef Wasercug was the editor, *Izraelita* seemed beleaguered by enemies on all sides, as the Polish nationalist press expressed anti–Jewish sentiments more and more often, and the Yiddish press aggressively supported Jewish political nationalism and attacked any manifestation of assimilation.

Through the late nineteenth century, thus, only two Jewish serials were published in Warsaw for considerable lengths of time, one in Hebrew, the other in Polish. Both had, for the time, creditable circulations, and *Ha-Zefirah* became one of the leading Jewish periodicals of the Empire. Warsaw's Jews also read non-Jewish titles, including Polish, Russian, and German ones, and Jewish serials from other cities. Only with the rise of Yiddish periodicals did a truly popular Jewish press develop.

The first attempt at a Yiddish title was the weekly *Varshoyer Yudishe Tsaytung* [Warsaw Jewish Newspaper], edited by an assimilationist, Hilary Glatsztern, in 1867–68. It had little success, and had only about 180 subscribers right before its demise.[25] In the 1880s and 1890s a number of annuals and irregular serials appeared in Yiddish. Isaac Leib Peretz and Mordecai Spector were particularly active as editors and publishers.[26] One way that editors tried to get around the local restrictions on Jewish serials was to print titles in Galicia which were aimed at readers in Russian Poland; an example was *Der Yud* [The Jew], which was essentially a Warsaw weekly but was printed in Kraków. The Yiddish press as such took its first significant steps in the Empire around the turn of the century. Titles included the underground publications of the socialist Bund and, in 1903, the first Yiddish daily in the Empire, *Der Fraynd* in St. Petersburg.

The weakening of the Russian government's hold on the press in 1905 led to the appearance of many new Yiddish titles. In Warsaw as of January 1, 1906, the authorities had given permission for twenty-eight Yiddish serials.[27] The city's first Yiddish daily was *Der Veg* [The Way], which began to appear in August 1905 and achieved an average print run of about fifteen thousand copies. It was founded by Zevi Prylucki, who had worked in St. Petersburg's Jewish press. The first Jewish daily to have a high circulation was *Yidishes Tageblat* [Jewish Daily Paper], which Samuel Jackan and the brothers Noah and Nehemiah Finkelstein established in May 1906. The *Tageblat's* two basic goals were to be cheap (one kopeck), and to win readers through aggressive and lively reporting and sensationalism. In these terms it was a success, printing in 1906 an average press run of 54,200 copies, which made it the most popular newspaper in any language anywhere in the partitioned Polish lands.[28]

In January 1908, Jackan and the Finkelsteins began to publish a new daily, *Haynt*. It lasted all the way to the fall of Warsaw in September 1939, and *Haynt* and its chief rival *Der Moment* are remembered as the two most famous Jewish periodicals of Poland. By

1914, Warsaw had the highest circulation Yiddish press outside of New York, with readership concentrated in these two dailies.[29] They featured a mix of Jewish nationalism, sensational crime stories and scandals, prizes, cutthroat competition, translations of famous novels by non-Jewish writers, high quality writing by such leading Jewish authors as Peretz and Sholem Aleichem, and also less edifying literature. Isaac Bashevis Singer remembered that his older siblings "read the daily papers, including the serialized novels. I heard them talking about veiled ladies, horrible secrets, and fatal passions."[30] A real boon for the Yiddish press was the Mendel Beilis ritual murder trial in Kiev in 1913, which drew enormous interest in Warsaw.[31]

Bernard Singer, who worked for Jackan, gives a vivid recollection of the early days of the Yiddish press.

> The spirit of competition, which rule in trade, dominated also in newspapers. Every reader was fought over. They tried to tear readers from the hands of competitors by gutter novel serials, by feuilletons. News was stolen from one another. *Haynt* gave prizes in the form of a group trip to Palestine. Its competitor *Moment* promised as prizes plots in Palestine. They scrambled for leading writers and popular journalists. The older generation was outraged by vulgar paragraphs. The editor of the newspaper *Haynt* would say to his employees: "A reader like a pig eats everything, and likes the taste of s[. . .] ." In a popular, often vulgar style surveys of foreign news were given, and feuilletons were sprinkled with Talmudic examples. Thus Jews, who had emerged not long before from the yeshiva, who had listened to politics in the shul or mikva, were ushered into the political arena.
>
> The Jewish dailies did not scorn the high school graduate, the autodidact, the reader of Polish and Russian newspapers. It was necessary to consider the respect of the newly won reader for serious learning. On Fridays the paper was transformed into a magazine.
>
> On the second page an article discussed the high values of Jewish ethics, on the third an erotic serial was printed, on the fourth there was an article about Spinoza, and on the fifth a scandal or brutal attack on a competing newspaper.[32]

These and other Jewish dailies largely depended on outside sources for news: Polish, Russian, and European telegraph agencies, Polish dailies such as *Kurjer Warszawski*, and even New York's Yiddish press. The Jewish journalistic profession was still new, younger than the Polish or Russian, and experienced journalists, editors, and publishers were few and far between.

Polish-language Jewish titles also appeared, but this did not become a large scale phenomenon until the interwar period.[33] The first Polish-language Jewish daily in Warsaw was *Przegląd Codzienny* [Daily Review], which was founded in 1913 to combat the Polish anti-Jewish boycott movement which followed the 1912 elections to the State Duma. A Polish-language Zionist weekly in 1906 was *Głos Żydowski*. After the authorities closed it, it was succeeded by *Życie Żydowskie*, which lasted into 1907.

Many fewer Jewish than Polish titles appeared. The censor for Jewish titles reported that there were seventeen in 1912, including three in Hebrew; this probably does not count Polish-language serials.[34] Information on circulations and print runs is sparse, but some 1906 data have been published. Among Jewish newspapers which printed at least one hundred issues, *Yidishes Tageblat* was far and away the largest; its average print run was 54,200. *Der Telegraf* [The Telegraf] printed 10,000; *Der Veg*, 9,000; and the only major Hebrew daily, *Ha-Yom* [The Day], just 5,000. Among weeklies which printed at least ten issues, *Di Bihn* [The Bee] printed an average of ten thousand copies, and three Polish titles (*Głos Żydowski, Życie Żydowskie,* and *Izraelita*) averaged one thousand each.[35] These figures indicate how much more accessible, or acceptable, Yiddish was for Jewish titles in Warsaw than Polish or Hebrew.

The rapid development of both the Polish and Jewish presses in Warsaw was of great significance for the history of both groups, and also for relations between them. The press provided a mass communications forum for the dissemination of information, ideas, and all too often, angry attacks. The press became particularly important in the elections in the city to the Russian State Duma in 1906-12, and in the unhappy aftermath of these elections—the Polish anti-Jewish boycott of 1912-14.

Chapter 6
The Elections to the Russian State Duma and the "Jewish Question," 1906–1912

The "Jewish question" was one of the dominant issues of Polish politics before World War I. It was an especially complex and heated issue in Warsaw. While Polish–Jewish relations constituted a significant issue through the whole period of Russian rule, it was only in the last few years before World War I that Warsaw became the scene for open and urgent debate on this as on many other political questions. Thanks to concessions made by the Russian government during the 1905 revolution, a certain amount of legal political activity could take place; one key concession was the establishment of the Russian State Duma, which served as a quasi-parliament. The most important political events in Warsaw before the war were the four Duma elections in 1906–07 and 1912.

The growing political significance of ethnicity was a particularly important development in this period in the Polish lands as elsewhere in Eastern Europe and the Russian Empire. The complex ethnic mix in Poland—there were many Jews, Germans, Lithuanians, Ukrainians, and Belorussians, as well as Poles—had for centuries been significant in the social and cultural arenas rather than in politics. The Polish "political nation" which had dominated the independent Polish–Lithuanian Commonwealth had consisted of the Polish or Polonized gentry and nobility. By the late nineteenth century, however, these groups had lost their leadership role in Russian Poland, as a result of the Russifying policies of the Russian government and the series of Polish defeats at the hands of the Russians, which culminated in the failed insurrection of 1863–64. Moreover, in these decades the region entered the age of mass based political nationalism. Because of these developments, the relatively open Polish elite was in decline at the same time that less tolerant and more ethnically exclusive brands of nationalism—Polish, Russian, and Jewish—were gaining strength. Ethnic political tensions and conflict became endemic in early twentieth century Congress Poland. Political groups largely followed ethnic lines; attempts to build coalitions involving significant numbers of both Poles and Jews had no lasting success. The "Jewish question" in particular took on enormous importance in Polish politics. This chapter examines Polish approaches to the "Jewish question" during the elections in Warsaw to the State Duma. Special attention is paid to the last election, in 1912, which had particularly lasting, and destructive, effects. We will concentrate on Polish strategies in the elections, and on the non-socialist, nationalist and progressive groups, for whom this was a crucial issue, and who set the agenda for the debate over the "Jewish question" in Polish politics. We will not focus on positions taken by Jewish groups in the electoral campaigns.

The "Jewish Question" from the 1860s to 1905

A brief review of the political side of Polish–Jewish relations from the 1860s to 1905 in Warsaw is necessary. In the second half of the nineteenth century, the "Jewish question" became one of the most important issues in Warsaw's political life. The patriotic movement of the early 1860s, which led to the January Insurrection of 1863–64, saw conscious attempts to improve ethnic relations. There was some Jewish support for and participation in the patriotic movement, and during the insurrection there were direct appeals from the Polish side for Jewish support. The Russian government granted emancipation to the Jews of Congress Poland in 1862 under terms more liberal than elsewhere in the Empire, largely in order to prevent any possible Polish–Jewish united front.

The several decades following the January Insurrection were a time of official repression and political quiescence in Warsaw. On the surface, the most influential political orientation was "Warsaw positivism," but this was much more a *Weltanschauung* than a political movement. Its leaders, such as *Prawda's* editor Aleksander Świętochowski and novelist Eliza Orzeszkowa, praised education, economic growth, secularism, and Jewish assimilation, while opposing the romantic, revolutionary tradition that had prevailed in Polish political thought since the end of the eighteenth century. The positivists proved more articulate than influential, and were unable to create a viable political movement. Also, their assimilationism was of an intolerant kind; Jews were expected to assimilate to Polish ethnic and political identity, and there was no tolerance for the concept of a continued separate Jewish identity in Poland.[1] This attitude sometimes fed into anti-Semitic tendencies such as those that developed in connection with the weekly *Głos* in the late 1880s and the National

League (*Liga Narodowa*), which became the basis for the National Democratic movement.²

The 1870s and 1880s also saw specifically anti-Semitic sentiment coalescing, in part because of the writings of Jan Jeleński, author of *Żydzi, niemcy i my* (Jews, Germans, and We], which went through several editions in the 1870s, and editor, from 1883, of the anti-Semitic weekly *Rola*.³

In 1881, a major pogrom took place in Warsaw.⁴ The rioting began on Christmas day, at the Church of the Holy Cross, and spread to other parts of the city in the next two days. It began with a sudden panic during church services; twenty to thirty people were killed, someone shouted that a Jewish thief had started it, and soon a wave of looting and robbery by bands of youthful Poles began. Casualties were light—it is unclear if there were any fatalities—but there were about a million rubles' worth of property damage. There were several thousand Jewish families robbed or ruined, and several thousand arrests; the police and army remained generally passive until the third day of the pogrom, which encouraged rumors that the Russian authorities were somehow involved in planning and implementing it.

The pogrom received wide coverage in Western and Central Europe. To many Poles and Jews alike in the city it was a shocking event. The other pogroms which swept the Empire in 1881 took place in smaller cities and towns in the Ukrainian or Belorussian provinces, and the people of Warsaw prided themselves on being more civilized and European than their eastern neighbors. Some Polish writers, such as Orzeszkowa, expressed horror and shock; other sought scapegoats for the events, whether the Russian authorities or the Jews themselves.

Despite positivism and the pogrom, the actual main political outlook in late nineteenth century Warsaw was avoiding trouble with the Russian authorities. In the 1890s, however, underground political groups began to form among both Poles and Jews, including a wide spectrum of nationalist, autonomist, and socialist elements. A number of political parties, which ranged from tiny circles of the intelligentsia to mass based socialist and nationalist movements, emerged during the 1905 revolution.

This surge of political action and violence which swept the Russian Empire lasted in Warsaw from late 1904 to 1907.⁵ Actions ranged from mass demonstrations to acts of terror—murder and robbery—carried out by radical "fighting squads" of the left and right. Hundreds of policemen and soldiers were killed or wounded in the city, and there were more than 360 executions of radicals in the Citadel. Many more participants in demonstrations, innocent bystanders, political activists, and terrorists were killed by gun, knife, or bomb on the city's streets as well.

The troubles began in late 1904 with protests against military conscription led by the socialists. On January 28, socialists organized a general strike in Warsaw which rapidly spread from factories to schools, offices, and public transport. Later general strikes in October and December, 1905, won less support than the first, which lasted for a month. The year saw hundreds die in street clashes with police and soldiers, and more than thirteen hundred strikes. Many new political groups as well as those with more narrow educational, cultural, or social welfare goals were founded in both the Polish and Jewish communities.

The 1905 revolution signaled the revival of political life in Congress Poland.[6] In its essence, the revolution was based on the mobilization of large numbers of people to high levels of political concern and action. This was evident in the widespread strikes, demonstrations, and violence, and in the intense political involvement of the press, as well as in the emergence of open and organized political parties out of the underground groups that had been slowly developing. The level of mobilization and violence was very high in Warsaw.

Near civil war developed in both Warsaw and Łódź between the National Democrats and the socialist groups. Both sides formed armed units—the socialists to battle the government and the right, and the National Democrats to combat the left. In 1906, there were fewer strikes and demonstrations than in 1905, but terror increased. It reached its peak on August 15, "bloody Wednesday," with a wave of bombings and shootings by the Polish Socialist Party's "Fighting Organization." About 160 people were killed or wounded in Warsaw, 38 of them police or soldiers.[7] Three days later, Governor-General Skalon was wounded in a bombing; nine days after that, his replacement, General Vonliarliarskii, was killed.

The government proved it could outlast the revolutionaries in Poland as elsewhere in the Empire, and in the end the hold of the Russian authorities seemed nearly as firm as before. But a much greater degree of freedom prevailed henceforth, as can be seen in the liveliness of the local press and in the continued existence of many of the new political groups. Those which survived had to be circumspect in expressing goals of Polish independence and reunification or of socialist revolution, but nonetheless they had much more latitude than before. Socialist losses were very heavy; all the major leftist groups moved back underground, and entered a period marked by exile and factionalism. The National Democrats emerged as the strongest organized political party in Warsaw and the region.

The National Democratic Party and movement (*Narodowa Demokracja*), represented the right wing of the Polish nationalist movement, borrowing many features from other European extreme nationalist parties, and held that nationality was the absolute factor in political life, eclipsing all others such as class.[8] It claimed to represent all ethnic Poles, and worked hard to develop student, worker, and peasant affiliates. Its dominant figure was Roman Dmowski. Always strongly nationalistic, after 1905 the movement came to see enemies everywhere: Germany, which it viewed as the main threat to Polish ethnic survival, far more dangerous than backward Russia; the Jews, whom it regarded as the main internal enemy of the Poles; socialists of all sorts, and also Polish conservatives and liberals. Despite its claims, National Democracy did not have a monopoly on the Polish nationalist movement. After 1905 Dmowski tried to lead his party in the direction of conciliation with the Russian government; this cost him many followers, especially after 1908. Still, the party remained more popular and better organized than the less extreme Polish nationalist parties.

These other groups consisted of small circles of the intelligentsia without much popular following. The main attempt to create a liberal party was the Progressive Democratic Union (*Związek Postępowo-Demokratyczny*), formed in 1905. Among its leaders were such prominent older positivists as Aleksander Świętochowski and Jewish editor and economist Stanisław Kempner. The main conservative group was the aristocratic Party of Realistic Politics, or the Realists (*Stronnictwo Polityki Realnej*).

The various socialist groups reached their peak at the time of the 1905 revolution, when their combined memberships in Warsaw reached the tens of thousands and they for a time controlled industrial districts. One of the main groups was the Polish Socialist Party, known from its Polish initials as the PPS (*Polska Partia Socjalistyczna*). It combined nationalism with class struggle, for the goal of an independent, socialist Poland; the faction which became intermittently involved in local electoral politics was the PPS–Left. The Social Democratic Party of the Kingdom of Poland and Lithuania (*Socjaldemokracja Królestwa Polskiego i Litwy–SDKPiL*) was allied with Russian social democracy. Socialism had a strong appeal to Warsaw's Poles and Jews alike; the Social Democrats drew members from both peoples, and the Polish Socialist Party had a separate Jewish section for a time, which was, however, much weaker than the Jewish Bund. All Socialist groups suffered severely from both government repression and internal factionalism after 1905.

The rise of Jewish political movements was very important in the history of Polish–Jewish relations.[9] Traditionally, the Jews in Poland had been a politically passive element, and had left politics to the Polish gentry, aristocracy, and crown; the entry of the Jews into political life was as radical a change as the entries of social groups such the peasantry and urban lower classes. The one goal that united politically active Jews of all movements was support for full Jewish equal rights. Some assimilationist Jews participated in Polish liberal and socialist parties, and a few on occasion cooperated with National Democrats in election campaigns. The influence of the assimilationists in Warsaw was far greater than their limited numbers might suggest; for example, they retained control of the *kehile* board from the 1870s to the 1920s. Nonetheless, the strongest specifically Jewish political groups after the turn of the century were the socialist Bund (*Der algemeyner yidisher arbeter bund in lite, rusland un poyln* [General Jewish Labor Union in Lithuania, Russia, and Poland]) and the Zionists. These two mutually antagonist and some smaller non–assimilationist groups shared the view that the Jews were a political nationality, and must be mobilized to act on their own behalf.

The "Jewish question" in the context of Polish politics actually concerned a complex range of issues. Most succinctly, it could be defined as the problems of how Poles should deal with the strong and growing Jewish presence, as well as of the role that Polish political leaders felt the Jews should play in Polish politics. Polish parties and movements responded in various and often inconsistent ways. Among major groups, only the National Democrats, who became increasingly hostile to the Jews, approached this "question" with energy; other, more liberal or leftist groups, which might have worked towards Polish–Jewish conciliation, tended to downplay or avoid it.

The strongly nationalist ideology of the National Democrats, and their extremely combative attitude towards the Jews and also towards liberal and leftist Polish groups with which Jewish elements often worked or cooperated, insured that this influential party would increasingly promote anti–Semitism. The party program rejected, further, the notion that any Jewish group had a legitimate political role to play in Poland, and expressed little faith in the idea that the Jews could or would assimilate to Polish identity, or if they did, that this would be a desirable development. An element of racism appeared early on in the party's approaches to the "Jewish question," and the personal anti–Semitism of Roman Dmowski, the party's dominant figure, also helped to push this movement towards distinctly anti–Semitic positions. Despite this, the National Democrats could show tactical flexibility; they sometimes made statements in favor of Jewish equal rights.

Polish liberal and socialist parties were much more open to Jewish (chiefly assimilationist) participation, or to cooperation with Jewish groups. They largely followed the line that assimilation would solve the "Jewish question." Some older liberal writers, such as Prus, Świętochowski, and Orzeszkowa, had showed in the 1870s and 1880s considerable admiration for the numerically small but highly visible, assimilated and Polonophile Jewish intelligentsia. Few Polish liberals showed sympathy for the unassimilated Jewish masses or for Jewish traditions, however; their liberalism in the "Jewish question" was normally of an intolerant sort.[10] Positive sentiments, moreover, had faded by the turn of the century, as it became clear that mass assimilation was not taking place and that Jewish nationalist sentiments were gaining strength. It was also very hard for Polish and Jewish socialists to find common ground, except in the case of thoroughly assimilated Jews joining Polish groups. There was no support among any Polish groups, including liberals and the left, for the notion of an ethnically conscious, politically mobilized, and nationalist Jewish presence in Poland, and indeed there was substantial antipathy towards it.

The First Three State Duma Elections, 1906–07

The voters of Warsaw elected two delegates to the State Duma. Voting was indirect. In the first two elections, held in the spring of 1906 and early 1907, the voters in the city's general and workers' curiae chose an electoral college, which in turn selected the delegates from its own ranks. In the last two elections, held in late 1907 and 1912, one delegate was elected from a separate Russian curia, and the other by the non–Russian, chiefly Polish and Jewish, general workers' curiae.

Eligible voters in the general curia, which chose eighty electors, consisted of resident men over twenty–four years old who had fit into one of the following categories for at least a year: owners of real estate or industrial or commercial enterprises; members of the city's professional or managerial classes, who paid taxes on "personal industrial occupations" (*lichnye promyslovye zaniatiia*, in Russian); persons with large rented apartments who paid taxes on them; residents of smaller apartments, renting "in their own names;" and some government pensioners. Among groups who were explicitly excluded, besides all women and men under twenty–five, were students, military personnel, foreign citizens, criminals, persons under indictment, high state officials, and the police. The general curia was thus overwhelmingly upper and middle class in composition.

Factory workers chose only three electors to sit with the eighty from the general curia, so that the slate which won in the general curia controlled the election. Resident male workers over twenty-four years old, employed in factories or railroad workshops with at least fifty male workers, chose representatives from their places of work. These representatives then chose the three electors.[11] This chapter concentrates on the general curia, in which the "Jewish question" was a decisive issue and in which developments of considerable importance to Polish-Jewish relations took place, and does not examine the campaigns in the Russian or workers' curiae.

The first and second Duma elections took place within a span of ten months. At the time of the first, in April 1906, there was a great deal of excitement. It seemed that major reforms, even a successful revolution, were distinctly possible. By the time of the second election (February 1907), the authorities were clearly gaining the upper hand. Still, this election also aroused popular interest and hope. The third election, in October 1907, was greeted with widespread apathy; it had become clear that the government was determined and able to keep the Duma from developing into a powerful force for change.

In early 1906, the National Democrats were initially the only major group to enter the campaign for the Duma seats from Poland. The main socialist groups and the Progressive Democrats opposed participation, as did the non-assimilationist Jewish press. Assimilationist Jewish leaders supported eventual participation with reservations.[12] The Union of the Russian People (*Soiuz Russkogo Naroda*, in Russian), which was both intensely anti-Polish and anti-Jewish, worked to mobilize local Russian voters.

It was a quiet campaign from mid-February, when public meetings began, to mid-April. National Democratic spokesmen justified their participation by maintaining that there had to be Polish representatives in the Duma. The main points in the party's program were autonomy for Congress Poland and solidarity of Polish Duma representatives. The "Jewish question" was rarely mentioned. National Democratic spokesmen at first downplayed the issue and made general statements in favor of equal rights.[13]

Voting was held in most of the Empire in early April, several weeks before it was scheduled for Congress Poland. The results in Russia were a complete surprise, as the liberal Russian Constitutional Democrats received the largest number of votes. In Warsaw the Progressive Democrats hastily organized a campaign. Like the National Democrats, they supported autonomy, but they opposed compulsory Polish solidarity in the Duma. They had significant Jewish support, and were willing to cooperate with the socialists.[14]

The Progressive Democrats formed an alliance with the Jewish Electoral Committee. The *kehile* board dominated the Committee, which called on Jews to choose Jewish electors when possible or at least Christians who supported Jewish equal rights. The Progressive Democrats and the Jewish Committee agreed that the former would run in seven of the twelve precincts, and the latter in the five which had the largest Jewish populations; and if the alliance won, one of the delegates would be a Pole, the other a Jew.[15]

The National Democrats responded to this challenge with furious energy. The daily *Dzwon Polski* [Polish Bell] in the last week of the campaign constantly repeated one basic theme: Warsaw is threatened by the "Jewish danger." *Dzwon Polski* warned that the Jews, acting energetically and in concert, had stolen a march on the passive and disunited Poles, and were picking up their voting cards in greater numbers than the Poles were.[16]

The National Democrats claimed that the unexpectedness of this was not an accident, but it had all been planned by the Jews; earlier statements by Jewish groups that they probably would not participate in the election had been aimed at lulling the Poles into overconfidence.[17] In addition, the "Judaized Progressive Democrats," who had the support of the "dark Jewish masses," had, in the words of one flier, "sold Warsaw to the Jews."[18] These attacks were interspersed with statements that the National Democrats still supported equal rights and regarded the assimilationists as members of the Polish nation.[19]

There were reports of violence and intimidation directed against Jewish voters on the day of the voting, April 25.[20] The National Democrats used their domination of most of the precinct electoral commissions, which supervised the voting, to harass Jewish voters.[21]

The National Democrats won 54 percent of the sixty-seven thousand votes cast, and nine of twelve precincts, for sixty electors. The Jewish list won in three precincts, with twenty electors; they and the Progressive Democrats had a combined share of 40 percent, chiefly in heavily Jewish areas.[22] On May 3, the electoral college chose the National Democratic candidates, Franciszek Nowodworski and Władysław Tyszkiewicz, to represent Warsaw. All but three of the thirty-seven delegates from Congress Poland were National Democrats or their allies.[23]

Dzwon Polski expressed no regrets that the "electoral struggle had been conducted under the slogan of the defense of Warsaw against the Jews." The paper blamed the Jews for the bitterness of the campaign, repeated the charges of Jewish deception, and stated that it had been necessary to show the Jews that the Poles were the masters of Warsaw.[24]

Within a few months, the imperial government disbanded the first Duma as too radical, and new elections were set for late February 1907. On December 9 in Warsaw, the formation of the "National Concentration" was announced. Besides National Democracy, this alliance consisted of the small Polish Progressive Party (*Polska Partia Postępowa*), which had split off from the Progressive Democrats some months before, and the Realists. (The Realists subsequently dropped out.) They agreed to solidarity of the Polish Duma delegation, and to support Polish autonomy, but otherwise retained their separate programs.[25]

The National Democrats dominated the Concentration's campaign efforts and public meetings, thanks to their wide popular support and strong press. Their candidates for Warsaw's seats were Roman Dmowski and Franciszek Nowodworski; three provincial seats were reserved for Progressive Party leaders.

The opposing Progressive Alliance that was formed in January consisted of the Progressive Democrats plus some weak leftist elements. It nominated Aleksander Świętochowski and Ludwik Krzywicki. The PPS boycotted the elections, while the Bund and the Social Democrats formed a separate alliance. This time the Zionists rather than the assimilationists took the lead in forming a Jewish Electoral Committee. Its program initially called for democratization of the Empire, autonomy for Poland on democratic principles, Jewish equal rights, and Jewish cultural and social autonomy. The Committee, though it tried to represent all Jews, did not have assimilationist backing, and had difficulty getting Hasidic support.[26]

On January 17, the Concentration issued an appeal "To Our Jewish Fellow Citizens." It promised Polish support for equal rights on the basis of Polish honor, conscience, and tradition.[27] The immediate response was that a group of fifty assimilationists formed a committee to support the Concentration.[28] It is doubtful whether this had much effect on Jewish voting, but it certainly caused an uproar. The Jewish Electoral Committee, meanwhile, was in disarray. In order to gain Hasidic participation, it had weakened its platform, particularly on Jewish national rights. It had also undertaken to work with the Progressive Alliance, something which many Zionists had been wary of doing.[29]

On the surface, it might have appeared that Polish approaches to the "Jewish question" had changed for the better. The Progressive Alliance stated that it supported "full and equal rights in the whole vast sphere of human and civil rights."[30] The Concentration officially said it favored equal rights, and seemed to be courting Jewish votes.

But these changes were superficial, and in the case of the Concentration only cosmetic. Openly anti-Jewish sentiments were simultaneously multiplying in the National Democratic campaign meetings and in the party's main newspaper, *Goniec*. Friendly words from the National Democrats about the "handful of Jewish Poles" that had joined the Concentration still appeared, but these were juxtaposed with statements affirming that Poles must be masters in their own land, and the Jews no more than followers.

The thrust of their campaign thus again became that the "Jewish danger" threatened Warsaw. Dmowski stated that if the Jews had not learned their lesson in the first election, they would this time.[31] The chief National Democratic themes included: the Progressive Alliance was dominated by the Jews; the Zionists planned to control Congress Poland and turn it into Palestine; the Progressive Alliance and the Jews were cooperating with the Russians; and the "dark Jewish masses" were picking up their voting cards in greater numbers than the Poles.

The campaign continued to go poorly on the other side. The Progressive Alliance and the Jewish Committee found it difficult to work together. Świętochowski hardly campaigned, and made it clear that he had not wanted to run at all.[32] Further, *Goniec* revealed that Świętochowski and Krzywicki had illegally registered as elector-candidates in precinct VIII, where the Progressive Alliance seemed sure of victory because of its large Jewish community, rather than in the heavily Polish precincts where they actually lived. *Goniec's* comment was that this was part of a plan; if the Progressive Alliance and the Jewish Committee won a majority of electors, they would elect two Jews for the Duma because Świętochowski and Krzywicki would be automatically disqualified.[33]

By the eve of the voting, *Goniec's* banner headlines cried, "Tomorrow Warsaw must decide who is her master: We, the Poles, or the Jewish nationalists," and "SAVE WARSAW."[34]

On voting day, February 19, National Democratic gangs "ruled the streets," and there were reports of electoral abuses, threats, and violence; Krzywicki was physically attacked while visiting polling places.[35] In the general curia, the Concentration won four precincts and fifty-two electors with 53 percent of the fifty-eight thousand votes cast; the Progressive Alliance and the Jewish Committee won four heavily Jewish precincts with twenty-eight electors and 45 percent of the votes.[36] All three workers' electors were from the Bund-Social Democratic alliance. Dmowski and Nowodworski were elected.

The second Duma lasted only about three months before the government dissolved it. The third election, late in 1907, aroused little popular interest. The government had changed the voting laws to insure that liberals, the left, and non-Russians would have fewer Duma representatives. In Congress Poland the Duma delegation was cut from thirty-seven to fourteen, with two reserved for new Russian curiae in the southeast and in Warsaw.

In Warsaw the National Democrats ran almost unopposed in the general curia. Dmowski was elected to head the small Polish Circle in the Duma. Warsaw's Russian seat went to Sergei Alekseev, a local leader of the Union of the Russian People.

The Fourth Election, 1912

The third Duma, with many more Russians and conservatives and rightists than the first two, was allowed by the government to serve its full term, to the summer of 1912. In these five years there were many changes in political alignments in Congress Poland. All Polish groups were weaker than in 1906-07; government repression, factionalism, and popular apathy all had taken their toll. Socialist groups were particularly badly divided, but the National Democrats were weaker as well. Dmowski in 1909 had resigned from the Duma because of strong opposition within his own party to his policy of conciliation with the Russian government; he saw Germany as a greater threat to Polish survival. National Democracy suffered many defections as a result, including its allied worker and youth groups. One defection in 1908 took with it the daily *Goniec*. Another, in 1911, called the Secession (*Secesja*), would play a major role in the 1912 election.

Polish-Jewish political relations in Warsaw worsened in these years. The National Democrats became more consistently anti-Semitic. The ties which had existed between Polish and Jewish liberals weakened considerably. Nationalist sentiment gained greater strength in the Jewish community.

One Duma issue which came up in 1911 and had major ramifications in the 1912 election was a plan to institute urban self-government in the Kingdom. The proposal brought before the Duma would have severely limited Jewish participation. In cities in which Jews were in the majority, they could make up no more than one-fifth of the city council; in others, no more than one-tenth. The Polish Circle supported the restrictions, which caused a great deal of anger in the Jewish community. In late 1912, this issue remained unresolved.[37]

In the summer of 1912, after the third Duma completed its five year term, it was announced that voting in the general curia for the fourth Duma would take place on October 15 in Warsaw, and that the electoral college would meet three weeks later to choose the delegate from the general and workers' curiae. One significant change in voter eligibility had been made since 1907. This was the introduction of Article 57 of the general imperial election law of June 3, 1907, which had not previously been applied in Poland. By this article, small apartment renters and pensioners had to register to vote in the general curia by making a formal declaration of their intention to vote and providing documentation proving their eligibility by August 14.[38] When the government applied this article during the elections to the third Duma elsewhere in the Empire, few people registered to vote.[39] The same thing happened now in Warsaw. Only about 1,300 out of 20,000 people affected registered.[40]

In mid-August the government released information on eligible and registered voters. Even though Warsaw's population on January 1, 1912, had been estimated at 57 percent Catholic and 36 percent Jewish, 55 percent of the approximately 45,000 voters in the general curia were Jews. Jewish voters were in a majority in eight of the fifteen precincts.[41] This news came as a shock. The National Democrats' *Gazeta Warszawska* held that the Jews had cleverly responded to the rule change by organizing registration drives in key precincts; *Kurjer Warszawski* explained that there were more Poles in the groups affected by rules changes than Jews.[42] In considering how to respond, the *Kurjer* held that Poles should form a united front, including the assimilationist Jews, to oppose any separate Jewish lists and insure the election of a Polish delegate. The *Kurjer* emphasized that this arrangement would not actually constitute a compromise with the Jews, for it was in the interest of most of the Jewish as well as the Polish community to prevent a Jewish nationalist victory.[43] It was probably assumed that the assimilationists would influence the votes of many of the orthodox Jews, as had happened as recently as the elections to the *kehile* board in the spring of 1912.

However, the National Democrats rejected the idea that any sort of agreement with Jewish voters was possible on acceptable terms. In a letter of September 12 to the pianist Ignacy Paderewski, a financial backer of National Democracy, Dmowski stated, "we do not believe in an agreement with the Jews on terms that are possible for Poles, [and] we are preparing for a sharp electoral struggle with the Jews."[44] In the party's view, expressed in *Gazeta Warszawska* and elsewhere, there were only two possible lines to follow, the Polish or the Jewish; and that to advocate an agreement with any Jewish group, including the assimilationists, was to follow the Jewish line. The *Gazeta* held that the only way to combat successfully the "Jewish danger" was for all Poles to rally around National Democracy. Moreover, the *Gazeta* claimed that the Polish dailies which opposed National Democracy, specifically *Nowa Gazeta, Goniec,* and *Kurjer Poranny,* were taking their cues directly from the Jewish press.[45]

A crucial meeting took place on the evening of September 20. All major Polish non-socialist groups in the city were represented: National Democracy, the Realists, the National Democratic Secession, the Progressive Party, and the Progressive Union (*Polski Związek Postępowy*), heir of the Progressive Democrats. The goal, according to *Kurjer Warszawski,* was to insure that a Polish delegate be elected by creating a Polish united candidacy in the face of the Jewish voter majority.[46]

Party differences, however, prevented unanimity. There was too much hostility between the National Democrats and the one side, and the Secession and the progressive groups on the other. A great deal of discussion centered around the role and actions of the Polish Circle in the Duma, with the National Democrats defending it and the Secession and the progressives attacking.

The issue which eventually broke up the meeting was the "Jewish question" (ironically, the meeting was held on Yom Kippur). All speakers opposed any compromise with the Jewish nationalists. However, speakers from all parties except the National Democrats agreed that the assimilationists were, politically, Poles; therefore, working with them would not represent an unacceptable "compromise with the Jews." (The only Jewish speaker seems to have been Kazimierz Natanson. He made the point, apparently not well received, that while the bulk of the Jewish voters were willing to elect a Pole, they would only support one who favored equal rights in urban self-government for the Jews.)

Dmowski and his supporters, by contrast, held that a Polish delegate chosen with Jewish votes would represent Jewish, not Polish interests, and thus be unacceptable: "For us a candidate will be Jewish who is supported by Jews, because he will fulfill their Jewish demands—regardless of whether the candidate is a Jew or a Pole by descent."[47] Further, the assimilationists must leave the choice of the delegate up to the Poles. National Democratic spokesman Franciszek Nowodworski proposed a resolution that no party should make an electoral agreement with the Jews. He was understood to be referring to the assimilationists as well as the nationalists. Representatives of the other parties and some non-party participants refused to vote on the resolution and left the meeting. Those who supported it, chiefly National Democrats, made up about half of those who had attended.

A week later the Secession, the two progressive groups, and *Kurjer Warszawski* announced that they had formed an electoral alliance.

This bloc, the National Concentration, chose Jan Kucharzewski as its candidate for the Duma. He was an historian, lawyer, and former National Democrat who had left the party some time before. The three dailies which were strongest in their support for the Concentration were *Kurjer Warszawski, Goniec,* and *Kurjer Poranny.* There were two major goals behind its formation: to create a united Polish effort, including the assimilationists, to oppose any Jewish list; and to defeat the National Democrats, who were preparing their own campaign with Dmowski as their candidate, and were waging bitter polemical warfare with their Polish opponents. At first *Kurjer Warszawski*, in a conciliatory tone, stated that the Concentration was not directed against anyone (a reference to Dmowski), but at the same time the other papers attacked Dmowski sharply; and soon the *Kurjer* joined in the attack when it became clear that the National Democrats would not cooperate with the Concentration.[48]

Dmowski announced his candidacy a few days after Kucharzewski so that there were two competing Polish nationalist lists. Dmowski was much better known than Kucharzewski, but by the same token he had many more enemies. His name was anathema in Jewish Warsaw, and also among many Poles, including some of his former allies. The Concentration had the support of most of the Polish press, but the National Democrats remained the strongest single party.

A coalition of non-assimilationist Jewish groups, meanwhile, put forward a list of electors at the end of September, although they did not designate their own Duma candidate. Their platform was based on three resolutions proposed by Nahum Sokolow: one Duma seat from the Kingdom must be held by a Jew (this would presumably be from Łódź, where the Jewish voter majority was larger than in Warsaw); "in Warsaw a Christian Pole who supports the principle of [Jewish] equal rights must be elected;" and if these two resolutions could not be fulfilled, a "Jewish candidacy should be put forward in Warsaw."[49] The Zionists led the campaign, but the police also reported that there was some assimilationist participation.[50] Most of the Jewish press actively backed this list. The major question was whether it would win the votes of the orthodox majority of the Jewish community.

Izraelita, which bitterly opposed the nationalists and identified itself as much as possible with Polish political interests, pleaded with Jewish voters that,

> Warsaw is a Polish city! The Jews must not benefit from their accidental voting majority! They must vote for a man of tested civic virtues, for a   fervent Polish patriot! A manifestation of Jewish separatism must not be allowed to

take place.

The weekly stated that while equal rights were of great importance, this could not be the only issue on which a decision should be made. It said that while it approved of the formation of the Concentration and hoped to support its efforts, it wanted to hear Kucharzewski's views, particularly on the "Jewish question," before committing itself. An open letter from a "Group of Jewish Poles" published in the Polish press made the same general points.[51]

Socialist groups in Warsaw concentrated their efforts on the workers' curia. The PPS–Left and the Bund united into the Socialist Electoral Alliance, claiming to represent the combined interests of the city's Polish and Jewish working classes. Its platform included calls for wider democracy and civil rights, autonomy for the Kingdom, an end to ethnic and religious discrimination against both Poles and Jews, and also, in the area of specific labor issues, freedom for unions to organize, better insurance, and the eight hour working day.[52] The Social Democrats, who at this time were undergoing a schism, refused to join the alliance and ran a rival campaign.

During the campaign and in later years Dmowski maintained that at first he had not intended to be a candidate. In the 1920s he wrote,

> I did not intend at this time to take the position of delegate, because the situation in the region enjoined me to local work. However, in the presence of the provocative behavior of the Jews I put forward my candidacy in order to conduct the elections under the banner of struggle with the Jews.[53]

One of his associates, Władysław Jabłonowski, recalled that he and others had attempted to dissuade Dmowski.

> The electoral moods in Warsaw had undergone such a basic change to the disadvantage of our party, that Dmowski's chances of election were quite small. We understood this and were against the candidacy. We could not, however, knock the idea out of Dmowski's head. . . . We all attempted to persuade him not to rush ahead with his candidacy. . . . However, Dmowski would not be convinced.[54]

The National Democrats waged an aggressive campaign, and presented the "struggle with the Jews" as the central issue. They also defended the actions of the Polish Circle in the Duma; but it was the "Jewish question" into which the party's fervor went.

Gazeta Warszawska attacked all the papers supporting the Concentration. One of its main weapons was to tie its opponents to the Jews. This was also a major thrust, along with attacks directly on the

Jews, of the National Democrats' campaign meetings and literature. The Concentration was referred to as the "Jewish–Polish Concentration," and its members as "Jewish hirelings."[56] A flier read,

> Fellow countrymen! Let us swear, that if the Jews win the election, we won't buy even a groschen's worth from them! Vote for the list supporting Roman Dmowski. Down with *Kurjer Warszawski*, which serves Jewish interests![56]

In late September the party began to publish a daily which quickly gained a large readership. This was the *Gazeta Poranna 2 grosze*, the "Dwugroszówka," which proclaimed, "We accept advertising only from Christians," and exhorted its readers to "buy only from Christians." Aimed at Warsaw's working and lower middle classes, the daily promulgated a harsh brand of anti–Semitism in large print and easily accessible style. As regards the election in the workers' curia, the daily bannered, "Workers! Don't elect Jewish flunkeys!"[57]

The bitterness of this campaign led the daily *Słowo*, controlled by the Realists, to state with disapproval that the National Democrats had organized their campaign "under the banner of militant anti–Semitism, with the obvious goal of gaining victory for Dmowski at any cost, and of mobilizing the whole society to a struggle with the Jews, to a furious struggle which would stop at nothing."[58]

Dmowski himself was praised abundantly in the National Democratic press. Kucharzewski was not attacked nearly as much as the groups and periodicals supporting him. Instead, the National Democrats depicted him as a political lightweight, as a bookish soul and inexperienced politician, in contrast to Dmowski's practical experience. Indeed, Kucharzewski was placed on the list of National Democratic elector–candidates, with *Gazeta Warszawska* stating that his views were acceptable.[59] Kucharzewski apparently never commented publicly on this.

In contrast with the directness of the National Democratic campaign, the Concentration lacked real unity or a consistent program. This was partly the result of the difficulties of a coalition campaign in a country where electoral politics were a novelty. Further, the Concentration was made up of several groups united chiefly by their opposition to the National Democrats and the Jewish nationalists, and Kucharzewski was indeed politically inexperienced, a little known compromise candidate who apparently came across as an intelligent man but not a skillful leader.

The papers supporting the Concentration continued to attack Dmowski. *Kurjer Warszawski* claimed that the plan of Dmowski's campaign was to split the Polish vote and give the victory to the

Jews, in order to gain support for his own extreme anti-Jewish views. He was also attacked as a demagogue with an exalted opinion of his personal place in Polish politics.[60]

In his campaign speeches Kucharzewski tried to downplay the "Jewish question," and instead to emphasize the issue of the role that Polish Duma delegates should play. However, the National Democrats' constant pounding on this issue forced Kucharzewski to deal with it more than he evidently would have liked. Even though willingness to work with the assimilationists had been a primary factor dividing the Concentration from the National Democrats, the specific views expressed by Kucharzewski on the "Jewish question," along with other developments in the Concentration's campaign, alienated real or potential Jewish support. Kucharzewski's views seem contradictory, and deserve careful examination.

In an interview published on October 2 in *Nowa Gazeta*, which had many Jewish readers, Kucharzewski stated, "I am a supporter of the *principle of Jewish equal rights*." On the specific issue of urban self-government, however, he felt that limitations would have to be put on Jewish participation. Without this, since Jews made up a majority in many Polish cities, they would be able to control the institutions of self-government. He said that this would be an unacceptable "privilege" for the Jews, and not "equal rights" at all: "the seizure of urban administration by the Jews would be tantamount to the removal of the Poles from the organization of their own economic and cultural life."[61] On a broader issue, he supported the abolition of the Pale of Settlement.

Kucharzewski gave his most important speech on October 8 at the Philharmonic Hall.[62] The greater part of the speech consisted of comments on Polish representation in the Duma. He began his discussion of the "Jewish question" as follows.

> I must touch upon the Jewish question, which is so extremely difficult and so embittered. This question presents itself today in an infinitely more difficult form than in Wielopolski's day. Too great a host of Jews has settled in our country. Moreover, these hundreds of thousands live, in the great majority, their own separate collective life, or adopt culture from someone else. Of course, sincerely assimilated individuals are members of the Polish nation.

He then stated that the Jewish role in the Polish economy was too strong, and therefore, "From the Polish side a systematic and energetic campaign is needed, to raise the competence of the nation and to support the Polish element in the economic sphere." He then condemned anti-Jewish acts and demagogy. One part of this speech was seen by many Jews as a piece of egregious insult; he took an imaginery tour of Warsaw with a Jewish companion, contrasting his own sentiments as a patriotic Pole on seeing the city's historical sites, with the ignorant and insensitive ones of his companion.[63]

On some general points, Kucharzewski's statements should have satisfied many Jewish voters, if certainly not all. He condemned anti-Semitic acts and demogogy, supported the abolition of the Pale (which, he pointed out, was an important reason behind heavy Jewish inmigration into the Kingdom), and supported Jewish equal rights in "principle." On a number of other points, including more specific issues, he alienated Jewish voters, among them assimilationists. His views appeared similar to Dmowski's, if less harshly expressed: the comment that "too great a host of Jews" had come into the Kingdom; promotion of the Polish position in the economy in the face of Jewish economic strength, which must have come perilously close to sounding like a call for a boycott; and support for limitations on Jewish participation in urban self-government. His views seemed hypocritical, or at the very least poorly developed and ingenuous.

Other developments in the Concentration's campaign also hurt it among Jewish voters. Groups of assimilationists who decided not to support the Concentration gave several reasons in open letters published on October 12 and 13 in *Kurjer Warszawski* and in *Nowa Gazeta*: Kucharzewski's position on urban self-government went counter to the principle of equal rights; the Concentration's lists of candidate-electors did not include any Jews; it was not allowing the assimilationists to participate in its campaign efforts outside the Jewish community; and the theme of the "Jewish danger" had been taken up by Concentration elements as well as by the National Democrats. *Izraelita* also stated that it could not support Kucharzewski, because it saw no "basic difference" between his views and Dmowski's. Meanwhile, the Jewish list stated that its electors would never support Kucharzewski, and also rejected a proposal to put forward a Jewish Duma delegate; they resolved instead to back some other Polish Christian.[64]

As a result of the assimilationists' withdrawal from the Concentration's campaign, *Kurjer Warszawski*, normally sympathetic to them, accused them of "muddying the waters," and of playing into the hands of both the National Democrats and the Jewish nationalists. *Gazeta Warszawska* claimed that it was part of a well-orchestrated Jewish plan to split the Polish vote.[65]

How complete the assimilationists' withdrawal was remains unclear, since they did not make up an organized group or party, and there were statements that the withdrawal concerned only active campaigning, not voting.[66] At about the same time, Kucharzewski picked up some support. The Realists gave him qualified support, calling on voters to choose the more conservative figures among the elector-candidates pledged to him.[67] Also, *Nowa Gazeta*, without much enthusiasm, said that it would support him and the Concentration, in order to defeat Dmowski.[68]

There was considerable maneuvering in the last few days before the voting. After the assimilationists' withdrawal, there was an appeal from some Concentration elements to form joint slates representing all Polish groups, from National Democrats through progressives and assimilationists, in those ethnically mixed precincts wherein the Jewish list could win with a plurality if the Polish vote were split. The National Democrats rejected the idea.[69] At about the same time, a "Democratic list" was announced, apparently first in the Yiddish daily *Der Fraynd*.[70] It was a non-party list made up chiefly of Jews, although it also included Ludwik Krzywicki.

The voting was held on October 15.

From the early morning the rain poured down in sheets, casting over the whole city an atmosphere of strange languor. Before the voting places small groups of people gathered, with umbrellas in their hands, debating without heat or animation. Whole masses of ephemeral election literature were distributed, but the citizens took them sluggishly, glancing with sleepy eyes at the multicolored cards and bright placards.[71]

Only about half of the eligible voters turned out. The voting was a victory for the Jewish list, which won eight of the fifteen precincts and gained forty-six electors; the Concentration won five precincts for twenty-three electors, and the National Democrats got eleven electors by winning in two precincts. The Jewish list had about 40 percent of the 23,000 votes cast in the general curia, the Concentration 30 percent, the National Democrats 27 percent, and 3 percent went to the Democratic list. Kucharzewski was among the winning electors, so he still had a chance at the Duma seat; Dmowski had lost, and was therefore out of the running.[72] Of the three electors who had already been chosen from the workers' curia, two were from the Social Democrats and the third from the PPS-Bund alliance. The latter was Eugeniusz Jagiełło, a political nonentity from the PPS-Left.[73]

Both the Jewish and the Polish electors soon made their positions known. On October 21, Kucharzewski said that he would make no "open or *secret* commitments" to the Jews to get their votes. On the next day, it was announced that the Concentration and National Democratic electors would all support his candidacy.[74] Presumably these two events were connected. The Jewish electors reaffirmed that they would not support him.

Kurjer Warszawski and *Gazeta Warszawska* spent the first few days after the voting blaming the Polish defeat on each other. These attacks largely ceased when the united Polish nationalist bloc of electors was formed. Henceforth, both *Gazeta Warszawska* and the "Dwugroszówka" paid little attention to the election. The former took the role of detached observer, prepared to say "we told you so" concerning Jewish acts and motives; the latter concentrated on attacking the Jews directly.

In the three weeks between the voting and the actual election of the delegate, the tone of *Kurjer Warszawski*, normally very low key, was angry. At first it expressed the hope that enough of the Jewish electors would support Kucharzewski to give him the victory. As it became clear that this was unlikely, the paper's tone grew harsher. It held that Polish society was united as never before, that the question of the delegate was for the Poles, not the Jews to decide, and that they had already settled it in favor of Kucharzewski. Neither the election of a Jewish delegate, nor the choice of a Polish socialist with Jewish votes (as was already rumored might happen) would be acceptable.[75]

One development in late October that caused a furor came when *Haynt* interviewed Russian Kadet Party leaders in St. Petersburg. Pavel Miliukov, Ivan Petrunkevich, Fedor Rodichev, and Maksim Vinaver (the last by birth a Warsaw Jew) stated that the Jewish and Polish electors must compromise on a liberal Pole who would support Jewish equal rights. By November 4, Vinaver had gone further and added that, since no Polish nationalist elector had been found who would make this commitment, the Jewish electors should support the socialist Jagiełło.[76]

On October 31, a long statement from the Jewish electors appeared in *Kurjer Warszawski*. Maintaining that Kucharzewski's program was "hostile to the interests of the Jewish population . . . and threatening in its consequences for the whole country," the electors stated that they could not allow his election. The statement implied that the Jewish electors looked to compromise with the Poles on a Polish delegate who would back Jewish equal rights, although no names were mentioned. The last paragraph read:

> Convinced of the necessity of joint action by the entire population of the country, we wish to believe that the "National Concentration," which emerged victorious from the contest

between the Polish groups, will not wish to adhere to the ruinous method of acting, "all or nothing." Only the uncompromising stand of the "National Concentration" can paralyze our good will and dictate to us the obligation of electing a candidate on our own and on our own responsibility.[77]

This statement was presumably intended as a moderate but firm call for compromise; however, it only inflamed the situation. The *Kurjer* stated,

> The proclamation of the Warsaw Jewish electors is, most clearly, the fruit of the intoxication which has swept over the Jewish nationalists because of their accidental winnings of a majority of the lists of electors in Warsaw and in Łódź.

The paper reaffirmed its support for Kucharzewski, and in particular for his stand on the urban self–government issue. Its comments included:

> If the Jews were opposing some sort of *party* candidacy, we would still be able somehow to understand it. . . . But today the Jews are opposing *all of Polish society*. They are talking about separate Jewish interests, about the obligation to fulfill them *in defiance of* Polish interests, and they say this now, when they certainly have nothing to gain. *They are making a demonstration*. They wish to harm the Poles at any cost, even though they will gain nothing from the election of their own delegate. They wish to show their strength . . .
>
> In language understandable to the whole world, this is called a declaration of war.[78]

During these weeks *Izraelita* expressed its views in alarmed tones. It stated that for the Jewish electoral majority to elect a Jew or even a Pole whom it found acceptable would be unjust, because the Jews were after all a minority in the Kingdom and in the city itself, and dangerous, because of the escalating scale of attacks on the Jews from the Polish parties and press. The key issue at hand, according to the weekly and also to the authors of open letters from "Groups of Jewish Poles" which appeared in Polish newspapers at the start of November, was internal peace in the Kingdom. *Izraelita* almost begged the Jewish electors to abstain:

> Being unable to give active support to a candidate favoring restrictions on Jews in self–government, let the electors, in the name of reason and justice, resolve *not* to prevent the election of a delegate whom a significant majority of the people of Warsaw wishes to have.[79]

Nowa Gazeta took a similar position, and published letters from "Groups of Jewish Poles" to the same effect from many cities of the Kingdom.[80]

The actual election took two days, November 7 and 8, and several rounds of voting. On the first day, Kucharzewski received the votes of the thirty-four Concentration and National Democratic electors. The Jewish electors split their votes among Jagiełło, Aleksander Lipsztadt (one of the Jewish electors), and three Concentration electors who were known to be supporters of Jewish equal rights. The last three all refused the candidacy. The two Social Democratic electors from the workers' curia did not take part at all.

By the time the Jewish electors and the Socialist Electoral Alliance had made an agreement whereby the former would vote for Jagiełło, the only Polish candidate willing to support unequivocally Jewish equal rights. On November 8, he was elected with the votes of forty-three Jewish electors, while the thirty-four Polish nationalists and two Jews opposed him. Lipsztadt had thirty-six Jewish votes for him, but all other votes opposed.[81] Bernard Singer, who was outside the city hall when the last round of voting took place, described the aftermath in his memoirs.

> Suddenly there was a shout inside the city hall. I saw the Secession elector and friend of the Jews, the noted surgeon Ignacy Baranowski, who was still shouting and waving his cane. I understand easily from his shouts that thanks only to the Jewish electors a representative of the left had gotten into the Duma.
>
> The Jews, silently, not looking around, with lowered heads, came down the steps. The expressions on their faces looked as though it were the Day of Atonement.
>
> The news of the election result ran quickly through the city; two hours later the first windows had been broken in the Jewish stores on Elektoralna Street.[82]

Kurjer Warszawski promptly denounced Jagiełło as the "Jewish delegate:" "Mr. Jagiełło received the seat from the hands of the Jewish nationalists. He will, then, be only their delegate." The reaction of this cautious and moderate newspaper seemed particularly ominous for the future of Polish-Jewish relations.

> Today's election by the Jews is the most flagrant demonstration imaginable. . . . Voting for Mr. Jagiełło, the Jews attempted to show that our national will means nothing here, that they can impose their will upon us, that they

will seize the first opportunity to give to the Polish nation a challenge to battle.

Let it be so. We stand in the presence of an accomplished fact.

We regard today's election as a symptom. The concrete fact is less important than what it represents. We have lost our seat despite the fact that we made the greatest efforts in order to save it for the national cause. In exchange we have gained a clear understanding of an important aspect of internal affairs, the knowledge of a danger which stands before us; we have recognized the features of internal enemies.

The Jews' triumph is momentary. We have a profound conviction that the Jews will pay dearly for it. Society must now begin quiet consideration, far from emotional outbursts, of systematic means of defense against enemies and means of struggle with a separatist and dangerous element.[82]

In further statements the *Kurjer* declared that separatism led by Russian Jews dominated the Jewish community, the Polish-born Jews as much as the Litvaks. It claimed that the whole election had been planned carefully by the Jews, and directed by "some Jew from Petersburg," presumably Vinaver.[84] Similarly, *Gazeta Warszawska* blamed Vinaver and the Kadets for giving the deciding word: "Who will be the delegate from our capital has been dictated from Petersburg for the first time."[85] The *Kurjer* stated that the assimilationists had revealed themselves to be a "*quantité negligeable*," and that they were to blame for the Polish defeat, because they could not or would not mobilize the Jewish community to oppose the Jewish nationalists.[86] The popular *Tygodnik Illustrowany* claimed that the assimilationists

either proved to be completely powerless in the election campaign, or also, were, on the quiet, in solidarity with the plan of the Jewish nationalists, which has ruined for a long time to come the possibility of any sort of Polish-Jewish understanding.[87]

Earlier criticism of the National Democrats was forgotten.

While the attacks by the *Kurjer* and other moderate Polish newspapers soon lessened in number and intensity, perhaps because of complaints by Jewish readers and advertisers, the National Democratic campaign against the Jews gained. The program of economic and social boycott of the Jews, which the National Democrats had used as a threat, won wide support in Polish society; the campaign's slogan was, *swój do swego po swoje* (stick to your own kind).

Besides "don't buy from Jews," the advocates of the boycott tried to limit or eliminate Jewish participation in Polish and regional organizational life. For example, the Polish leadership of the Warsaw City Credit Association (*Towarzystwo Kredytowe Miejskie*) initially tried to cut the share of Jewish representatives to 20 percent, and subsequently to remove them entirely, but the Russian authorities prevented this, stating that it was a matter for the State Duma to resolve. There were splits in the Association for Polish Culture (*Towarzystwo Kultury Polskiej*) over the issue of Jewish participation. Another part of the boycott campaign was that Polish students would stand outside Jewish-owned stores and harass shoppers. Certain acts of violence against individual Jews that took place in this period in various towns, including arson and murder, were laid to the boycott. The campaign was most intensive in Warsaw and the other large cities of Congress Poland.[88]

The central instrument of the National Democratic efforts was the popular daily *Gazeta Poranna 2 grosze*, which by the end of 1912 was regularly printing editions of 40,000 copies—a "quantity unheard of for a Polish newspaper in Warsaw."[89] It gave a great deal of space to covering the boycott, including lists of Jewish-owned firms, other companies with Jewish partners or investors, and the like. The daily expanded from four to eight pages and was filled to overflowing with advertising.

While National Democracy led the boycott, it was not alone. Former positivist writers such as Aleksander Świętochowski and Andrzej Niemojewski published some of the harshest anti-Jewish attacks. *Prawda*, once an outpost of pro-assimilationist positivism, and Świętochowski's newer journal *Kultura Polska* [Polish Culture] published pieces attacking the Jews.[90] Among Catholic leaders supporting the boycott was Father Godlewski of the Christian Workers' Union (*Chrześcijański Związek Robotniczy*) and the journal *Przegląd Katolicki* [Catholic Review].[91]

The Russian authorities rarely involved themselves or interfered in the boycott's excesses. The *oberpolitseimeister* wrote that the election had led to a "significant worsening of Polish–Jewish relations, not only in Warsaw but in the whole region." He went on to note in his report for 1912 that the boycott "continues to gain strength and will not soon die out," and that "almost all Polish periodicals have taken on an anti-Semitic coloring."[92]

The economic results of the boycott campaign are impossible to evaluate with any certainty. The chief of the local *Okhrana* (secret police) reported in 1913 that it had "ruined mostly the impoverished Jewish population."[93] There seems no likelihood that more prosperous parts of the community suffered any direct economic harm. While the "don't buy from the Jews" side of the boycott won wide vocal support, it may have been honored more in the breach than in the observance; and in any case, the place of Jews in commerce and trade as so well established in Poland that, regardless of the progress Poles were making in this period, it could hardly have helped "Polish" at the expense of "Jewish" trade in such a short time.

There was little direct and open Polish opposition to the boycott. Some conservatives and socialists condemned or spoke against it, but they normally treated it as a rather minor issue. The great Polish linguistics scholar Jan Baudouin de Courtenay came to the city to speak against the campaign.[94] But the voices of boycott opponents were rarely heard above the attacks of the National Democrats and other proponents.

There was unhappiness among the Polish left about the electoral outcome, despite its success in getting a Polish socialist into the Duma. One member of the PPS–Left, Roman Jabłonowski, recalled:

> We accepted with great reserve the accidental election of Jagiełło as delegate from Warsaw. . . . The fact that the socialists from the SDKPiL and the PPS–Left had not achieved unity for the elections was for us the basic matter, harmful and contrary to the postulates of unity. The question of the anti–Semitic uproar which had arisen during the elections was something secondary.[95]

The Social Democrats claimed that socialist parties could not legitimately accept bourgeois votes in such a fashion. Jagiełło was admitted to the Social Democratic faction in the Duma with Menshevik support over Bolshevik opposition.[96]

The true importance of the boycott campaign lay in the area of ethnic political relations. To a significant degree, the National Democrats used it as a tool to recoup their political losses. Writing some years later, Dmowski noted cynically that after the election, "The atmosphere cleared up right away."[97] National Democracy continued to find the "Jewish danger" a useful rallying cry and weapon against both Polish and Jewish opponents after 1912. They had, indeed, lost this Duma seat, and Dmowski himself had suffered a major personal defeat. Yet National Democracy still dominated Polish representation in the Duma, and remained the strongest Polish nationalist group in the Kingdom. Further, the party could claim that its extremist view of the "Jewish danger" had been vindicated; Polish divisions had opened the way to a Jewish electoral majority in the greatest of Polish cities, and Jewish political leaders had sent a socialist to the Duma, depriving the city of Polish representation in that body. (The Russian seat went, as before, to Sergei Alekseev of the Union of the Russian People.) The Polish nationalist elements which had opposed Dmowski and the National Democrats before October 15, 1912, after November 8 essentially came around to the party's views on the "Jewish question."

The most important single aspect of the election campaign of 1912 and the subsequent boycott was that the level of polemics in the "Jewish question" was sharply raised, and anti-Semitism became a more significant factor than before in the Polish nationalist movement in Congress Poland. After 1912, it was possible to speak of an emerging anti-Semitic consensus among the broad Polish nationalist movement in the Kingdom, including the National Democrats, the progressive parties, and many non-party nationalists; in sum, those who had supported Jan Kucharzewski and Roman Dmowski alike.

Frank Golczewski, in his clear analysis of the boycott, notes that it also had an economic side, an attempt by Polish businessmen to use political strife to their own advantage. Yet he also states that the greatest significance of the boycott was in the rising tensions between Poles and Jews.[98]

Conclusions

In the last years before World War I there were crucial changes in Polish attempts to answer the "Jewish question" in Congress Poland. These changes were evident in the State Duma campaigns and results, which in their turn also led to the hardening of lines and the intensification of feelings. Tension and conflict became the essential features of Polish-Jewish political relations in the city.

Most Polish nationalist groups, despite their disagreements on many points, were coming to regard the Jews as politically and economically negative factors in Poland, and moreover as a huge and unabsorbable element. The idea of a separate, nationalist, politically mobilized Jewish community in Poland was perceived as deeply threatening. National Democracy won notoriety as the most anti-Semitic party, but more moderate and liberal elements, which had not seemed explicitly anti-Semitic before, were also coming to the same conclusion that the Jews were an alien and threatening force. Further, views became more extreme between 1906–07 and 1912. National Democracy, whether for immediate tactical or ideological reasons, became more consistently hostile to the Jews, no longer displaying even the limited willingness to make use of the assimilationist Jews that it had shown in the campaign before the second Duma election. Other nationalist elements, specifically those that supported

Kucharzewski in 1912, promulgated views that turned out to be not much more generous than National Democracy's, despite the fact that they counted on assimilationist support and evidently felt betrayed by the negative assimilationist response to Kucharzewski before the voting on October 15.

Particularly striking was the shift in the attitude of Polish progressive parties. The Progressive Democrats went through the 1906–07 elections in alliance with Jewish groups, included Polish liberals who had supported the Jewish assimilationists for decades, and did well only in heavily Jewish precincts. It seemed conceivable that Polish progressives might help to bridge the gap between Polish and Jewish political groups. By 1912, however, they had pulled away from their former Jewish assimilationist allies, and the potential Polish progressive–Jewish assimilationist bridge was no longer possible. Further to the left on the Polish political spectrum, socialist groups remained open to Jews (indeed, they included many leaders from assimilationist families), but these groups saw class struggle or Polish independence as their main goals, more important than damping ethnic conflict. It also became clear in these years that the Jewish assimilationists did not speak for most of the Jewish community, and could not serve as an effective bridge, either. Indeed, nationalist and autonomist sentiments were gaining strength in Jewish Warsaw, including among members of thoroughly assimilated families.

Study of the 1906–12 elections shows that the "Jewish question" in Polish politics in early twentieth century Warsaw meant both the general problem of how Poles should deal with the Jewish presence, and more specific issues such as equal rights for Jews and the voice that Jews should have in the politics of Poland and of its cities.

This discussion has examined specific events rather than the general causes of Polish–Jewish conflict. Important general factors were the centuries of living side by side, yet alien to each other; traditional tensions and conflicts between the two groups; the rising anti-Semitism of the time in all Eastern and Central Europe; a significant history of anti-Semitism in Poland; the generally repressive and specifically anti-Polish and anti-Jewish policies and atmosphere of the Russian Empire; the rise of competing mass nationalist movements, a development which profoundly changed both Polish and Jewish politics; the economic and professional competition of particular social groups; Polish fears and frustrations after a century of foreign rule, as well as in the face of the increased social visibility and political assertiveness of the Jews. All these were significant.

But specific and concrete political choices were also important. By no means the least important part of the "Jewish question" was the use by the National Democrats of the Jews as a weapon against their more moderate or liberal Polish opponents. National Democracy's leaders, particularly Roman Dmowski, chose the Jews as their chief target, and also as their weapon against more liberal Poles. National Democracy fanned the flames of ethnic conflict in Warsaw far higher than they would otherwise have risen. Other Polish nationalists ended up joining the developing anti–Semitic consensus of 1912–14 as well, laying the groundwork for the harsh anti–Semitism of interwar Poland.

Conclusions

Warsaw, Varshe, Varshava: the historic Polish capital; the greatest Jewish center in Europe; the third city of the Russian Empire. Warsaw was all of these.

In the decades before World War I, Warsaw experienced enormous growth, intensive socioeconomic change, and a significant degree of political mobilization. It was a multi-ethnic city, largely Polish and Jewish in its composition and heritage, but under repressive Russian rule. The two resident ethnic groups followed mostly divergent paths of communal development. Few leaders recognized any significant commonality of interests between them; separation and separatism on both sides prevailed in most spheres of life.

Much of the responsibility for this must be placed on the Polish nationalist leadership. Chauvinistic nationalism with anti-Semitism as one of its chief components became an important element in the Polish nationalist movement. This was true especially in the case of the influential National Democratic Party. But as study of the State Duma elections and their aftermath reveals, a consensus was developing among the broader Polish nationalist leadership centered in Warsaw that the Jews were an alien and inimical element that must be consciously opposed in the political, economic, and cultural spheres. This consensus included progressive groups and others who opposed National Democracy and its leading figure, Roman Dmowski, as well as among National Democracy itself.

As a community, Warsaw remained deeply split along ethnic lines. Boundaries between the Poles and the Jews were, to be sure, shifting, chiefly as a result of Jewish acculturation and assimilation. More Jews were using the Polish language, and moving away from traditional Jewish ways of life and belief; Polish culture and patriotism appealed to a significant section of the Jewish community. But this Polish orientation had competition. German culture was very influential among the "enlightened" segment of Warsaw's Jews until the late nineteenth century. Russian culture was gaining strength by the early years of the twentieth century, due partly to the "Litvak invasion," but also due to Russification and the opportunities that learning Russian might offer. Still, the greatest challenge to traditional Jewish life came from within the Jewish community, as Jewish nationalist, socialist, and other primarily secularist movements developed. Many Jews were experiencing a significant degree of acculturation with respect to the non-Jewish ethnic communities of the region, without, however, undergoing identificational assimilation.

The larger Polish and Jewish populations and their leaders remained essentially alien to, and separate from, one another. Jewish acculturation and assimilation, oppression of both Poles and Jews at the hands of the Russian authorities, and daily contact and intensive socioeconomic change did not lead to a sense of shared community, nor to a significant weakening of ethnic boundaries. Residential patterns, economic activities, politics, and the popular press were among the factors that served to emphasize and exacerbate ethnic distinctiveness and conflict in the city. Indeed, instead of a "melting pot" effect encouraging the assimilation of diverse groups under the pressures of intensive change, "the accompaniments of economic development—increased social mobilization and communication—appear to have increased ethnic tensions and to [have been] conducive to separatist demands."[1] Warsaw represents a case in which the chief result of change was conflict rather than accommodation. It shows the importance of examining the continued strength and significance of ethnic boundaries, which persist regardless of extensive contact, mobility, and social and economic change.[2]

This was an era of the intensive politicization of ethnicity in Eastern Europe. Ethnic political relations worsened profoundly in these decades in Warsaw. This was in part a result of the strongly anti-Polish and anti-Jewish atmosphere and policies of the Russian Empire, which served to encourage ethnic conflict and competing nationalisms; and also the general rise of anti-Semitic politics all over Central and Eastern Europe. But it also had specific local causes. A significant history of Polish anti-Semitic activity set the stage, and the choices of influential Polish nationalist leaders—most obviously, again, National Democracy's leadership in 1905–14—insured that anti-Jewish sentiment and agitation would play an important part in the Polish nationalist movement.

During the 1912 election campaign, candidate Jan Kucharzewski caused a furor in Jewish Warsaw by a speech in which he took an imaginary tour of Warsaw with a Jewish companion. Anger over this statement came from assimilationist as well as non-assimilationist Jewish sources. His comments, which may well have been a significant factor in costing him the election, have the feel of casual throwaway

Conclusions 109

lines at the end of a long speech. No doubt Kucharzewski himself was surprised at the response. But particularly instructive were the words of Isaac Leib Peretz, who said in a Jewish campaign meeting that the Jews had a part to play in Warsaw, just as did the Poles, and would also fight to lead the city in new paths.[3] This was, perhaps, the crux of the matter; the question of whose city Warsaw was, and would become. Jews felt it was their city as well as the Poles', and that they had the right to be involved in deciding its future. But important elements of the Polish nationalist leadership rejected this view.

In the mid-1970s, before the recent rise in interest in Polish-Jewish studies began, the distinguished Polish historian Stefan Kieniewicz wrote of pre-1914 Warsaw: "Today's generation can imagine only with difficulty the sharpness of the conflicts of the time—in an epoch, when out of every five citizens of Warsaw, two were Jews, [and] three were Christians. . ."[4]

An understatement at the time, it is still one today, at the end of the 1980s. but there has definitely been progress in research in Poland as well as in Israel, North America, and Western Europe, which is helping us to reconstruct more clearly the Warsaw of a century ago.

WARSAW BEFORE THE FIRST WORLD WAR

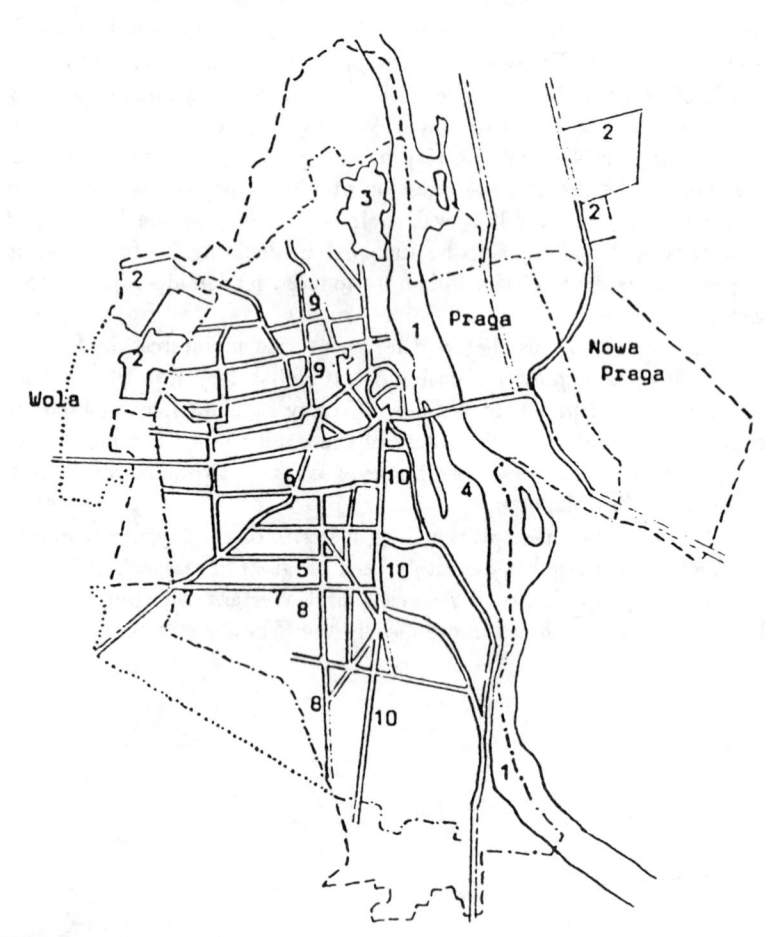

KEY

—·—· 1864 boundaries
——— Areas added 1887
···· Areas added 1900
1. Vistula River
2. Cemetaries
3. Citadel
4. Powiśle
5. Warsaw-Vienna Station
6. Grzybów Square
7. Jerozolimskie Avenue
8. Marszałkowska Street
9. Nalewki Street
10. Krakowskie Przedmieście/Nowy Świat/Ujazdowskie Avenue

Notes

Notes to Introduction

[1] The most important recent Polish work is Stefan Kieniewicz, *Warszawa w latach 1795-1914* (Warsaw, 1976), vol. 3 of the series *Dzieje Warszawy*. Early major surveys were: A. Załęski, et al., "Warszawa," *Słownik geograficzny Królestwa Polskiego i innych krajów słowiańskich* (Warsaw, 1880-1904); and Stefan Dziewulski and Henryk Radziszewski, *Warszawa*, 2 vols. (Warsaw, 1913-15). The multivolume series *Studia warszawskie*, which appeared in twenty-five volumes in 1968-79, is a mine of valuable articles. *Rocznik Warszawski* regularly publishes information on Polish "Varsaviana" studies. Older reviews of works on the history of Warsaw are, Stanisław Herbst, "Historia Warszawy: stan i potrzeby badań," *Rocznik Warszawski*,1 (1960), 8-34; and Juliusz W. Gomulicki, "Trzysta lat książki o Warszawie (1643-1944)," in *Z dziejów książki i bibliotek w Warszawie*, ed. Stanisław Tazbir (Warsaw, 1961), pp. 130-202. The main work on the Jewish community, covering up to the 1890s, remains Jacob Shatzky, *Geshikhte fun yidn in Varshe*, 3 vols. (New York, 1947-53). An older, interesting work is Hilary Nussbaum, *Szkice historyczne z życia żydów w Warszawie od pierwszych śladów pobytu ich w tem mieście do chwili obecnej* (Warsaw, 1881). Studies in English of Warsaw's history in this period include my Ph.D. dissertation, "Political and Social Change in Warsaw from the January 1863 Insurrection to the First World War: Polish Politics and the 'Jewish Question,' " University of Michigan, 1981; and my "Warsaw: Poles and Jews in a Conquered City," in *The City in Late Imperial Russia*, ed. Michael F. Hamm (Bloomington, Ind., 1986), pp. 122-51. Edward D. Wynot continues the city's history through the interwar period in his *Warsaw between the World Wars: Profile of the Capital City in a Developing Land, 1918-1939* (Boulder, Colo., 1983). The best recent surveys in English of Polish history in the partitions era are Piotr Wandycz, *The Lands of Partitioned Poland, 1795-1918* (Seattle, Wash., 1974); and R. F. Leslie, et al., *The History of Poland since 1863* (Cambridge, Eng., 1980).

² Polish literature on the "Jewish question" is a vast and still largely uncharted area. It was one of the most important ethnic issues in Congress Poland, and it permeated many spheres of public life. For orientation, the reader can consult Pawel Korzec, *Juifs en Pologne: la question juive pendant l'entre-deux-guerres* (Paris, 1980), pp. 21–49; Frank Golczewski, *Polnisch-jüdische Beziehungen 1881–1922: Eine Studie zur Geschichte des Antisemitismus in Osteuropa* (Wiesbaden, 1981); and pp. 175–82 of Gershon David Hundert and Gershon Bacon, *The Jews in Poland and Russia: Bibliographical Essays* (Bloomington, Ind., 1984). Books on Jewish history in the Russian Empire have little to say on events in Congress Poland, an unfortunate omission. The study of the history of the Jews of Congress Poland is, however, a rapidly growing field, thanks in large part to such efforts as the series of conferences on Poles and Jews begun at Columbia University in 1983, and the journals *Gal-Ed: On the History of the Jews in Poland* (published at Tel Aviv University since 1973); and *Polin: A Journal of Polish-Jewish Studies*, (published in Oxford since 1986). A recent work is Michael J. Ochs, "St. Petersburg and the Jews of Russian Poland, 1862–1905," Ph. D. dissertation, Harvard University, 1986.

³ In recent years there have been many important western studies of individual cities in the Russian Empire and Eastern Europe before World War I, including: James H. Bater, *St. Petersburg: Industrialization and Change* (London and Montreal, 1976); Gary B. Cohen, *The Politics of Ethnic Survival: Germans in Prague, 1861–1914* (Princeton, N.J., 1981); Marsha L. Rosenblit, *The Jews of Vienna, 1867–1914: Assimilation and Identity* (Albany, N.Y., 1983); Joseph Bradley, *Muzhik and Muscovite: Urbanization in Late Imperial Russia* (Berkeley, Cal., 1985); Steven J. Zipperstein, *The Jews of Odessa: A Cultural History, 1794–1881* (Stanford, Cal., 1985); Patricia Herlihy, *Odessa: A History, 1794–1914* (Cambridge, Mass., 1986); and two very important collections edited by Michael F. Hamm, the aforementioned *The City in Late Imperial Russia*, as well as *The City in Russian History* (Lexington, Ky., 1976).

Notes to Chapter 1

¹ Major articles dealing with the early years of Warsaw include, Aleksander Gieysztor, Stanisław Herbst, and Eugeniusz Szwankowski, "Kształty Warszawy," *Biuletyn Historii Sztuki i Kultury*, 9, no. 1–2 (1947), 148–210, and Aleksander Gieysztor, "Początki

życia miejskiego nad środkową Wisłą i geneza Warszawy," *Rocznik Warszawski*, 7 (1966), 45–50.

[2] On the 1792 count, see Samuel Szymkiewicz, *Warszawa na przełomie XVIII i XIX wieku w świetle pomiarów i spisów* (Warsaw, 1959). The census counted 81,000 people, but scholars have revised the totals to 98–116,000. Andrzej Zahorski, *Warszawa za Sasów i Stanisław Augusta* (Warsaw, 1970), covers the eighteenth century.

[3] Aleksandr Shcherbatov, *General-fel'dmarshal Kniaz' Paskevich: ego zhizn' i dieiatel'nost*, supplement to vol. 5 (St. Petersburg, 1896), 284.

[4] Kieniewicz, *Warszawa 1795–1914*, pp. 33–35 and 108–12, summarizes data on Warsaw's population from the 1790s to the 1860s. Załęski, et al., "Warszawa," *Słownik geograficzny*, XIII, 24, presents data on the population in 1864.

[5] Emanuel Ringelblum, *Żydzi w Warszawie: część pierwsza, od czasów najdawniejszych do ostatniego wygnania w roku 1527* (Warsaw, 1932), remains an important work for the history of the Jews in medieval Warsaw. See also the first volume of Shatzky, *Varshe*. Bernard D. Weinryb, *The Jews of Poland: A Social and Economic History of the Jewish Community from 1100 to 1800* (Philadelphia, 1973), is a very important study. On the Jews in eighteenth century Warsaw, see Artur Eisenbach, "Żydzi warszawscy i sprawa żydowska w XVIII wieku," *Warszawa w XVIII wieku*, fasc. 3, *Studia warszawskie*, vol. 22 (Warsaw, 1975), pp. 229–98.

[6] Artur Eisenbach, *Kwestia równouprawnienia Żydów w Królestwie Polskim* (Warsaw, 1972), is the most important study of the Jews in Congress Poland up to 1862.

[7] Adam Wein, "Żydzi poza rewirem żydowskim w Warszawie (1809-1862)," *Biuletyn Żydowskiego Instytutu Historycznego*, no. 41 (1962), pp. 59–60.

[8] Artur Eisenbach, et al., eds., *Żydzi a powstanie styczniowe: Materiały i dokumenty* (Warsaw, 1963), pp. 77–82.

[9] See Edward C. Thaden, with the collaboration of Marianna Foster Thaden, *Russia's Western Borderlands, 1710–1870* (Princeton, N.J., 1984); and S. J.Zyzniewski, "Russian Policy in the Congress Kingdom of Poland, 1863–1881," Ph.D. dissertation, Harvard University, 1956.

[10] Załęski, et al., "Warszawa," *Słownik geograficzny*, XIII, 22, lists forces from the quiet early 1890s, including a guards division, two cavalry guards regiments, and seven artillery batteries, plus a Kuban Cossack unit. Troops in the fortifications included seven

artillery battalions, four infantry, and one reserve battalion. Numerous staffs for units stationed in the region were also headquartered in the city.

[11] Kieniewicz, *Warszawa 1795-1914*, p. 191.

[12] For the reports of the *oberpolitseimeisters*, see Halina Kiepurska and Zbigniew Pustuła, eds., *Raporty warszawskich oberpolicmajstrów (1892-1913)* (Wrocław, 1971).

[13] An anecdotal but occasionally interesting memoir of a Russian's boyhood in Warsaw is in the papers of Ivan Shumilin, in the Bakhmeteff Archive of Russian and East European History and Culture, Columbia University Libraries; folder "Staraia Varshava," box 6.

[14] Dziewulski and Radziszewski, *Warszawa*, II, 368-439; Załęski, et al., "Warszawa," *Słownik geograficzny*, XIII, 31-36. In addition, see Stefan Górski, "Gospodarka finansowa miasta Warszawy," *Praca*, nr. 6 (supplement to *Biblioteka Warszawska*, vol. 262, nr. 3, June 1906).

[15] Roman Podoski, "Rozwój Warszawy znów zagrożony!" *Kurjer Warszawski*, 10 March 1913.

[16] *Goroda Rossii v 1910 godu* (St. Petersburg, 1914); pp. 774-883 cover Congress Poland.

[17] Jerzy Cegielski, *Stosunki mieszkaniowe w Warszawie w latach 1864-1964* (Warsaw, 1968), p. 85. The second set of percentages is from 1919, but concerns the city within its 1914 boundaries.

[18] Kiepurska and Pustuła, *Raporty oberpolicmajstrów*, p. 32.

[19] "Wiadomości bieżące," *Kurjer Warszawski*, 9 Nov. 1911.

[20] Bolesław Prus, *Kroniki*, III (Warsaw, 1954), 132-33.

[21] Shumilin Papers, "Staraia Varshava."

[22] Ludwik Krzywicki, "W roku 1878," in his *Wspomnienia*, II (Warsaw, 1958), 561.

[23] Dziewulski and Radziszewski, *Warszawa*, II, 132, 139-40.

[24] *Ibid.*, II, 136-40. Cegielski, *Stosunki*, p. 90n., notes the title of a contemporary pamphlet attacking the improvements: "Kanalizacja miasta Warszawy jako narzędzie judaizmu i szarlataneryj w celu zniszczenia rolnictwa polskiego oraz wytępienia ludności słowiańskiej nad Wisłą" (Canalization of the city of Warsaw as a tool of Judaism and charlatanry with the goal of the destruction of Polish agriculture and extermination of the Slavic population along the Vistula).

[25] Kiepurska and Pustuła, *Raporty oberpolicmajstrów*, pp. 27-28.

[26] Krzywicki, "1878," p. 561.

[27] Dziewulski and Radziszewski, *Warszawa*, II, 72.

[28] Cegielski, *Stosunki*, p. 99.

29 *Goroda Rossii.*
30 Dziewulski and Radziszewski, *Warszawa,* II, 92-114. Detailed information on public works can be found in the second volume of that work, and in Adolf Suligowski, "Warszawa i jej przedsiębiorstwa miejskie," *Ekonomista,* year 3 (1903), nr. 1, pp. 219-56, and nr. 2, pp. 1-50.
31 Prus, *Kroniki,* VI, 13.
32 Kieniewicz, *Warszawa 1795-1914,* pp. 249-50.
33 Isaac Bashevis Singer, *In My Father's Court* (New York, 1966), p. 17.
34 Paweł Hostowiec, "Wronia i Sienna," *Kultura,* nr. 5/43 (May 1951), pp. 45-46.
35 Kiepurska and Pustuła, *Raporty oberpolicmajstrów,* p. 11.
36 *Ibid.,* pp. 67, 69.
37 For the Russian view, see S. V. Rozhdestvenskii, *Istoricheskii obzor dieiatel'nosti Ministerstva Narodnago Prosvieshcheniia 1802-1902* (St. Petersburg, 1902), pp. 586-92, 681-88. There is a vast literature in Polish on the topic. Contemporary works include Władysław Studnicki, *Polityka Rosji względem szkolnictwa zaboru rosyjskiego* (Kraków, 1906), and Adolf Suligowski, *Miasta analfabetów,* 2nd ed. (Kraków, 1905).
38 Corrsin, "Political and Social Change," pp. 197-205, reviews the development of the University. Its annual reports can be found in *Varshavskiia Universitetskiia Izviestiia.*
39 Shatzky, *Varshe,* III, 225. See also Dioniza Wawrzykowska-Wierciochowa, "Udział kobiet w tajnym i jawnym ruchu społeczno-kulturalnym w Warszawie w latach 1880-1914," in Tazbir, *Z dziejów książki,* pp. 283-319. Girls' schools were less rigorously watched, and parents would have been concerned about their sons' career prospects rather than their daughters'.
40 Stanisław Orłowski, ed., *Dziesięciolecie Wolnej Wszechnicy Polskiej: Sprawozdanie działalności Towarzystwa Kursów Naukowych, 1906-1916* (Warsaw, 1917). See also Corrsin, "Political and Social Change," pp. 207-19.
41 *Prepis' 1897,* LI, Table 15.
42 Shatzky, *Varshe,* III, 212-22, and Hilary Nussbaum, *Z teki weterana Warszawskiej Gminy starozakonnych* (Warsaw, 1880), pp. 59-63. For information on the social context of Jewish religious education, see Shaul Stampfer, "*Heder* Study, Knowledge of Torah, and the Maintenance of Social Stratification in Traditional East European Society," *Studies in Jewish Education,* 3 (1988), 271-89. On Jewish education in general in Warsaw, see *Z dziejów Gminy Starozakonnych w Warszawie,* I (Warsaw,

1907), on the efforts of the *kehile*, Shatzky, *Varshe*, III, 212-50, and Shatzky's papers at the Yivo Institute for Jewish Research in New York.

[43] For an example of a *kheyder* inspection, see Bernard Singer, *Moje Nalewki* (Warsaw, 1959), p. 30; and for a Polish school, see Eve Curie, *Madam Curie: A Biography* (Garden City, N.Y., 1937), pp. 17-21.

[44] Shatzky, *Varshe*, III, 219.

[45] Mendel Mozes, "Der Moment," *Fun noentn ovar*, 2 (1957), 50-52, reviews a controversy in the Yiddish daily *Der Moment*.

[46] Shatzky, *Varshe*, III, 221.

[47] Shatzky, *Varshe*, III, 231-35; and *Z dziejów Gminy*, I, 145-252, which also shows that the *kehile* even supported an agricultural school in the Grójec district near Warsaw (I, 253-67).

[48] See Jolanta Niklewska, "Prywatne szkolnictwo średnie z wykładowym językiem polskim w Warszawie w latach 1905-1915," *Rocznik Warszawski*, 16 (1981), 263-81; Ryszard Wroczyński, "Ruch oświatowy w Królestwie Polskim w początkach XX wieku," in Tazbir, *Z dziejów książki*, pp. 230-82.

[49] On language restrictions on Jewish schools after 1905, see Niklewska, "Prywatne szkolnictwo," p. 264. *Sprawozdanie Zarządu Warszawskiej Gminy Starozakonnych za lata 1912-1916* (Warsaw, 1918) discusses language issues (pp. 27-28). On the use of Yiddish in a Polish progressive educational group, see I. W-g., "Żargon w polskiej instytucji oświatowej," *Izraelita*, 17 May 1907 (concerning the *Stowarzyszenie Kursów dla Dorosłych Analfabetów*, the Association of Courses for Adult Illiterates).

Notes to Chapter 2

[1] Józef Konczyński, *Ludność Warszawy: studium statystyczne, 1877-1911* (Warsaw, 1913), and Maria Nietyksza, *Ludność Warszawy na przełomie XIX i XX wieku* (Warsaw, 1971), are detailed studies of Warsaw's population.

[2] The censuses are: *Rezul'taty odnodnevnoi perepisi naseleniia goroda Varshavy v 1882 godu. Rezultaty spisu jednodniowego ludności miasta Warszawy 1882 roku*, 3 vols. (Warsaw, 1883-85), and *Pervaia vseobshchaia perepis' naseleniia Rossiiskoi Imperii*, LI (St. Petersburg, 1904). For discussions from a very critical Polish perspective of the organization and processing of the 1897 census, see Stefan Szulc, *Wartość materjałów statystycznych dotyczących stanu ludności byłego Królestwa Polskiego* (Warsaw, 1920), pp. 3-22, and Nietyksza, *Ludność*, pp. 218-28. Nietyksza regards

the 1882 census as more trustworthy than the 1897 count but this point of view seems to be based mostly on a preference for a local, Polish product, as opposed to a Russian imperial one. The 1882 census has rarely been thoroughly analyzed, while the 1897 count has been examined repeatedly in critical detail. A useful recent collection is Ralph S. Clem, ed., *Research Guide to the Russian and Soviet Censuses* (Ithaca, N.Y., and London, 1986). Samples of the 1897 questionnaire can be found in Szulc, *Wartość*, p. 5, and A. I. Gozulov, *Perepisi naseleniia SSSR i kapitalisticheskikh stran* (Moscow, 1936), pp. 189–206. N. Ia. Vorob'ev, *Vsesoiuznaia perepis' naseleniia 1926 goda*, 2nd ed. (Moscow, 1957), pp. 83–94, has explanations of the questions asked, apparently the ones given to the census takers. Copies of the 1882 census schedule have evidently been lost.

[3] *Perepis' 1897*, LI, Table 1.

[4] Nietyksza, *Ludność*, p. 27.

[5] *Ibid.*, pp. 29–30.

[6] *Ibid.*, p. 65.

[7] *Rezul'taty 1882*, I, Table 21.

[8] *Perepis' 1897*, LI, Table 11. For other discussions of data on origins and in-migration, see Nietyksza, *Ludność*, pp. 32–47, and Adam Szczypiorski, "Imigracja do Warszawy w XIX wieku," *Studia Demograficzne*, I, nr. 1 (1961), 61–86. The 1897 census asked, "Were you born here, and if not here, then where exactly (province, district, city)?" (Vorob'ev, *Vsesoiuznaia perepis'*, p. 89). Richard H. Rowland, "Urban In-Migration in Late Nineteenth Century Russia," Ph.D. dissertation, Columbia University, 1971, pp. 76–85, raises questions about the 1897 census' birthplace data.

[9] For surveys of religious groups in Congress Poland, see Zygmunt Morżkowski, "Sprawy kościelne," in *Opis ziem zamieszkanych przez Polaków pod względem geograficznym, etnograficznym, historycznym, artystycznym, przemysłowym, handlowym i statystycznym*, II (Warsaw, 1904), 314–32; and Witold Pruss, "Społeczeństwo Królestwa Polskiego w XIX i początkach XX wieku," *Przegląd Historyczny*, 68 (1977), 259–86, and "Skład wyznaniowo-narodowościowy Warszawy w XIX i początkach XX wieku," in *Społeczeństwo Warszawy w rozwoju historycznym*, eds. Józef Kazimierski, et al. (Warsaw, 1977), pp. 372–88. The Mariavites are listed in Table 2-3 with the Catholics. The 1882 and 1897 Protestant figures include only the Lutheran and Reformed churches. Smaller Protestant groups are counted with Others; it is unclear whether they are listed as Protestants or Others in

1914. The Ukrainian Catholic church was banned, and its followers were probably counted as Orthodox; in 1882, 93 Uniates were listed as Others. Twenty-four Karaites in 1882 and 21 in 1897 are included as Others, as are 77 Old Believers in 1882 and 406 in 1897. Dissenting Orthodox, called *edinovertsy* in 1897, appear with the Orthodox in 1897 but are not mentioned in 1882.

10 Eisenbach, *Kwestia równouprawnienia*, pp. 61–64.

11 Szulc, *Wartość*, pp. 106–09, summarizes age and sex data for the Kingdom. See also Nietyksza, *Ludność*, pp. 80–94. Much of the following discussion is drawn from my article in *Polin: A Journal of Polish-Jewish Studies*, 3 (1988), 122–41; "Aspects of Population Change and Acculturation in Jewish Warsaw at the End of the Nineteenth Century: The Censuses of 1882 and 1897." My thanks go to the editors for permission to quote so extensively from this essay.

12 Many sources refer to the unreliability of these data, for example: Szulc, *Wartość*, pp. 22–49; Nietyksza, *Ludność*, pp. 228–33; Irena Gieysztorowa, *Wstęp do demografii staropolskiej* (Warsaw, 1976); Bohdan Wasiutyński, *Ludność żydowska w Królestwie Polskiem* (Warsaw, 1911), pp. 1–4, 77; B. Bornstein, *Analiza krytyczna danych statystycznych dotyczących ruchu naturalnego ludności byłego Królestwa Polskiego* (Warsaw, 1920); Stefan Szulc, *Ruch naturalny ludności w Polsce w latach 1895–1935* (Warsaw, 1936), and his "Statystyka urodzeń ludności żydowskiej w miastach," *Miesięcznik Statystyczny*, 6 (1923), 28–31; I. Bornstein, "Z zagadnień statystyki ruchu naturalnego ludności żydowskiej w Polsce," *Sprawy Narodowościowe*, 11 (1937), 405–19; Szyja Bronsztejn, *Ludność żydowska w Polsce w okresie międzywojennym: studium statystyczne* (Wrocław, 1963), pp. 36–39; and Konczyński, *Ludność*, passim. Attempts were made to improve the reliability of the data on the Jews; see *Sprawozdanie Zarządu Gminy*, which also notes that the older data "did not have and could not have the least value for research" (p. 63).

13 Herlihy, *Odessa*, p. 246; George W. Barclay, *Techniques of Population Analysis* (New York, 1958), notes that it is "especially useful where there is no adequate registration of births" (p. 25).

14 *Rezul'taty 1882*, I, Table 10; *Perepis' 1897*, LI, Table 25.

15 Władysław Schoenaich, "Statystyka urodzeń i śmiertelność dzieci wśród ubogiej ludności chrześcijańskiej i żydowskiej w Łodzi," *Ekonomista*, year 14 (1914), no. 1, pp. 132–44.

16 On low Jewish infant and child mortality in Poland and elsewhere, see Wasiutyński, *Ludność*, pp. 87–89; Jacob Lestschinsky, *Probleme der Bevölkerungs-Bewegung bei den Juden* (Padua,

Italy, 1926); Arjeh Tartakower, "Stan liczebny i rozwój naturalny ludności żydowskiej w Polsce," in *Żydzi w Polsce odrodzonej*, eds. Ignacy Schiper, et al., II (Warsaw, 1934), 215; U. O. Schmelz, *Infant and Early Childhood Mortality among Jews of the Diaspora* (Jerusalem, 1971); Lucjan Dobroszycki, "The Fertility of Modern Polish Jewry," in *Modern Jewish Fertility*, ed. Paul Ritterband (Leiden, 1981), pp. 64–77; Franciszek Makysmilian Sobieszczański, *Rys historyczno-statystyczny wzrostu i stanu miasta Warszawy od najdawniejszych czasów aż do 1847 roku*, ed. Konrad Zawadzki (Warsaw, 1974), p. 207; and *Wyniki spisu z 1921 na terenie miasta stołecznego Warszawy: zestawienie i rozbiór krytyczny* (Warsaw, 1928) pp. 26–27. Jacques Silber, "The Demographic Characteristics of the Jewish Population in Russia at the End of the Nineteenth Century," *Jewish Social Studies*, 42 (1980), 268–80, reviews evidence supporting relatively low Jewish birth and death rates in the larger Empire. Nietyksza, *Ludność*, pp. 98–120, examines the data on natural increase, including Catholic–Jewish differences. I would like to thank Shaul Stampfer and Bronislaw Bloch for some illuminating discussions on these and related points.

[17] According to official statistics, in 1887 the city's live birth rate was 37.8 per thousand and the death rate 24.9. Among Catholics these rates were 41.3 and 27.1; among Jews 28.4 and 21.9. In 1911 the official city birth rate was 27.5 and the death rate 19.4; for Catholics 31.9 and 23.3; for Jews 22.6 and 14.8. (Dziewulski and Radziszewski, *Warszawa*, I, Tables 22–24 in statistical appendix.) See the sources cited in note 12 on questions of the value of these figures.

[18] "Warszawa," *S. Orgelbranda encyklopedja powszechna z ilustracjami i mapami* (1898–1903 edition), XV, 151, presents totals of illegitimate births by faith. For additional data on this issue, see *Dvizhenie naseleniia goroda Varshavy za dvadtsatiletnii period (1882-1901)* (Warsaw, 1901), tables 3, 4, and 15; Dziewulski and Radziszewski, *Warszawa*, I, 428, 432; and Konczyński, *Ludność*, pp. 70–77, 90–94. Konczyński notes that, in 1909, out of 1,000 legitimate newborns, 213.9 infants died, compared to a death rate of 646.3 among illegitimate ones (pp. 91–93).

[19] *Rezul'taty 1882*, I, 38–39.

[20] Edward Strzelecki, "Ludność Warszawy na przełomie XIX i XX wieku," in Tazbir, *Z dziejów książki*, pp. 211–12.

[21] "Z tygodnia," *Izraelita*, 17 Feb. 1882.

[22] Jacob Shatzky, "Institutional Aspects of Jewish Life in Warsaw in the Second Half of the Nineteenth Century," *Yivo Annual of*

Jewish Social Science, 10 (1955), 23. The Yiddish text is in his *Varshe*, III, 125. Zalewski was probably city statistician Witold Załęski.

[23] "Z tygodnia," *Izraelita*, 8 July 1881.

[24] "Z tygodnia," *Izraelita*, 21 Oct. 1881.

[25] "Z tygodnia," *Izraelita*, 10 Feb. 1882.

[26] Vorob'ev, *Vsesoiuznaia perepis'*, p. 90.

[27] I deal at length with language issues in, "Language Use in Cultural and Political Change in Pre-1914 Warsaw: Poles, Jews, and Russification," forthcoming in *Slavonic and East European Review*.

[28] Some Polish scholars have questioned the 1897 language data, but only insofar as these, they feel, artifically decrease the Polish-speaking share of the population. See Szulc, *Wartość*, p. 21, and Nietyksza, *Ludność*, pp. 126, 222. I discuss this issue in detail in "Language Use."

[29] Nahum Sokolow, "Zanik mysnagdyzmu," *Izraelita*, 11 Nov. 1898. Shatzky, *Varshe*, III, 30, 35, refers to the acculturation of the Misnagdic community in these decades.

[30] Cited by Shatzky, *Varshe*, III, 20. There are no hard data on the relative sizes of the different parts of the Jewish population. Assimilationist author Hilary Nussbaum, in his *Szkice historyczne*, p. 131, estimated that two-thirds of the Jewish population was Hasidic (writing in 1881), and later writers have followed him.

[31] For useful definitions of acculturation and assimilation see Milton M. Gordon, *Assimilation in American Life: The Role of Race, Religion, and National Origins* (New York, 1964), pp. 71, 77. On the Jews in Poland, recent studies include Ezra Mendelsohn, "A Note on Jewish Assimilation in the Polish Lands," in *Jewish Assimilation in Modern Times*, ed. Bela Vago (Boulder, Colo., 1981), pp. 141-49; Joseph Lichten, "Notes on the Assimilation and Acculturation of Jews in Poland, 1863-1943," in *The Jews in Poland*, eds. Chimen Abramsky, et al. (Oxford and New York, 1986), pp. 106-29; Alina Cała, "The Question of the Assimilation of Jews in the Polish Kingdom (1864-1897): An Interpretive Essay," *Polin: A Journal of Polish-Jewish Studies*, I (1986), 130-50; Aleksander Hertz, *Żydzi w kulturze polskiej* (Paris, 1961); Celia Heller, *On the Edge of Destruction: Jews of Poland between the Two World Wars* (New York, 1977); and my, "Aspects of Population Change and of Acculturation." Mendelsohn summarizes clearly the distinction between the two concepts: ". . . the different though related processes of acculturation (by which is meant the Jews' adoption of the external characteristics of the

majority culture, above all its language) and assimilation (by which is meant the Jews' efforts to adopt the national identity of the majority, to become Poles, Hungarians, Romanians 'of the Mosaic faith,' or even to abandon their Jewish identity altogether)" (*The Jews of East Central Europe between the World Wars* (Bloomington, Ind., 1983), p. 2).

[32] Cała, "Question," p. 130.

[33] For a memoir by Grosser, see "From Pole to Jew," in *The Golden Tradition: Jewish Life and Thought in Eastern Europe*, ed. Lucy Dawidowicz (New York, 1967), pp. 435–41. For examples of the new positions some of these Polonized, young Jewish nationalists took, see the collection *Safrus: książka zbiorowa poświęcona sprawom żydostwa*, ed. Jan Kirszrot (Warsaw, 1905), and the weeklies *Głos Żydowski* and *Życie Żydowskie* (1906–07).

[34] An interesting, if uneven, study is Maria Brzezina, *Polszczyzna Żydów* (Warsaw, 1986). Chone Shmeruk, *The Esterke Story in Yiddish and Polish Literature* (Jerusalem, 1985), goes far beyond its narrow title into the realm of Polish–Jewish historical sociolinguistics.

[35] Mendelsohn, *Jews of East Central Europe*, pp. 67–68, argues that, by the 1930s, it appeared that Polish would soon replace "modern Yiddish and Hebrew culture and schools." Jacob Lestschinsky, "Di shprakhn bay yidn in umophengikn poyln," *Yivo bleter*, 22 (1943), 147–62, analyzes the relevant statistics, which seem to show the continued strength of Yiddish in interwar Poland; yet he also refers to political agitation before the 1931 census distorting the results and leading many people to claim Yiddish or Hebrew as native languages, as a nationalist statement rather than a reflection of actual language use. A very important article is Chone Shmeruk, "Hebrew–Yiddish–Polish: A Trilingual Jewish Culture," in *The Jews of Poland between Two World Wars*, Israel Gutman, et al., eds. (Cambridge, Mass., 1989), pp. 265–91. My thanks go to the Tauber Institute for the Study of European Jewry at Brandeis University for making available to me, at Professor Shmeruk's suggestion, a copy of this essay prior to publication.

[36] Brzezina, *Polszczyzna*, discusses these points (pp. 141–42). Cała, "Question," p. 138, notes that while many more Jews had learned Polish by the end of the nineteenth century, this did not necessarily mean that they had abandoned Yiddish. Shmeruk, *Esterke Story*, pp. 47–48, touches on the Jews' spoken and written command of Polish.

[37] The "Litvak invasion" was a key aspect of the "Jewish ques-

tion," and one that deserves a great deal more study than it has received; comments on it in Polish historiography do not delve past the anecdotal level. The reader can start with Golczewski, *Polnisch-jüdische Beziehungen*, pp. 96–101, for orientation. The rise and significance of the Russian Jewish community in Warsaw is a constant theme in Shatzky, *Varshe*, III. Wasiutyński, *Ludność*, pp. 6–7, estimates that at least one hundred thousand Jews came to Congress Poland in the period 1893–1909, but the data are so uncertain that any estimate can only be a wild guess.

[38] Samuel Hirszhorn, "Litwaki," *Głos Żydowski*, 29 April 1906.

[39] B. Singer, *Nalewki*, p. 66; he is citing a Polish Hasidic saying that Hirszhorn also uses.

[40] Shatzky, *Varshe*, III, 228, and B. Singer, *Nalewki*, p. 142, provide examples. Shatzky also notes (III, 268n.) that in the 1870s Russian textbooks began to appear in Warsaw for Yiddish-speakers. To some extent Jewish schools using Russian appeared because of official pressure; see Niklewska, "Prywatne szkolnictwo," pp. 264–65, and *Sprawozdanie Zarządu Gminy*, pp. 27–28.

[41] K., "Stare prawdy," *Izraelita*, 20 Jan. 1882. This claim may have been premature.

[42] Shatzky notes that, "Warsaw *Maskilim* . . . held until 1861 that only German was a language of culture (*kulturshprakh)" (Varshe*, III, 297). Raphael Mahler, *Hasidism and the Jewish Enlightenment: Their Confrontation in Galicia and Poland in the First Half of the Nineteenth Century* (Philadelphia, 1985), discusses the importance of German to the Haskalah, as does Shmeruk, *Esterke*. *Daytsh* (German) long remained a common term for *oyfgeklerte* (enlightened) Jews.

[43] At least 1,470 Jews exclusive of small children accepted Christianity in Warsaw in 1800–1903; Witold Pruss, "Społeczeństwo," p. 282.

[44] Lewental was a member of the *kehile* board until 1886. On Bloch's Warsaw connections and his interest in Jewish matters, see Shatzky, *Varshe*, III, 80–88, 104–05 (on his response to the pogrom). On Kraushar, see Jacob Shatzky, "Alexander Kraushar and His Road to Total Assimilation," *Yivo Annual of Jewish Social Science*, 7 (1952), 146–74.

[45] Mahler, *Hasidism and the Jewish Enlightenment*, explains the emphasis of the Haskalah on Hebrew. Nahum Sokolow presents his views on the role of Hebrew in, *Zadania inteligencji żydowskiej* (Warsaw, 1890), pp. 41–47, and "Hebrajszczyzna i oświata żydowska," *Izraelita*, 19 Feb. 1897.

[46] B. Singer, *Nalewki*, pp. 127, 145.

[47] Mendelsohn, *Jews of East Central Europe*, p. 32: "The language a Polish Jew might speak in his home . . . certainly tells us something about his degree of acculturation and assimilation. But his answers do not enable us to predict with total accuracy his attitude toward his Jewishness and toward the dilemma of being a Jew in Poland."

[48] Adam Skierko, "The Jews in Poland," in *Polish Encyclopedia*, II (Geneva, Switz., 1922–26), 935. In Jacob Shatzky's papers at the Yivo Institute for Jewish Research, folder 73, there is a reference to an aptly named work from 1900—"Werytus," *Warszawa w 2000 roku: zżydzenie stolicy polskiej*. I have been unable to locate it, however. In 1911, anti–Semitic publisher Szczepan Jeleński (son of Jan Jeleński) reprinted Julian Niemcewicz's *Rok 3333, czyli, sen niesłychany*, with the same theme of the "Judaization" of the city. (Russian officials also expressed concern about this as early as the 1860s; Shatzky, *Varshe*, III, 11, 18, 24.) Much of the apparent increase in the Jewish population of Poland actually resulted from improved record keeping.

[49] "Przegląd prasy," *Kurjer Warszawski*, 13 December 1911.

Notes to Chapter 3

[1] Irena and Jan Kosim, "Fritza Wernicka opis Warszawy z 1876 roku, I," *Warszawa XIX wieku*, fasc. 1, *Studia warszawskie*, vol. 9 (Warsaw, 1970), p. 304. My translation is from the Kosims' Polish translation. Wernick, from Elbląg, published his comments in *Schlesische Zeitung* and *Danziger Zeitung*. The Baedeker firm's *Russia with Teheran, Port Arthur, and Peking: Handbook for Travellers* (Leipzig, London, and New York, 1914), ws the primary pre-war English-language guide to the city (see pp. 9–25 on Warsaw).

[2] I. B. Singer, *Father's Court*, p. 59.

[3] Kosim, "Fritza Wernicka opis, I," p. 306.

[4] "Warszawa," *S. Orgelbranda encyklopedja*, XV, 146.

[5] Antoni Słonimski, *Wspomnienia warszawskie* (Warsaw, 1957), pp. 6–7.

[6] "Warszawa," *S. Orgelbranda encyklopedja*, XV, 148.

[7] Kosim, "Fritza Wernicka opis, I," p. 308.

[8] "Warszawa," *S. Orgelbranda encyklopedja*, XV, 150.

[9] Ibid., XV, 149.

[10] Aleksander Jankowski, "Rzut oka po kraju," in *Opis ziem zamieszkanych przez Polaków*, II, 132.

[11] "Warszawa," *S. Orgelbranda encyklopedja*, XV, 151.

[12] Stefan Żeromski, *Dzienniki*, II (Warsaw, 1954), 267; entry for 13 June 1887.
[13] Janowski, "Rzut oka," p. 129.
[14] Bolesław Prus, *The Doll*, trans. David Welsh (New York, 1972), pp. 73-74.
[15] Adolf Suligowski, "Warszawa i jej przedsiębiorstwa miejskie," *Ekonomista*, year 3 (1903), vol. 2, p. 23.
[16] Krzywicki, "W roku 1878," p. 557.
[17] See Stanisław Herbst, *Ulica Marszałkowska*, 2nd ed. (Warsaw, 1978).
[18] I. B. Singer, *Father's Court*, pp. 226-27.
[19] B. Singer, *Nalewki*, p. 7.
[20] Isaac Bashevis Singer, *The Family Moskat* (New York, 1950), p. 22.
[21] Jan Detko, "Antynomie warszawskie," *Przegląd Humanistyczny*, 22 (1978), nr. 7/8, pp. 1-13, and nr. 9, pp. 45-59.
[22] B. Singer, *Nalewki*, p. 86.
[23] Kosim, "Fritza Wernicka opis, I," p. 326. See also Eugeniusz Szwankowski, "Praga w latach 1814-1880," in *Dzieje Pragi*, eds. Józef Kazimierski, et al. (Warsaw, 1970), pp. 161-74.
[24] Janowski, "Rzut oka," p. 138.
[25] Kiepurska and Pustuła, *Raporty oberpolicmajstrów*, pp. 28-29, 32.
[26] Jan Berger, "Z dziejów Saskiej Kępy," *Rocznik Warszawski*, 15 (1979), 344-49.
[27] Janusz Strzeszewski, "Sprawa inkorporacji przedmieść w polityce wielkomiejskiej," *Ekonomista*, year 17 (1917), no. 1, p. 123.
[28] "Zebranie przedwyborcze VII cyrkułu," *Praca Polska*, 8 March 1906, morning edition.
[29] Detko, "Antynomie," *Przegląd Humanistyczny*, 22 (1978), nr. 7/8, p. 7; from B. Londyński, *Rycerze Czarnego Dworu* (Warsaw, 1888).
[30] See Shatzky, *Varshe*, III, 91-92; Cegielski, *Stosunki*, p. 43, 150-54; and "Wiadomości bieżące," *Kurjer Warszawski*, 4 July 1912.
[31] *Perepis' 1897*, LI, Tables 12 and 14.
[32] Janowski, "Rzut oka," pp. 130-31.
[33] Shatzky, *Varshe*, III, 61-67.
[34] Krzywicki, "1878," p. 563; see also Shatzky, *Varshe*, III, 21.
[35] For detailed and methodologically creative studies, see Bronisław Bloch, "Spatial Evolution of the Jewish and General Population of Warsaw, 1792-1939," in *Papers in Jewish Demography, 1973*, U. O. Schmelz, et al., eds. (Jerusalem, 1977), pp. 209-34,

and "Urban Ecology of the Jewish Population of Warsaw, 1897–1939," in *Papers in Jewish Demography, 1981*, U. O. Schmelz, et al., eds. (Jerusalem, 1983), pp. 381–99. Also very informative is Peter J. Martyn, "The Undefined Town within a Town: A History of Jewish Settlement in the Western Districts of Warsaw," *Polin: A Journal of Polish-Jewish Studies*, 3 (1988), 17–45.

Notes to Chapter 4

[1] Kieniewicz, *Warszawa 1795–1914*, p. 224. Witold Pruss, *Rozwój przemysłu warszawskiego w latach 1864–1914* (Warsaw, 1977) is a very thorough study of factory industry; Barbara Grochulska and Witold Pruss, eds., *Z dziejów rzemiosła warszawskiego* (Warsaw, 1983), covers craft industry.

[2] Kieniewicz, *Warszawa 1795–1914*, p. 232.

[3] Jan Stanisław Bystroń, *Warszawa*, 2nd ed. (Warsaw, 1977), pp. 276–77; and Dziewulski and Radziszewski, *Warszawa*, II, 190–211.

[4] B. Singer, *Nalewki*, p. 8.

[5] Jankowski, "Rzut oka," p. 131.

[6] For studies which use older, less trustworthy employment data, see Ignacy Schiper, *Dzieje handlu żydowskiego na ziemiach polskich* (Warsaw, 1937), and Adam Szczypiorski, "Struktura zawodowa i społeczna Warszawy w pierwszym okresie epoki kapitalistycznej (1864–1882)," *Kwartalnik Historii Kultury Materialnej*, 8 (1960), 75–102.

[7] For discussions of the 1897 census see Szulc, *Wartość*, pp. 5, 21; Gozulov, *Perepisi*, pp. 203–06; and Vorob'ev, *Vsesoiuznaia 1926*, pp. 92–93.

[8] Barclay, *Techniques*, p. 275.

[9] For another classification scheme and discussion of the categories see Nietyksza, *Ludność*, pp. 131–37, 232–36.

[10] Janina Żurawicka, *Inteligencja warszawska w końcu XIX wieku* (Warsaw, 1978), p. 92. Nietyksza, *Ludność*, p. 133, states that administrative personnel in private business were listed by the branch of industry or commerce in which they were employed, but this was apparently not the case.

[11] For an attempt to analyze the ethnic composition of the working class of Poland, see Anna Żarnowska, *Klasa robotnicza Królestwa Polskiego 1870–1914* (Warsaw, 1974), pp. 70–101.

[12] Shatzky, *Varshe*, III, 36–53, covers "Jewish factories and Jewish labor."

[13] *Ibid.*, III, 42.

14 In his novel *Jakób Izraelewicz* (1886); cited by Shatzky, *Varshe*, III, 33.
15 Shatzky, *Varshe*, III, 45.
16 Vladimir Medem, *The Life and Soul of a Legendary Jewish Socialist*, translation of his *Fun mayn leben* by S. A. Portnoy (New York, 1979), p. 485.
17 Shatzky, *Varshe*, III, 39.
18 Julian Marchlewski, "Antysemityzm a robotnicy," in his *Ludzie, czasy, idee*, Z. Marchlewska, et al., eds. (Warsaw, 1973), p. 372.
19 Shatzky, *Varshe*, III, 52.
20 Such families are discussed in Shatzky, *Varshe*, III, 68–94; and Schiper, *Dzieje handlu*.
21 Żurawicka, *Inteligencja*, p. 92.
22 Cezary Łagiewski, "Ruch współdzielozy," in *Dzieje gospodarcze Polski porozbiorowej w zarysie*, ed. Stanisław A. Kempner, II (Warsaw, 1922), 309–18, provides basic information on the cooperative movement.
23 David Engel, *In the Shadow of Auschwitz: The Polish Government-in-Exile and the Jews, 1939–1942* (Chapel Hill, N.C., 1987), p. 15. Engel refers to an important summary of the basic Polish nationalist position on the Jews in the early twentieth century; Franciszek Bujak, *The Jewish Question in Poland* (Paris, 1919).
24 While this may well have been the case, the data are too sparse and uncertain to provide strong support for this viewpoint. These views may have been based in part on the wishes of individual authors to find signs of a Jewish "process of productivization," and a movement "from commerce in the direction of manufacturing and craft industry" (these phrases are from Schiper, *Dzieje handlu*, pp. 495, 499; see also Leon Wengierow, "Przyczynek do stanu ekonomicznego żydów w Królestwie Polskim," in Kirszrot, *Safrus*, pp. 308–17). Shatzky, *Varshe*, III, 53–61, discusses Jews in trade in Warsaw.
25 For general discussions of the Polish intelligentsia, see Jan Szczepański, *Inteligencja i społeczeństwo* (Warsaw, 1957), "Inteligencja a pracownicy umysłowi," *Przegląd Socjologiczny*, 13, no. 2 (1959), pp. 7–23, and "Struktura inteligencji w Polsce," *Kultura i Społeczeństwo*, 4, no. 1–2 (1960), pp. 19–48; Halina Kiepurska, *Inteligencja zawodowa Warszawy 1905–1907* (Warsaw, 1967); Ryszard Czepulis-Rastenis, ed., *Inteligencja polska pod zaborami* (Warsaw, 1978); and Żurawicka, *Inteligencja*. This is just a sample; there is a vast literature, historical and sociological, on the Polish intelligentsia.

[26] Ludwik Krzywicki, "Stanisław Ciszewski," in his *Wspomnienia*, II, 496; see also Żurawicka, *Inteligencja*, p. 119.

[27] Shatzky, *Varshe*, III, 70.

[28] Żurawicka, *Inteligencja*, pp. 107-08, 115-17.

[29] *Perepis' 1897*, XXI, Table 22.

[30] Cited in Żurawicka, *Inteligencja*, pp. 49-50.

[31] *Ibid.*, p. 124. On Jewish participation in medicine, see Shatzky, *Varshe*, III, 192-211.

Notes to Chapter 5

[1] Two major titles, *Gazeta Handlowa* and *Nowa Gazeta*, have often been referred to as Jewish newspapers, because both had Jewish publishers and editors and many Jewish readers. However, they had much more of a Polish liberal orientation with strong ties to the assimilationist Jews, than an expressly Jewish one. Jewish publishers were very active in the Polish press, also, and some indisputably Polish titles (such as *Kurjer Warszawski*) were very popular among Jewish readers. It appears that the boundaries were less firm than in the interwar period.

[2] One example is that *Yidishes Tageblat* had a Polish police reporter; Moshe Grosman, " 'Haynt': ershter period, 1908-1915," *Fun noentn ovar*, 2 (1957), 7. There were also business contacts between Polish and Jewish publishers and firms. Jerzy Or (Ohr), a convert, specialized in providing Polish serials with news from the Jewish press, "with his own provocative comments," added (Florian Sokolow, *Nahum Sokolow: Life and Legend* (London, 1975), p. 73.

[3] Prus, *Kroniki*, XX, 13.

[4] For a survey, see Jerzy Łojek, ed., *Prasa polska w latach 1864-1918*, vol. II of *Historia prasy polskiej* (Warsaw, 1976). Several in-depth studies by Zenon Kmiecik are *Prasa warszawska w okresie pozytywizmu (1864-1885)* (Warsaw, 1971); *Prasa polska w rewolucji 1905-1907* (Warsaw, 1980); and *Prasa warszawska w latach 1908-1918* (Warsaw, 1981).

[5] Stefan Lewandowski, "Rozwój produkcji wydawniczej w okresie kształtowania się kapitalistycznej struktury społecznej w Warszawie," in *Społeczeństwo Warszawy w rozwoju historycznym*, Józef Kazimierski, et al., eds. (Warsaw, 1977), p. 244.

[6] For 1870—Zenon Kmiecik, "Wydawnictwa periodyczne w Królestwie Polskim w latach 1868-1904," *Rocznik Historii Czasopiśmiennictwa Polskiego*, 4, No. 2 (1986), pp. 142-43. Dailies from 1870 were: *Kurjer Codzienny, Kurjer Warszawski, Gazeta*

Warszawska, Gazeta Polska, Gazeta Handlowa, and weeklies were *Kłosy, Tygodnik Illustrowany, Bluszcz, Gazeta Rolnicza,* and *Tygodnik Mód i Powieści.* For 1909—Jerzy Myśliński, "Nakłady prasy w Królestwie Polskim w 1909 roku," *Rocznik Historii Czasopiśmiennictwa Polskiego,* 9 (1970), 119. Dailies from 1909 were *Kurjer Warszawski, Goniec, Kurjer Poranny, Nowa Gazeta,* and *Kurjer Polski,* and weeklies were *Tygodnik Illustrowany, Wiarus, Pracownik Polski, Gazeta Świąteczna,* and *Świat.*

7 Franciszka Ramotowska, "Warszawskie komitety cenzury w latach 1832–1915," *Warszawa XIX wieku,* fasc. 2, *Studia warszawskie,* vol. 9 (Warsaw, 1971), deals mostly with the earlier period. For an interesting 1904 document which shows the concerns of the Russian government about the Polish press, see Marek Tobera, "Z archiwum Warszawskiego komitetu cenzury," *Kwartalnik Historii Prasy Polskiej,* 25, no. 1 (1986), 119–23.

8 See Teresa Ostrowska, *Polskie czasopiśmiennictwo lekarskie w XIX wieku (1800–1900): zarys historyczno-bibliograficzny* (Wrocław, 1973).

9 Kmiecik, *Prasa 1905–07,* p. 24.

10 Kmiecik, *Prasa w okresie pozytywizmu,* tables 4 and 5 following p. 262.

11 See Kmiecik, *Prasa 1908–18,* pp. 197–223, and his *Program polityczny "Głosu Warszawskiego" (1908–1909) i "Gazety Warszawskiej" (1909–1915)* (Warsaw, 1980); and Stanisław Kozicki, *Historia Ligi Narodowej (okres 1887–1907)* (London, 1964), pp. 281–84.

12 Czesław Lechicki, "Polskie czasopiśmiennictwa katolickie w latach 1833–1914," *Kwartalnik Historii Prasy Polskiej,* 22, no. 1 (1983), 19–42.

13 Jerzy Myśliński, *Prasa polska socjalistyczna w okresie zaborów* (Warsaw, 1982).

14 For surveys of the Jewish press see Shatzky, *Varshe,* III, 307–21, and Marian Fuks, *Prasa żydowska w Warszawie, 1823–1939* (Warsaw, 1979). An extensive and very informative review of Fuks, correcting many errors and pointing out additional sources, is Chone Shmeruk, "A Pioneering Study of the Warsaw Jewish Press," *Soviet Jewish Affairs,* 11, no. 3 (1981), 35–53. Shmeruk's "Aspects of the History of Warsaw as a Yiddish Literary Centre," *Polin: A Journal of Polish–Jewish Studies,* 3 (1988), 142–55, and his "Hebrew–Yiddish–Polish" should also be consulted.

15 Michael C. Steinlauf, "The Polish–Jewish Daily Press," *Polin: A Journal of Polish–Jewish Studies,* 2 (1987), 236, notes the "great prestige" attached to Hebrew titles, but also that there were

"never enough Hebrew readers in Poland to make a Hebrew daily a viable competitor of a Yiddish or even a Polish-Jewish daily."

[16] Fuks, *Prasa*, pp. 21-40, Shatzky, *Varshe*, I, 290-91, and Israel Zinberg, *Istoriia evreiskoi pechati v Rossii v sviazi s obshchestvennymi techeniiami* (Petrograd, 1915), pp. 13-15.

[17] Fuks, *Prass*, p. 41, and Shmeruk, "Pioneering Study," pp. 41-42n.

[18] Fuks, *Prasa*, pp. 41-62, and Shatzky, *Varshe*, II, 254-55.

[19] Zinberg, *Istoriia*, p. 86; see also Shatzky, *Varshe*, III, 307-11, and Fuks, *Prasa*, pp. 103-23. Its title is often transliterated as *Hatsfira* or *Ha-tsefira*.

[20] Nahum Sokolow, "Sredi dvukh pokolenii (Ieguda-Leib Kantor), III," *Evreiskaia Zhizn'*, 6 March 1916.

[21] *Ibid.* Kmiecik, "Wydawnictwa periodyczne," pp. 146, 148, provides the five thousand figure for 1896 and 1900, taking his data from official records. Shatzky, *Varshe*, III, 310, gives ten thousand for 1891, without citing any source.

[22] Some sources err on the weekly's last years, giving 1908 or 1912. It did not appear from December 1908 to April 1910, except for one issue in November 1909. After it was published from April 1910 to November 1913, the 21 November issue announced that *Izraelita* was closing and that its subscribers would henceforth receive *Widnorkąg* [Horizon]. *Izraelita* was revived during World War I.

[23] Kmiecik, "Wydawnictwa periodyczne," pp. 143, 150, 156. For its history see Fuks, *Prasa*, pp. 85-102, and Shatzky, *Varshe*, III, 318-21. The journal's 25 December 1908 issue provides interesting looks backward.

[24] For Sokolow's coverage of the 1897 congress, see his, "Kongres syjonistów w Bazylei," *Izraelita*, 10, 17, and 24 Dec. 1897.

[25] Zinberg, *Istoriia*, p. 112; see also Fuks, *Prasa*, pp. 62-84.

[26] Fuks, *Prasa*, pp. 127-29, Shatzky, *Varshe*, III, 316-18, and Shmeruk, "Aspects," pp. 148-49.

[27] Fuks, *Prasa*, p. 296.

[28] *Ibid.*, p. 298; Grosman, " 'Haynt,' " p. 5.

[29] Aleksander Hafftka, "Prasa żydowska w Polsce (do 1918 roku)," in Schiper, *Żydzi w Polsce odrodzonej*, II, 157, cites one hundred thousand and sixty thousand for *Haynt's* and *Moment's* circulations. It is difficult to credit that such extraordinary circulations were the norm before World War I, although it may have been true for such special events as the Mendel Beilis trial in 1913.

[30] I. B. Singer, *Father's Court*, p. 161.

[31] Mozes, "Der Moment," pp. 247-48.

[32] B. Singer, *Nalewki*, p. 161.

Notes to Chapter 6

[1] Stanislaus A. Blejwas, *Realism in Polish Politics: Warsaw Positivism and National Survival in Nineteenth Century Poland* (New Haven, 1984), surveys the movement. For a selection of Świętochowski's essays, see his *Liberum veto*, eds. Samuel Sandler and Maria Brykalska, 2 vols. (Warsaw, 1976). Orzeszkowa's most important single essay on the "Jewish question," is "O żydach i kwestyi żydowskiej," in her *Pisma*, IX (Warsaw, 1913), 1–77 (written in 1882, after the Warsaw pogrom). Blejwas also notes that the positivists' strongly assimilationist, intolerant approach to the Jews "bore a similarity" to the anti–Polish measures of the Russian government ("Polish Positivism and the Jews," *Jewish Social Studies*, 46 (1984), 32).

[2] My thanks go to Professor Israel Oppenheim, for making available to me his manuscript, "The Jewish Question in *Głos* [The Voice], 1886–1894 (Origins of the Polish Right's Attitude toward the Jewish Question)."

[3] On Jeleński, see Andrzej Jaszczuk, *Spór pozytywistów z konserwatystami o przyszłość Polski, 1870–1903* (Warsaw, 1986), pp. 202–29, and the collection *Ćwierćwiecze walki: księga pamiątkowa "Roli"* (Warsaw, 1910).

[4] See Shatzky, *Varshe*, III, 95–109; Golczewski, *Polnisch–jüdische Beziehungen*, pp. 41–51; Karolina Beylin, *Dni powszednie Warszawy w latach 1880–1900* (Warsaw, 1967), pp. 47–55; and Isaac Grünbaum, "Die Pogrome in Polen," in *Die Judenpogrome in Russland*, I (Köln and Leipzig, 1910), 134–51.

[5] Halina Kiepurska, *Warszawa w rewolucji 1905–1907* (Warsaw, 1974), covers this period in detail. See also Kiepurska and Pustuła, *Raporty oberpolicmajstrów*, pp. 54–91.

[6] Standard surveys of Polish political history are Wandycz, *Lands of Partitioned Poland*, and Wilhelm Feldman, *Dzieje polskiej myśli politycznej, 1864–1914*, 2nd ed. rev. by Józef Feldman (Warsaw, 1933).

[7] Kiepurska and Pustuła, *Raporty oberpolicmajstrów*, pp. 71, 74.

[8] Among the most useful works on this movement and its ideology are: Stanisław Kozicki, *Historia Ligi*; Roman Zimand, "Uwagi o teorii narodu na marginesie analizy nacjonalistycznej teorii narodu," *Studia Filozoficzne*, 4 (1951), 3–39; Janusz Jerzy Terej, *Idee, mity, realia: szkice do dziejów Narodowej Demokracji* (Warsaw, 1971); and Roman Wapiński, *Narodowa Demokracja, 1893–1939: ze studiów nad dziejami myśli nacjonalistycznej* (Wrocław,

1980). My thanks go (again) to Professor Israel Oppenheim for providing me with the manuscript of his "The 'National Democrats'—Endecja—Attitude to the Jewish Question at the Outset (1895–1905)." For the writing of the movement's dominant leader, Roman Dmowski, see especially his *Myśli nowoczesnego Polaka* (L'vov, 1902); *Niemcy, Rosya i kwestya polska* (L'vov, 1908); and *Polityka polska i odbudowanie państwa*, 2nd ed. (Warsaw, 1926). An important ideological essay by another party leader is, Zygmunt Balicki, *Egoizm narodowy wobec etyki*, new ed. (L'vov and Warsaw, 1914). For the party program from this era, see "Program Stronnictwa Demokratyczno–Narodowego w zaborze rosyjskim," *Przegląd Wszechpolski*, vol. 9, no. 3 (Oct. 1903), pp. 721–58.

9 The most comprehensive study on Jewish politics in the Russian Empire is Frankel, *Prophecy and Politics*. Ezra Mendelsohn discusses Jewish politics in partitioned Poland in the introduction of his *Zionism in Poland: The Formative Years, 1915–1926* (New Haven and London, 1981), especially pp. 12–36.

10 Concerning the essentially intolerant assimilation of the Polish liberals, and the turn to anti-Semitism that many of them took, see: Korzec, *Juifs en Pologne*, pp. 39–42; Golczewski, *Polnisch-jüdische Beziehungen*, pp. 92–96; and Blejwas, *Realism*. The changes in attitudes expressed by many of these writers on the "Jewish question" from the optimistic 1870s to the much more pessimistic pre-World War I years is striking.

11 This is a summary of the very complicated election laws. The relevant legislation is, *Polnoe Sobranie Zakonov*, 3rd collection, XXV, law 26662, 6 August 1905, and law 27029, Dec. 11, 1905.

12 On initial Jewish approaches, see Ad. J. Cohn, "W sprawie wyborów," *Izraelita*, Jan. 19, 1906; Ż. W., "W sprawie wyborów," *Głos Żydowski*, Feb. 1, 1906.

13 For examples, see in *Praca Polska:* "W sprawie wyborów," Feb. 12, 1906, evening edition; E. Maliszewski, "Czy wybierać Żyda na posła?," Feb. 16, evening edition; and in *Dzwon Polski*, "W kwestji żydowskiej," April 14, morning edition, and "Kłamstwa wśród żydów," April 21, evening edition.

14 "Odezwa Związku P.–D.," *Prawda*, April 21, 1906. For the party's platform, see "Zasady programu Związku Postępowo–Demokratycznego," *Prawda*, Nov. 22, 1905.

15 In *Izraelita:* "Odgłosy," and "Kronika," April 20, 1906, and "Odgłosy," April 27; in *Głos Żydowski*, "Kronika wyborcza," April 20, and "Kronika wyborcza," April 29.

16 "Wybory w Warszawie," *Dzwon Polski*, April 20, 1906, morn-

ing edition; "Ostatnia chwila," *Dzwon Polski*, April 23, morning edition.
[17] "Zwartą ławą," *Dzwon Polski*, April 22, 1906, morning edition.
[18] "Wybory," *Prawda*, May 5, 1906.
[19] "Demokracja narodowa a żydzi," *Dzwon Polski*, April 24, 1906, morning edition.
[20] Kiepurska, *Warszawa 1905-1907*, p. 289; "Wybory," *Prawda*, May 5, 1906; Bolesław Prus, *Kroniki*, XVIII, 541.
[21] I. Frenkiel, "Refleksje powyborcze," *Izraelita*, May 4, 1906.
[22] Ignacy Chabelski, "Wybory w Warszawie w świetle cyfr," *Praca*, no. 5 (supplement to *Biblioteka Warszawka*, vol. 262, no. 2, May 1906), pp. 28–40.
[23] Dmowski did not run because of residency requirements. All three workers' electors chosen were supporters of National Democracy. The socialists had implemented an effective boycott in the workers' curia, so that of 114 factories which could choose plenipotentiaries to vote for the three electors, only at nine did workers participate; Kiepurska, *Warszawa 1905-1907*, p. 287.
[24] "Po wyborach warszawskich," *Dzwon Polski*, April 27, 1906, evening edition.
[25] "Kroniki," *Tygodnik Illustrowany*, Dec. 16, 1906.
[26] In *Życie Żydowskie*: "Nasze hasła wyborcze," and "Z życia," Nov. 16, 1906, "Komunikat," Dec. 14, and "Koło polskie i sprawa żydowska," Dec. 28, in *Izraelita*: "Kronika," Dec. 21., and Civis, "Sprawy wyborcze. Żydzi wobec 'Koncentracji Narodowej,'" Jan. 4, 1907.
[27] "Odezwa Komitetu Centralnego do współobywateli żydów," *Goniec Wieczorny*, Jan. 17, 1907.
[28] The Zionists later maintained that the *kehile* board had backed the Concentration: "Do dymisji!," *Życie Żydowskie*, March 1, 1907.
[29] In *Izraelita*: "Kronika," Jan. 11, 1907; in *Życie Żydowskie*: "Żydowski Komitet Wyborczy," and "Z życia," Jan. 4., Z. B., "Zebranie przedwyborcze," Jan. 11, "Przedwyborcze zebranie sjonistyczne," Feb. 8, and "Odezwa żydowskiego komitetu wyborczego," Feb. 15.
[30] "Z prasy polskiej," *Izraelita*, Jan. 25, 1907.
[31] "Wybory," *Goniec Wieczorny*, Jan. 28, 1907.
[32] Barbara Petrozolin-Skowrońska, "Z dziejów liberalizmu polskiego: partie liberalno-demokratyczne inteligencji w Królestwie Polskim 1905-1907," *Dzieje Najnowsze*, 3 (1971), no. 3, p. 24; Poseł Prawdy (Świętochowski), "Liberum veto," *Prawda*, Feb. 2, 1907.

[33] Żk, "Licha farsa," *Goniec Wieczorny*, Feb. 6, 1907.
[34] *Goniec Poranny*, Feb. 18, 1907, and "Dodatek Nadzwyczajny" to *Goniec*, Feb. 19.
[35] Kiepurska, *Warszawa 1905-1907*, p. 375; "Pamiętnik," *Prawda*, Feb. 23, 1907.
[36] "Kronika," *Życie Żydowskie*, Feb. 22, 1907.
[37] See Adolf Suligowski, *Projekt przyszłego samorządu miejskiego* (Warsaw, 1911); Edward Chmielewski, *The Polish Question in the Russian State Duma* (Knoxville, 1970), pp. 138-60; Mirosław Wierzchowski, *Sprawy polskie w III i IV Dumie Państwowej* (Warsaw, 1966), pp. 196-201; and A. Ia. Avrekh, *Stolypin i Tret'ia Duma* (Moscow, 1968), pp. 92-108.
[38] *Polnoe Sobranie Zakonov*, 3rd collection, XXVII, law 29242, June 3, 1907; see also "Od magistratu miasta Warszawy," *Kurjer Warszawski*, July 16, 1912.
[39] Alfred Levin, *The Third Duma: Election and Profile* (Hamden, Conn., 1973), pp. 77-78.
[40] "Przegląd prasy polskiej," *Izraelita*, Aug. 30, 1912.
[41] "Przed wyborami," *Gazeta Warszawska*, Sept. 12, 1912.
[42] "Żydzi i wybory," *Gazeta Warszawska*, Sept. 7, 1912; "Nowa sytucja," *Kurjer Warszawski*, Aug. 18.
[43] "Nowa sytuacja;" "O wybory w Warszawie," Aug. 21, 1912, and "Ugoda czy kompromis?" Aug. 26., all in *Kurjer Warszawski*.
[44] Halina Janowska, et al., eds., *Archiwum polityczne Ignacego Paderewskiego*, I (Warclaw, 1973), 39.
[45] "Śmierć Narodowej Demokracji!" *Gazeta Warszawska*, Aug. 28, 1912. See also "Walka z Demokracją Narodową," Aug. 29-30 and Sept. 1-2., and "Żydzi i wybory," Sept. 6-7.
[46] "Zebranie obywatelskie," *Kurjer Warszawski*, Sept. 21, 1912. Other views can be found in *Gazeta Warszawska*, "Nieudana próba," and "Zebranie w Resursie Kupieckiej," Sept. 21, and in *Nowa Gazeta*, "Znamienne zebranie," Sept. 21, afternoon edition.
[47] "Nieudana próba."
[48] "Kandydat Warszawy," *Kurjer Warszawski*, Sept. 29, 1912; "Kandydatura grup połączonych," *Nowa Gazeta*, Oct. 1, afternoon edition.
[49] "Ruch wyborczy," *Izraelita*, Oct. 4, 1912. See also Archiwum Państwowe miasta stołecznego Warszawy, Zarząd Oberpolicmajstra Warszawskiego, sygnatura 21, k. 78-79.
[50] Zarząd Oberpolicmajstra Warszawskiego, sygnatura 21, k. 78-79, 149-50, 194-95, and 220, has information on Jewish public meetings.

Notes

51 In *Izraelita*: "Czego żądacie?" Sept. 27, 1912, and "Kandydat Warszawy," Oct. 4; see also "Przed wyborami," *Kurjer Warszawski*, Oct. 2, morning supplement.
52 *PPS-Lewica, 1906-1918: materiały i dokumenty*, ed. Feliks Tych, II (Warsaw, 1962), 250–94.
53 Dmowski, *Polityka polska*, p. 105.
54 Cited in Andrzej Micewski, *Roman Dmowski* (Warsaw, 1971), p. 191.
55 Zarząd Oberpolicmajstra Warszawskiego, sygnatura 21, k. 222–25.
56 *Ibid.*, k. 214.
57 *Gazeta Poranna*, Sept. 25, 1912.
58 "Wobec wyborów," *Słowo*, Oct. 10, 1912.
59 "Zebranie przedwyborcze w Filharmonii," *Gazeta Warszawska*, Oct. 7. 1912.
60 "Pan Dmowski nie pozwala! . . .," Oct. 2, 1912, "Kandydat na szczudłach," Oct. 3, and "W niewoli tłumu," Oct. 7, all in *Kurjer Warszawski*, provide examples.
61 Józef Wasercug, "Kandydatura grup połączonych," *Nowa Gazeta*, Oct. 2, 1912, afternoon edition.
62 "Zebranie przedwyborcze," *Kurjer Warszawski*, Oct. 9, 1912.
63 These last comments in particular came back to haunt him. See Feldman, *Dzieje polskiej myśli*, p. 370; Hirszhorn, *Historia Żydów*, p. 304; and Leo Belmont and Jerzy Huzarski, *Zwycięztwo Romana Dmowskiego* (Warsaw, 1913).
64 "Przed wyborami," Oct. 12, 1912, morning supplement, and "Przed wyborami," Oct. 13, both in *Kurjer Warszawski*; in *Nowa Gazeta*, "Żydzi–Polacy wobec wyborów," Oct. 11, afternoon edition, "Ruch wyborczy," Oct. 12, morning edition, "Wobec wyborów," Oct. 12, afternoon edition, and "Ruch wyborczy," Oct. 13, morning edition; "Ruch wyborczy," *Izraelita*, Oct. 11; and Zarząd Oberpolicmajstra Warszawskiego, sygnatura 21, k. 149–50, 194–95.
65 "Przed wyborami," *Kurjer Warszawski*, Oct. 13, 1912; "Już się wyjaśniło," *Gazeta Warszawska*, Oct. 12.
66 "Ruch wyborczy," *Nowa Gazeta*, Oct. 13, 1912, morning edition.
67 "Wobec wyborow," *Słowo*, Oct. 10, 1912.
68 "Wobec wyborów," *Nowa Gazeta*, Oct. 12, 1912, afternoon edition.
69 "Przed wyborami," Oct. 12, 1912, morning supplement, and "Przed wyborami," Oct. 13, both in *Kurjer Warszawski*, and in *Nowa Gazeta*, "Ruch wyborczy," Oct. 12, morning edition, and "Ruch wyborczy," Oct. 13, morning edition.

[70] "Do obywateli miasta Warszawy," *Nowa Gazeta*, Oct. 14, 1912, afternoon edition.
[71] "Na dobie," *Tygodnik Illustrowany*, Oct. 19, 1912.
[72] From *Nowa Gazeta:* "Wybory," Oct. 17, 1912, morning edition, and "Wybory," Oct. 17, afternoon edition.
[73] For a brief biography of this obscure figure, see Jan Tomicki, "Jagiełło Eugeniusz," *Polski słownik biograficzny*, X, 313–14, and also Zarząd Oberpolicmajstra Warszawskiego, sygnatura 21, k. 307–08, for a police report.
[74] "Głosy publiczne," *Kurjer Warszawski*, Oct. 21, 1912; and "Wybory," *Nowa Gazeta*, Oct. 22, afternoon edition.
[75] For examples of the paper's point of view, see *Kurjer Warszawski:* "Wróg czy obywatel?" Oct. 20, 1912, "Po wyborach w Warszawie," Oct. 17, and "Jutrzejsza odpowiedź," Nov. 6.
[76] In *Kurjer Warszawski:* "Znamienny krok," Oct. 27, 1912, and "Rady p. Winawera," Nov. 4; *Gazeta Warszawska*, "Interwencja 'Kadetów,' " Oct. 24–25; and in *Nowa Gazeta*, "Wybory," Oct. 28, afternoon edition, and "Wybory," Nov. 4, afternoon edition.
[77] "Odezwa żydowska," *Kurjer Warszawski*, Oct. 31, 1912, morning supplement.
[78] "W otwarte karty," *Kurjer Warszawski*, Oct. 31, 1912.
[79] "O mandat z Warszawy," *Izraelita*, Oct. 25, 1912. See also, in *Kurjer Warszawski*, "Wybory," Nov. 1, and "Wybory," Nov. 3.
[80] See issues of *Nowa Gazeta* for Nov. 3–7.
[81] In *Nowa Gazeta:* "Wybory," Nov. 8, 1912, morning edition; and "Wybór posła miasta Warszawy," Nov. 8, afternoon edition.
[82] B. Singer, *Nalewki*, pp. 165–66. Singer, who was working for *Haynt*, comments on negotiations at the newspaper for this Jewish nationalist–socialist accommodation. *Haynt* played a central role in Jewish efforts; Y. Davidsohn, "Der 'Haynt' un Yagello," *Haynt yubilei-bukh, 1908–1928* (Warsaw, 1928), pp. 12–13.
[83] "Wybory," *Kurjer Warszawski*, Nov. 8, 1912.
[84] "Wczorajszy wybór," *Kurjer Warszawski*, Nov. 9, 1912, morning supplement.
[85] "Finis coronat . . .," *Gazeta Warszawska*, Nov. 8, 1912. There is no serious evidence that Vinaver, or any other Kadets, actually played any direct part.
[86] "Co mówią fakty?" *Kurjer Warszawski*, Nov. 10, 1912.
[87] "Żydowski poseł Warszawy," *Tygodnik Illustrowany*, Nov. 16, 1912.
[88] On the boycott, see Samuel Hirszhorn, *Historia Żydów w Polsce od sejmu czteroletniego do wojny europejskiej (1788–1914)* (Warsaw, 1921), pp. 309–33; Schiper, *Dzieje handlu*, pp. 532–42; and

Golczewski, *Polnische-jüdische Beziehungen*, pp. 106–20. The election of a Jewish Duma delegate from Łódź, Mayer Bomash, does not seem to have been a major issue.

[89] Zarząd Oberpolicmajstra Warszawskiego, sygnatura 21, k. 378–80.

[90] For a particularly bitter piece by Świętochowski, see his "Żydo-Polska," *Tygodnik Illustrowany*, Feb. 22, 1913.

[91] Hirszhorn, *Historia Żydów*, p. 326.

[92] Kiepurska and Pustuła, *Raporty oberpolicmajstrów*, p. 119.

[93] Kiepurska and Pustuła, *Raporty oberpolicmajstrów*, p. 126.

[94] Jan Baudouin de Courtenay, *W 'kwestji żydowskiej'* (Warsaw, 1913).

[95] Roman Jabłonowski, *Wspomnienia 1905–1928* (Warsaw, 1962), pp. 138–39.

[96] A. Badayev, *The Bolsheviks in the Tsarist Duma* (New York, 1973), pp. 30–31; V. I. Lenin, *Polnoe sobranie sochinenii*, 5th ed. (Moscow, 1958–69), XXII, 238–40, and XLVIII, 122–23, 128–29.

[97] Dmowski, *Polityka polska*, p. 105. For his comments shortly after the election, see his *Upadek myśli konserwatywnej w Polsce* (Częstochowa, 1938), pp. 63–65 and 118–27 (originally published in 1914).

[98] Golczewski, *Polnisch-jüdische Beziehungen*, pp. 115–17.

Notes to Conclusions

[1] Walker Connor, "Nation–Building or Nation–Destroying?" *World Politics*, 24 (1972), 132. This article examines Karl Deutsch's work on nationalism and social change, the most important of which is *Nationalism and Social Communication: An Inquiry into the Foundations of Nationality*, 2nd ed. (Cambridge, Mass., 1966).

[2] The views of anthropologist Fredrik Barth on the importance of boundaries are especially relevant. In the "Introduction," to Fredrik Barth, ed., *Ethnic Groups and Boundaries: The Social Organization of Cultural Differences* (Bergen–Olso and London, 1969), pp. 9–10, he states:

> First, it is clear that boundaries persist despite a flow of personnel across them. In other words, categorical ethnic distinctions do not depend on an absence of mobility, contact, and information, but do entail social processes of exclusion and incorporation whereby discrete categories are maintained *despite* changing participation and membership in the course of individual life histories. Secondly, one finds

that stable, persisting, and often vitally important social relationships are maintained across such boundaries, and are frequently based precisely on the dichotomized ethnic statuses. In other words, ethnic distinctions do not depend on an absence of social interaction and acceptance, but are quite to the contrary often the very foundations on which embracing social systems are built. Interaction in such a social system does not lead to its liquidation through change and acculturation; cultural differences can persist despite inter-ethnic contact and interdependence.

John A. Armstrong uses this emphasis on boundaries in a historical perspective in his *Nations before Nationalism* (Chapel Hill, N.C., 1982). William G. Lockwood has argued that ethnic boundaries based on faith are particularly strong, more so than those based on language; "Religion and Language as Criteria of Ethnic Identity: An Exploratory Comparison," in *Ethnicity and Nationalism in Southeastern Europe*, eds. Sam Beck and John W. Cole (Amsterdam, 1981), pp. 71–82.

[3] I. L. Pertz, "Oyf a farval–farzamlung," in his *Ale verk*, XI (New York, 1948), 305–10. The text is not dated, but it clearly came after Kucharzewski's October 8th speech at the Philharmonic.

[4] Stefan Kieniewicz, "Społeczeństwo Warszawy w okresie rozbiorów," in Kazimierski, *Społeczeństwo Warszawy*, p. 72.

List of Tables

Table 1-1 Warsaw's Budget, 1883 and 1914
Table 2-1 Growth of Warsaw's Population, 1882-1914
Table 2-2 Birthplaces of Warsaw's Population, 1882 and 1897
Table 2-3 Religious Composition of Warsaw's Population, 1882-1914
Table 2-4 Age Breakdowns by Faith in Warsaw, 1882, and in Warsaw and Congress Poland, 1857
Table 2-5 Faith and Native Language, 1897
Table 3-1 Religious Composition by Precinct, 1882-1910
Table 3-2 Religious Composition of the Suburbs, 1893 and 1909
Table 4-1 Faith and Employment, 1882

Table 4-2 Faith and Employment, 1882: Percentages, All Persons, by Faith Group within Employment Category
Table 4-3 Native Language and Employment in Warsaw, 1897
Table 4-4 Native Language and Employment in Warsaw, 1897: Percentages, All Persons, by Native Language within Employment Category
TAble 4-5 Intelligentsia by Faith, 1882, Employed and Dependents Combined
Table 4-6 Intelligentsia by Native Language, 1897: Employed and All Persons

Table 1–1

Warsaw's Budget, 1883 and 1914

1. 1883

Category	Thousands of rubles	Percentage of total
Sewers, water mains, other special projects	609	25.4%
Streets, bridges, etc.	462	19.3%
Police, courts, fire, administration, etc.	868	36.2%
Charity and hospitals	75	3.1%
Education	71	3%
Debt service	107	4.5%
Other	203	8.5%
Total	2,395	100.%

Source: Załęski, "Warszawa," *Słownik geograficzny*, XIII, 34.

Table 1–1 continued

2. 1914

Sewers, water mains	972	6.6%
"External appearance of the city"	2,649	16.5%
Police, fire, courts, administration, etc.	1,963	12.3%
Charity and hospitals	2,091	13.1%
Education	749	4.7%
Debt service	2,791	17.4%
"Reversible and extraordinary" (*wydatki zwrotne, nadzwyczajne*)	3,549	22.2%
Other	1,247	7.8%
Total	16,011	100.1%[a]

[a] Rounding error.

Source: Dziewulski and Radziszewski, *Warszawa*, II, 436–39.

Table 2-1

Growth of Warsaw's Population, 1882–1914

Year	Total	1882=100
1882	382,964	
1897	624,189	163
1914	884,584	231

Sources: 1882—*Rezul'taty 1882*, I, 2: 1897—*Perepis' 1897*, LI, Table 7; 1914—Kiepurska and Pustuła, *Raporty oberpolicmajstrów*, p. 123.

Table 2-2
Birthplaces of Warsaw's Population, 1882 and 1897

1. Birthplaces of Warsaw's Residents, 1882

Place	Men	Women	Total
Warsaw City	94,183	107,261	201,444
	51.9%	53.2%	52.6%
Warsaw province	19,401	23,760	43,161
	10.7%	11.8%	11.3%
Elsewhere in Polish Kingdom[a]	45,978 25.4%	54,111 26.8%	100,089 26.1%
Elsewhere in Russian Empire	12,915 7.1%	8,541 4.2%	21,456 5.6%
Austria-Hungary	3,576 2.0%	2,345 1.2%	5,921 1.5%
Germany	4,838	4,763	9,601
	2.7%	2.4%	2.5%
Other	471	821	1,292
	0.3%	0.4%	0.3%
Total	181,362	201,602	382,964

Source: *Rezul'taty 1882*, I, Table 27.

[a] Includes 3,065 men and 3,378 women born in the Kingdom, but without the province of birth designated.

Table 2–2 (continued)

2. Birthplaces of Warsaw's Actual Population, 1897

Place	Men	Women	Total
Warsaw City	148,657	165,736	314,393
	48.3%	52.4%	50.4%
Warsaw province	39,778	47,308	87,086
	12.9%	15.0%	14.0%
Elsewhere in Polish Kingdom[a]	65,338	77,781	143,119
	21.2%	24.6%	22.9%
Elsewhere in Russian Empire	48,570	19,393	67,963
	15.8%	6.1%	10.9%
Austria-Hungary	2,424	1,723	4,147
	0.8%	0.5%	0.7%
Germany	2,461	3,217	5,678
	0.8%	1.0%	0.9%
Other[b]	706	1,097	1,803
	0.2%	0.3%	0.3%
Total	307,934	316,255	624,189

Source: *Perepis' 1897*, LI, Table 7.

[a] Includes 4 men and 6 women born "in the Vistula provinces in general."
[b] Includes 19 men and 58 women born "abroad in general."

Table 2-3

Religious Composition of Warsaw's Population, 1882-1914

Year	Catholics	Jews	Orthodox	Protestants	Others	Total
1882	223,127	127,917	13,640	17,643	637	382,964
	58.1%	33.4%	3.6%	4.6%	0.2%	
1897	347,565	210,526	46,787	17,943	1,358	624,189
	55.7%	33.7%	7.5%	2.9%	0.2%	
1914	487,950	337,024	36,650	19,922	2,203	883,749[a]
	55.2%	38.1%	4.1%	2.3%	0.2%	

Sources: 1882—*Rezul'taty 1882*, I, Table 10; 1897— *Perepis' 1897*, LI, Table 12; 1914—Kiepurska and Pustuła, *Raporty oberpolicmajstrów*, p. 123.

[a] The same source gives the total population as 884, 584, without explaining the discrepancy.

Table 2-4

Age Breakdowns by Faith in Warsaw, 1882, and in Warsaw and Congress Poland, 1897

1. Years of Birth, 1882

Years	Total	Catholics	Jews
1862-82	163,788 (42.8%)	83,835 (37.6%)	67,823 (53%)
1832-61	171,979 (44.9%)	108,405 (48.6%)	47,693 (37.3%)
Pre-1832	45,672 (11.9)	30,012 (13.5%)	11,940 (9.3%)
Unknown	1,525 (0.4%)	875 (0.4%)	461 (0.4%)
Totals	382,964	223,127	127,917

2. Ages, 1897 (Warsaw only)

Ages	Total	Catholics	Jews
0-19	256,592 (41.1%)	134,412 (38.7%)	106,652 (50.7%)
20-49	292,917 (46.9%)	165,835 (47.7%)	81,915 (38.9%)
Over 49	74,093 (11.9%)	47,045 (13.5%)	21,707 (10.3%)
Unknown	587 (0.1%)	273 (0.1)	238 (0.1)
Totals	624,189	347,565	210,526

3. Ages, 1897 (Entire Congress Kingdom; percentages only)

Ages	Total	Catholics	Jews
0-19	49.1%	49.7%	53.7%
20-49	38.1%	36.8%	35.3%
Over 49	12.7%	13.4%	11%

("Unknown" shares come out to less than 0.1% in each case)

Sources: *Rezul'taty 1882*, I, Table 10; *Perepis' 1897*, LI, Table 25; Szulc, *Wartość*, pp. 106-09.

Table 2-5
Faith and Native Language, 1897

Faith Language	Catholic	Jewish	Orthodox	Protestant[a]	Others	Total, by language
Polish	343,386	28,781	1,435	8,615	89	382,306 61.2%
Yiddish	212	176,263	39	20	5	176,539 28.3%
Russian	1,174	4,552	35,823	404	434	42,387 6.8%
German	1,052	869	50	7,888	78	9,937 1.6%
Others	1,741	61	9,440	1,016	752	13,020 2.1%
Total, by faith	347,565	210,526	46,787	17,943	1,358	624,189

Source: *Perepis' 1897*, LI, Table 14.

[a]Includes Lutheran and Reformed churches.

Table 3-1

Religious Composition by Precinct, 1882–1910

Area		1882	1897	1910
Center	Catholics	53,092	65,457	73,276
		70.5%	67.6%	64.6%
	Jews	15,910	22,049	32,562
		21.1%	22.8%	28.7%
	Others	6,280	9,348	7,559
		8.3%	9.7%	6.7%
	Total	75,282	96,854	113,397
South	Catholics	62,228	75,551	98,727
		78.3%	71.2%	73.2%
	Jews	7,527	7,997	23,380
		9.5%	7.5%	17.3%
	Others	9,666	22,581	12,698
		12.2%	21.3%	9.4%
	Total	79,421	106,129	134,805
South-west	Catholics	63,940	121,787	157,259
		56.7%	60%	62.2%
	Jews	39,733	62,555	78,525
		35.2%	30.8%	31%
	Others	9,174	18,485	17,075
		8.1%	9.1%	6.8%
	Total	112,847	202,827	252,959
North-west	Catholics	36,053	51,808	48,471
		36.6%	32.1%	23.9%

Table 3-1 continued

	Jews	57,431	102,490	149,195
		58.3%	63.6%	73.7%
	Others	5,094	6,968	4,756
		5.2%	4.3%	2.3%
	Total	98,578	161,266	202,429
Praga	Catholics	7,814	32,872	47,177
		48%	57.6%	60.8%
	Jews	7,316	15,435	22,399
		44.9%	27%	28.9%
	Others	1,160	8,806	8,013
		7.1%	15.4%	10.3%
	Total	16,290	57,113	77,589

Sources: 1882—*Rezul'taty 1882*, I, Table 11; 1897— *Perepis' 1897*, LI, Table 12; 1910—Konczyński, *Ludność*, p. vi in statistical appendix.

Precincts

Center: 1882—I/XI, II/III; 1897—I, II; 1910—I, II, XII.
South: 1882—IX, X; 1897—same; 1910—IX, X, XIII.
Southwest: 1882—VII, VIII; 1897—VI, VII, VIII, XI; 1910—same.
Northwest: 1882—IV, V/VI; 1897—III, IV, V; 1910—same.
Praga: 1882—XII; 1897—same; 1910—XIV, XV

Table 3-2

Religious Composition of the Suburbs, 1893 and 1909

Year	Total	Catholics	Jews	Others
1893	61,955	50,339	8,508	3,108
		81.3%	13.7%	5%
1909	162,995	120,616	26,793	15,586
		74%	16.4%	9.6%

Sources: 1893—*Sostoianie naseleniia v desiati guberniiakh Tsarstva Pol'skago k pervomu ianvaria 1893 goda*, Trudy Varshavskago Statisticheskago Komiteta, No. 11 (Warsaw, 1894), pp. 2-5 and 144-47; 1909—*Tablitsy sostoianiia naseleniia v desiati guberniiakh Tsarstva Pol'skago k pervomu ianvaria 1909*, Trudy Varshavskago Statisticheskago Komiteta, No. 39, Part 1 (Warsaw, 1910), pp. 2-3.

Table 4-1

Faith and Employment, 1882:

Employed and Dependents Combined

Category	Total	Catholics	Jews	Others
Industry	125,367	80,741	35,992	8,634
Trade	63,963	11,036	50,714	2,213
Servants	50,209	40,380	7,294	2,535
Govt. Service and professions	44,182	24,625	13,111	6,446
Laborers	35,064	24,011	8,790	2,263
Property owners and capitalists	18,496	12,139	4,796	1,561
Transport and communications	16,850	12,569	3,136	1,145
Pensioners	6,713	5,688	99	926
Agriculture	1,245	1,061	80	104
Others, unknown	14,544	9,213	3,760	1,571
Total, civilians	376,633	221,463	27,772	27,398
Army and navy	6,331	1,664	145	4,522
Total	382,964	223,127	127,917	31,920

Source: *Rezul'taty 1882*, III, Tables 12 and 13.

Table 4–1 continued

Faith and Employment, 1882: Percentages, All Persons Except Military, by Employment Category within Faith Group

Category	Total	Catholics	Jews	Others
Industry	33.3%	36.5%	28.2%	31.5%
Trade	17%	5%	39.7%	8.1%
Servants	13.3%	18.2%	5.7%	9.3%
Govt. Service and Professions	11.7%	11.1%	10.3%	23.5%
Laborers	9.3%	10.8%	6.9%	8.3%
Property owners and Capitalists	4.9%	5.5%	3.8%	5.7%
Transport and Communications	4.5%	5.7%	2.5%	4.2%
Pensioners	1.8%	2.6%	0.1%	3.4%
Agriculture	0.3%	0.5%	0.1%	0.4%
Others, unknown	3.9%	4.2%	2.9%	5.7%
Total, civilians	100%	100.1%[a]	100.2%[a]	100.1%[a]

[a]Rounding error.

Table 4-2

Faith and Employment, 1882: Percentages, All Persons by Faith Group within Employment Category

Category	Catholics	Jews	Others	Total
Industry	64.4%	28.7%	6.9%	100%
Trade	17.3%	79.3%	3.5%	100.1%[a]
Servants	80.4%	14.5%	5%	99.9%[a]
Govt. Service and Professions	55.7%	29.7%	14.6%	100%
Laborers	68.5%	25.1%	6.5%	100.1%[a]
Property Owners and Capitalists	65.6%	25.9%	8.4%	99.9%[a]
Transport and Communications	74.6%	18.6%	6.8%	100%
Pensioners	84.7%	1.5%	13.8%	100%
Agriculture	85.2%	6.4%	8.4%	100%
Others, unknown	63.3%	25.9%	10.8%	100%
Total, civilians	58.8%	33.9%	7.3%	100%
Army and navy	26.3%	2.3%	71.4%	100%
Total	58.3%	33.4%	8.3%	100%

Source: See Table 4-1.

[a]Rounding error.

Table 4-3
Native Language and Employment in Warsaw, 1897: Employed and All Persons

Category	Total Employed	Total All	Polish Employed	Polish All
Industry	89,510	214,048	62,870	145,010
Service, Labor	72,766	123,248	57,181	98,590
Trade	36,253	115,293	13,899	38,633
Government, Professions	18,644	42,438	11,697	26,785
Transport, Communications	12,093	38,693	8,871	28,846
Property owners, Pensioners	17,441	36,044	13,351	26,539
Agriculture	936	2,142	774	1,737
Others, Unknown	15,844	21,872	11,487	15,087
Total, Non-Military	263,487	593,778	180,130	381,227
Military	27,878	30,411	658	1,079
Total	291,365	624,189	180,788	382,306

Table 4-3 continued

Category	Yiddish Employed	Yiddish All	Others Employed	Others All
Industry	22,888	61,467	3,752	7,571
Service, Labor	12,185	19,712	3,400	4,946
Trade	20,299	71,732	2,055	2,928
Government, Professions	1,862	6,006	5,085	9,647
Transport, Communications	1,643	6,284	1,579	3,563
Property Owners, Pensioners	2,053	5,716	2,037	3,789
Agriculture	76	269	86	136
Others, Unknown	2,381	4,552	1,976	2,233
Total, Non-Military	63,387	175,738	19,970	36,813
Military	705	801	26,515	28,531
Total	64,092	176,539	46,485	65,344

Source: *Perepis' 1897*, LI, Table 22.

Table 4-3 continued
Native Language and Employment in Warsaw, 1897:
Percentages, All Persons Except Military, by
Employment Category within Language Group

Category	Total	Polish	Yiddish	Other
Industry	36%	38.1%	35%	20.6%
Service, Labor	20.8%	25.9%	11.2%	13.5%
Trade	19.4%	10.1%	40.8%	13.4%
Govt., Professions	7.1%	7%	3.4%	26.2%
Transport, Comm.	6.5%	7.6%	3.6%	9.7%
Property Owners, Pensioners	6.1%	7%	3.3%	10.3%
Agriculture	0.4%	0.5%	0.2%	0.4%
Others, unknown	3.7%	3.9%	2.6%	6.1%
Total, non-military	100%	100.1%[a]	100.1%[a]	100.1%[a]

[a]Rounding error.

Table 4-4

Native Language and Employment in Warsaw, 1897: Percentages, All Persons, by Native Language within Employment Category

Category	Polish	Yiddish	Other	Total
Industry	67.7%	28.7%	3.5%	99.9%[a]
Service, Labor	80%	16%	4%	100%
Trade	33.5%	62.2%	4.3%	100%
Govt., Professions	63.1%	14.2%	22.7%	100%
Transport, Comm.	74.6%	16.2%	9.2%	100%
Property Owners, Capitalists	73.6%	15.9%	10.5%	100%
Agriculture	81.1%	12.6%	6.3%	100%
Others, unknown	69%	20.8%	10.2%	100%
Total, non-military	64.2%	29.6%	6.2%	100%
Military	3.5%	2.6%	93.8%	99.9%[a]
Total	61.2%	28.3%	10.5%	100%

Source: See Table 4-3.

[a]Rounding error.

Table 4-5
Intelligentsia by Faith, 1882
Employed and Dependents Combined

Category	Total	Catholics	Jews	Others[a]
Private Admin.	14,530	6,641	6,851	1,038
		45.7%	47.2%	7.2%
Govt. Service, Police	11,925	8,604	165	3,156
		72.2%	1.4%	26.5%
Education	6,975	2,444	3,615	916
		35%	51.8%	13.1%
Health	4,502	2,853	1,073	576
		63.4%	23.8%	12.8%
The Arts	2,867	2,030	505	332
		70.8%	17.6%	11.6%
Religion	1,605	656	607	342
		40.9%	37.8%	21.3%
Private Law Practice	1,315	1,030	223	62
		78.3%	17%	4.7%
Literature, Press	463	367	72	24
		79.3%	15.6%	5.2%

Source: See Table 4-1.

[a]The Orthodox made up 22.1% (2,630) in the govenment service and police category, and 15.7% (252) in religion; they were under 10% in all others.

Table 4-6

Intelligentsia by Native Language, 1897: Employed and All Persons

Category	Total Employed	Total All	Polish Employed	Polish All
Administration, Courts, Police	5,648	13,887	2,980	8,564
			52.8%	61.7%
Education	4,482	8,772	2,233	3,842
			49.8%	43.8%
Health, Sanitation	3,634	7,108	2,811	5,362
			77.4%	75.4%
Scholarship, Literature, Art	2,072	4,780	1,653	3,874
			79.8%	81%
Religious Service	1,043	3,283	500	1,112
			47.9%	33.9%
Public and Class Service	719	2,162	596	1,835
			82.9%	84.9%
Private Law Practice	597	1,775	548	1,640
			91.8%	92.4%
Service in Charitable Institutions	449	675	376	556
			83.7%	82.4%

Table 4-6 continued

Category	Yiddish Employed	Yiddish All	Others[a] Employed	Others[a] All
Administration, Courts, Police	47	164	2,621	5,159
	0.8%	1.2%	46.4%	37.1%
Education	821	2,459	1,428	2,471
	18.3%	28%	31.9%	28.2%
Health, Sanitation	353	902	470	844
	9.7%	18.9%	12.9%	11.9%
Scholarship, Literature, Art	121	324	298	582
	5.8%	6.8%	14.4%	12.2%
Religious Service	434	1,871	109	300
	41.6%	57%	10.5%	9.1%
Public and Class Service	49	190	74	137
	6.8%	8.9%	10.3%	6.3%
Private Law Practice	19	65	30	70
	3.2%	3.7%	5%	3.9%
Service in Charitable Institutions	18	31	55	88
	4%	4.1%	12.2%	13%

Source: See Table 4-3.

[a]The Russian–speaking group was above 10% in Administration, courts, and police (4,192 employed plus dependents, 30.2%); Education (1,744 19.9%); and Health and Sanitation (727, 10.2%).

Appendix: Employment Categories, 1882 and 1897

Employment Categories from the 1882 Census

Category	Census Category Number
Industry	
Mining	V 5
Processing of stones and minerals	VI 6–15
Metalworking	VII 16–33
Machine and instrument production	VIII 34–43
Chemical production	IX 44–46
Fuel and lighting industry	X 47–52
Textile products	XI 53–58
Production of paper and leather	XII 59–68
Wooden and carved articles	XIII 69–82
Comestibles	XIV 83–97
Clothing and cleaning	XV 98–113
Construction	XVI 114–22
Printing occupations	XVII 123–26
Art in industrial applications	XVIII 127–30
Trade	
Trade in general	XIX 131–52
Streeet peddling	XX 153
Insurance	XXI 154
Restaurants and hotels	XXV 159–61
Servants	XXVI 162

Government service and the professions
    Officials (state and private)   XXIX 165–69
    Ministry of Justice and legal practice   XXX 170–76
    Religious service   XXXI 177
    Education   XXXII 178
    Health   XXXIII 179–85
    Literature and the press   XXXIV 186
    The Arts   XXXV 187–89

Unskilled laborers   XXVII 163

Property owners and capitalists   XXXVI 190–92

Transport and communications
    Post, telegraph, and telephone   XXII 155
    Railroads   XXIII 156
    Transport occupations (land and water transport except railroads; messengers)   XXIV 157–58

Pensioners   XXXVI 193

Agriculture
    Agriculture   I 1
    Gardening   II 2
    Forestry   III 3
    Fishing   IV 4

Others and unknown
    Living on social charity   XXXVI 194
    Prostitution   XXXVI 195
    Beggars   XXXVI 196
    Young people studying away from their families   XXXVI 197
    Undetermined occupation   XXXVII 198
    People under detention   XXXVIII 199

Army and navy   XXVIII 164–65

Intelligentsia Categories, 1882, in Greater Detail

Officials	XXIX
State officials, surveyors, and engineers	166
Private officials	167
Lower police ranks	168
Messengers and those in lower private service	169
Ministry of Justice and legal practice	XXX
Officials of the Ministry of Justice	170
Judges	171
Lawyers	172
Lawyers' assistants	173
Private plenipotentiaries	174
Notaries	175
Lawyers' and notaries' clerks	176
Religious service	XXXI 177
Education	XXXII 178
Health	XXXIII
Doctors	179
Dentists	180
Midwives	181
Veterinarians	182
Doctors' assistants	183
Nurses	184
Lower hospital service	185
Literature and the press	XXXIV 186
The Arts	XXXV
Plastic arts	187
Musicians, music teachers	188
Theater, and singing and dancing teachers	189

Source: *Rezul'taty 1882,* III, pp. 20–27.

Employment Categories from the 1897 Census

Category	Census Category Number
Industry	
Mining	22
Metal smelting	23
Processing of fibrous substances (including textiles)	24
Processing of animal products (leather, furs, saddles, harnesses)	25
Woodworking	26
Metalworking	27
Processing of mineral substances (ceramics)	28
Chemical and related production	29
Wine making, beer and mead brewing	30
Production of other drinks and intoxicants	31
Procesing of plant and animal substances for consumption	32
Tobacco processing and products from tobacco	33
Printing	34
Production of physical, optical, surgical, and musical instruments, watches, toys, etc.	35
Jewelry, portraits, religious objects, luxury items, etc.	36
Production of articles of clothing	37
Construction, repair, and maintenance of dwellings and construction in general,	38
Construction of carriages of wooden vessels	39
Other and undetermined industries	40
Private service and day labor	13
Trade	
Credit and public commercial institutions, including banks and insurance	46
Brokerage	47
Trade in general	48
Trade in livestock	49
Trade in grain products	50

Trade in other agricultural products	51
Trade in construction materials and fuel	52
Trade in household articles	53
Trade in various metal goods, machines, and weapons	54
Trade in fabrics and articles of clothing	55
Trade in leather, skins, etc.	56
Trade in luxury, scholarly, artistic, and religious items	57
Trade in other items	58
Street peddling	59
Inns, hotels, furnished rooms, clubs, restaurants	60
Public house trade	61

Government service and the professions

Administration, courts, and police	1
Public and class service	2
Private legal practice	3
Orthodox religious service	5
Religious service in other Christian denominations	6
Religious service in non-Christian faiths	7
Functionaries at churches, cemeteries, etc., and servants and guards at the	8
Education	9
Literature, scholarship, and the arts	10
Health and sanitation	11
Service in charitable institutions	12

Transport and communications

Water transport	41
Railroads	42
Carting	43
Other means of land transport	44
Post, telegraph, and telephone	45

Persons living on the income from capital and property, from relatives, and on pensions 14

Agriculture

Agriculture 17
Apiculture and sericulture 18
Livestock raising 19
Forestry and forest industries 20
Fishing and hunting 21

Others and unknown

Persons supported publicly, by social institutions, or by private persons 15
Persons deprived of freedom and serving prison sentences 16
Establishments concerned with cleanliness and bodily hygiene 62
Persons of undertermined occupations 63
Prostitution 64
Unknown 65

Armed Forces

Intelligentsia Categories, 1987, in Greater Detail

Administration, courts, and police: Officials of the administrative, justice, and surveying ministeries; employees in the offices of the administrative and justice ministries, and servants and guards at them; court officials and employees at palaces; foreign ambassadors and people working at embassies and missions; police and firement. 1

Public and class service (rural and urban): elected employees, hired employees, servants, messengers, and guards, etc., in institutions of public and class service, atamans, communal mayors, village elders, etc. 2

Private legal practice: notaries, lawyers, employees, servants, and messengers in the offices of notaries and lawyers. 3

Orthodox religious service: monks, novices, clergy, psalmreaders, church singers, etc., reciters of the deceased, collectors of alms for churches. 5

Religions service in other Christian denominations: monks and clergy. 6

Religious service in non-Christian faiths: clergy of higher and lower ranks. 7

Functionaries at churches, chapels, mosques, synagogues, cemeteries, etc., and servants and guards at them. 8

Education: supervisors, teachers, other officials, employees, guards, and servants in educational institutions; private teachers; governors and governesses working for private persons; teachers of arts and crafts. 9

Literature, scholarship, and the arts: scholars, writers, engineers, technologists, artists, musicians, theatrical artists and actors, employees in scholarly and artistic institutions and theatres, museums, and at periodicals, servants in scholarly and artistic institutions and theatres. 10

Health and sanitation: supervisors at medical institutions, civilian doctors; army and navy doctors; midwives; veterinarians; druggists, pharmacists, dentists; doctors' assistants, pharmacy students, etc.; nurses and orderlies in hospitals; sick-nurses and servants in hospitals and pharmacies; hospital attendants; persons engaged in healing with the right to do so (quacks, etc.). 11

Service in charitable institutions 12

Source: *Perepis' 1897*, LI, Table 20.

Selected Bibliography

This bibliography includes those monographs, essays, and journal articles, which were the most important for my work, but certainly very far from all that I used, consulted, or footnoted. I have left out several categories of materials, including manuscripts and archival collections, newspapers and periodical articles, articles in encyclopedias and other reference works (with a few exceptions), and a great many titles which, while they were useful, are of secondary interest to the essential themes for this study.

Abramsky, Chimen et al., eds. *The Jews in Poland.* Oxford, 1986.

Balicki, Zygmunt. *Egoizm narodowy wobec etyki.* New ed. L'vov, 1914.

Baudouin de Courtenay, Jan. *W 'kwestji żydowskiej'.* Warsaw, 1913.

Belmont, Leo, and Huzarski, Jerzy. *Zwyciężtwo Romana Dmowskiego.* Warsaw, 1913.

Beylin, Karolina. *Dni powszednie Warszawy w latach 1880-1900.* Warsaw, 1967.

──── . *W Warszawie w latach 1900-1914.* Warsaw, 1972.

Blejwas, Stanislaus A. "Polish Positivism and the Jews." *Jewish Social Studies*, 46 (1984), 21-37.

──── . *Realism in Polish Politics: Warsaw Positivism and National Survival in Nineteenth Century Poland.* New Haven, Conn., 1984.

Bloch, Bronislaw. "Spatial Evolution of the Jewish and General Population of Warsaw, 1792-1939," in *Papers in Jewish Demography, 1973*, edited by U. O. Schmelz et al., pp. 209-34. Jerusalem, 1977.

──── . "Urban Ecology of the Jewish Population of Warsaw, 1897-1938," in *Papers in Jewish Demography, 1981*, edited by U. O. Schmelz et al., pp. 381-99. Jerusalem, 1983.

Brzezina, Maria. *Polszczyzna Żydów.* Warsaw, 1986.

Bujak, Franciszek. *The Jewish Question in Poland.* Paris, 1919.

Bystroń, Jan Stanisław. *Warszawa.* 2nd ed. Warsaw, 1977.

Cała, Alina. "The Question of the Assimilation of Jews in the Polish Kingdom (1864-1897): An Interpretive Essay." *Polin: A Journal of Polish-Jewish Studies*, 1 (1986), 130-50.

Selected Bibliography

Cegielski, Jerzy. *Stosunki mieszkaniowe w Warszawie w latach 1864–1964*. Warsaw, 1968.
Clem, Ralph S., ed. *Research Guide to the Russian and Soviet Censuses*. Ithaca, N.Y., 1986.
Corrsin, Stephen D. "Aspects of Population Change and of Acculturation in Jewish Warsaw at the End of the Nineteenth Century: The Censuses of 1882 and 1897." *Polin: A Journal of Polish-Jewish Studies*, 3 (1988), 122–41.
──────. "Language Use in Cultural and Political Change in Pre-1914 Warsaw: Poles, Jews, and Russification." *Slavonic and East European Review*, in press. ──────. "Polish-Jewish Relations before the First World War: The Case of the State Duma Elections in Warsaw." *Gal-Ed*, 11 (1989), 31–53.
──────. "Political and Social Change in Warsaw from the January 1863 Insurrection to the First World War: Polish Politics and the 'Jewish Question.' " Ph.D. dissertation, University of Michigan, 1981.
──────. "Warsaw: Poles and Jews in a Conquered City," in *The City in Late Imperial Russia*. Edited by Michael F. Hamm, pp. 122–51. Bloomington, Ind., 1986.
'Cwierćwiecze walki: księga pamiątkowa 'Roli.' Warsaw, 1910.
Detko, Jan. "Warszawskie antynomie." *Przegląd Humanistyczny*, 22 (1978), nr. 7–8, pp. 1–13, nr. 9, pp. 45–59.
Dmowski, Roman. *Myśli nowoczesnego Polaka*. L'vov, 1902.
──────. *Niemcy, Rosya i kwestya polska*. L'vov, 1908.
──────. *Polityka polska i odbudowanie państwa*. 2nd ed. Warsaw, 1926.
──────. *Upadek myśli konserwatywnej w Polsce*. Częstochowa, 1938.
Drozdowski, Marian M., and Zahorski, Andrzej. *Historia Warszawy*. 2nd ed. Warsaw, 1975.
Dziewulski, Stefan, and Radziszewski, Henryk. *Warszawa*. 2 vols. Warsaw, 1913–15.
Eisenbach, Artur. *Kwestia równouprawnienia Żydów w Królestwie Polskim*. Warsaw, 1972.
──────. *Z dziejów ludności żydowskiej w Polsce w XVIII i XIX wieku: studia i szkice*. Warsaw, 1983.
──────. "Żydzi warszawscy i sprawa żydowska w XVIII wieku." *Wars- zawa w XVIII wieku*, fasc. 3, pp. 229–98. *Studia warszawskie*, vol. 22. Warsaw, 1975.
Feldman, Wilhelm. *Dzieje polskiej myśli politycznej, 1864–1914*. 2nd ed. revised by Józef Feldman. Warsaw, 1933.
Frankel, Jonathan. *Prophecy and Politics: Socialism, Nationalism, and the Russian Jews, 1862–1917*. Cambridge, Eng., 1981.

Fuks, Marian. *Prasa żydowska w Warszawie, 1823-1939.* Warsaw, 1979.

Golczewski, Frank. *Polnisch-jüdische Beziehungen: eine Studie zur Geschichte des Antisemitismus in Osteuropa.* Wiesbaden, 1981.

Gomulicki, Juliusz W. "Trzysta lat książki o Warszawie (1643-1944)," in *Z dziejów książki i bibliotek w Warszawie.* Edited by Stanisław Tazbir, pp. 130-202. Warsaw, 1961.

Goroda Rossii v 1910 godu. St. Petersburg, 1914.

Grochulska, Barbara, and Pruss, Witold, eds. *Z dziejów rzemiosła warszawskiego.* Warsaw, 1983.

Grosman, Moshe. " 'Haynt': ershter period, 1908-1915." *Fun noentn ovar*, 2 (1957), 3-67.

Grunbaum, Isaac. "Die Pogrome in Polen," in *Die Judenpogrome in Russland.* Vol. 1, pp. 134-51. Koln and Leipzig, 1910.

Haynt yubiley-bukh, 1918-1928. Warsaw, 1928.

Herbst, Stanisław. "Historia Warszawy: stan i potrzeby badań." *Rocznik Warszawski*, 1 (1960), 8-34.

———. *Ulica Marszałkowska.* 2nd ed. Warsaw, 1978.

Hertz, Aleksander. *Żydzi w kulturze polskiej.* Paris, 1961.

Hirszhorn, Samuel. *Historia Żydów w Polsce od sejmu czteroletniego do wojny europejskiej (1788-1914).* Warsaw, 1921.

Ihnatowicz, Ireneusz. *Burżuazja warszawska.* Warsaw, 1972.

Jankowski, Aleksander. "Rzut oka po kraju," in *Opis ziem zamieszkanych przez Polaków pod wzgledem geograficznym, etnograficznym, historycznym, artystycznym, przemysłowym, handlowym i statystycznym.* Vol. 2, pp. 314-32. Warsaw, 1904.

Jaczczuk, Andrzej. *Spór pozytywistów z konserwatystami o przyszłość Polski, 1870-1903.* Warsaw, 1986.

Jeleński, Jan. *Żydzi, niemcy i my.* 3rd ed. Warsaw, 1877.

Karl Baedeker (firm). *Russia, with Teheran, Port Arthur, and Peking.* Leipzig, 1914.

Kieniewicz, Stefan. "Społeczeństwo Warszawy w okresie rozbiorów," in *Społeczeństwo Warszawy w rozwoju historycznym.* Edited by Józef Kazimierski et al., pp 49-76. Warsaw, 1977.

———. *Warszawa w latach 1795-1914.* Warsaw, 1976.

Kiepurska, Halina. *Warszawa w rewolucji 1905-1907.* Warsaw, 1974.

———, and Pustuła, Zbigniew, eds. *Raporty wrszawskich oberpolicmajstrów (1892-1913).* Wroclaw, 1971.

Kirszrot, Jan, ed. *Safrus: książka zbiorowa poświęcona sprawom żydowstwa.* Warsaw, 1905.

Kmiecik, Zenon. *Prasa pelska w rewolucji 1905-1909.* Warsaw, 1980.

———. *Prasa warszawska w latach 1908-1918.* Warsaw, 1981.

———. *Prasa warszawska w okresie pozytywizmu (1864-1885)*. Warsaw, 1971.
———. *Program polityczny "Głosu Warszawskiego" (1908-1909) i "Gazety Warzawskiej" (1909-1915)*. Warsaw, 1980.
Konczyński, Józef. *Ludność Warszawy: studium statystyczne, 1877-1911*. Warsaw, 1913.
Korzec, Pawel. *Juifs en Pologne: la question juive pendant l'entredeux-guerres*. Paris, 1980.
Kosim, Irena and Jan. "Fritza Wernicka opis Warszawy z 1876 roku." *Warszawa XIX wieku*, fasc. 1, pp. 297–338, and fasc. 2, pp. 317–49, *Studia warszawskie*, vol. 6, 9, Warsaw, 1970–71.
Kozicki, Stanisław. *Historia Ligi Narodowej (okres 1887-1907)*. London, 1964.
Krzywicki, Ludwik. *Wspomnienia*. 3 vols. Warsaw, 1947–59.
Leslie, R. F., ed. *The History of Poland Since 1863*. Cambridge, Eng., 1980.
Lichten, Joseph. "Notes on the Assimilation and Acculturation of Jews in Poland, 1863-1943," in *The Jews in Poland*. Edited by Chimen Abramsky et al., pp. 106–29. Oxford, 1896.
Lojek, Jerzy, ed. *Prasa Polska w latach 1864-1918*. Vol. 2 of *Historia prasy polskiej*. Warsaw, 1976.
Martyn, Peter J. "The Undefined Town within a Town: A History of Jewish Settlement within the Western Districts of Warsaw." *Polin: A Journal of Polish-Jewish Studies*, 3 (1988), 17–45.
Mendelsohn, Ezra. *The Jews of East Central Europe between the World Wars*. Bloomington, Ind., 1983.
———. "A Note on Jewish Assimilation in the Polish Lands," in *Jewish Assimilation in Modern Times*. Edited by Bela Vago, pp. 141–49. Boulder, Colo., 1981.
Mozes, Mendl. " 'Der Moment.' " *Fun noentn ovar*, 2 (1957), 241–69.
Narodnoe obrazovanie v 10 guberniiakh Tsarstva Pol'skago za 90 let, 1816-1906. Vol. 28 of *Trudy Varshavskago Statisticheskago Komiteta*. Warsaw, 1907.
Nietyksza, Maria. *Ludność Warszawy na przełomie XIX i XX wieku*. Warsaw, 1971.
Nussbaum, Hilary. *Szkice historyczne z życia żydów w Warszawie od pierwszych śladów pobytu ich w tem mieście do chwili obecnej*. Warsaw, 1880.
———. *Z teki weterana Warszawskiej Gminy Starozakonnych*. Warsaw, 1880.
Ochs, Michael J. "St. Petersburg and the Jews of Russian Poland, 1862-1905." Unpublished Ph.D. dissertation, Harvard University, 1986.

Orzeszkowa, Eliza. *Pisma.* Vol. 9. Warsaw, 1913.

Pervaia vseobshchaia perepis' naseleniia Rossiiskoi Imperii. 89 vols. St. Petersburg, 1899–1905.

Pietrzak-Pawłowska, Irena, ed. *Wielkomiejski rozwój Warszawy do 1918 roku.* Warsaw, 1973.

Plan goroda Varshavy, s prilozheniem alfavitnago ukazatelia ulits. Warsaw, 1914.

"Program Stronnictwa Demokratyczno–Narodowego w zaborze rosyjskim." *Przegląd Wszechpolski,* 9, nr. 3 (Oct. 1903), pp. 721–58.

Prołopopov, D. "Po okrainam. I. Varshava." *GorodskoeDielo,* Aug. 15, 1910, pp. 1028–39.

Prus, Bolesław. *The Doll.* Translated by David Welsh. New York, 1972.

―――. *Kroniki.* Edited by Zygmunt Szweykowski. 20 vols. Warsaw, 1953–70.

Prus, Witold. *Rozwój przemysłu warszawskiego w latach 1864–1914.* Warsaw, 1977.

―――. "Skład wyznaniowo–narodowościowy Warszawy w XIX i początkach XX wieku," in *Społeczeństwo Warszawy w rozwoju historycznym.* Edited by Józef Kazimierski et al., pp. 372–88. Warsaw, 1977.

―――. "Społeczeństwo Królestwa Polskiego w XIX i początkach XX wieku." *Przegląd Historyczny,* 68 (1977), 259–86 and 487–512.

Rezul'taty odnodevnoi perepisi naseleniia goroda Varshavy v 1882 godu. Rezultaty spisu jednodiowego ludności miasta Warszawy 1882 roku. 3 vols. Warsaw, 1883–85.

Ringelblum, Emanuel. *Żydzi w Warszawie: część pierwsza, od czasów najdawniejszych do ostatniego wygnania w roku 1527.* Warsaw, 1932.

Rozhdestvenskii, S. V. *Istoricheskii obzor dieiatel'nosti Ministerstva Narodnago Prosveshcheniia, 1802–1902.* St. Petersburg, 1902.

Schiper, Ignacy. *Dzieje handlu żydowskiego na ziemiach polskich.* Warsaw, 1937.

―――et al., eds. *Żydzi w Polsce odrodzonej.* 2 vols. Warsaw, 1933–34.

Shatzky, Jacob. "Aleksander Kraushar and His Road to Total Assimilation." *Yivo Annual of Jewish Social Science,* 7 (1952), 146–74.

―――. *Geshikhte fun yidn in Varshe.* 3 vols. New York, 1947–53.

Shmeruk, Chone. "Aspects of the History of Warsaw as a Yiddish Literary Centre." *Polin: A Journal of Polish–Jewish Studies,* 3 (1988), 142–55.

―――. *The Esterke Story in Yiddish and Polish Literature.* Jerusalem, 1985.

———. "Hebrew-Yiddish-Polish: A Trilingual Jewish Culture," in *The Jews of Poland between Two World Wars*. Edited by Israel Gutman et al., pp. 265–91. Cambridge, Mass., 1989.

———. "A Pioneering Study of the Warsaw Jewish Press." *Soviet Jewish Affairs*, 11, nr. 3 (1981), pp. 35–53.

Singer, Bernard. *Moje Nalewki*. Warsaw, 1959.

Singer, Isaac Bashevis. *In My Father's Court*. New York, 1966.

Słonimski, Antoni. *Wspomnienia warszawskie*. Warsaw, 1957.

Sokolow, Nahum. *Zadania intelligencji żydowskiej: szkic programu*. Warsaw, 1890.

Sprawozdanie Zarządu Warszawskiej Gminy Starozakonnych za lata 1912–1916. Warsaw, 1918.

Strzelecki, Edward. "Ludność Warszawy na przełemie XIX i XX wieku," in *Z dziejów książki i bibliotek w Warszawie*. Edited by Stanisław Tazbir, pp. 207–22. Warsaw, 1961.

Suligowski, Adolf. *Miasto analfabetów*. 2nd ed. Krakow, 1905.

———. "Warszawa i jej przedsiębiorstwa miejskie." *Ekonomista*, year 3 (1903), vol. 1, pp. 219–56, vol. 2, pp. 1–50.

Szczypiorski, Adam. "Imigracja do Warszawy w XIX wieku." *Studia Demograficzne*, 1 nr. 1 (1961), pp. 61–86.

———. "Struktura zawodowa i społeczna Warszawy w pierwszej okresie epoki kapitalistycznej (1864–1882)." *Kwartalnik Historii Kultury Materialnej*, 8 (1960), 75–102.

Szulc, Stefan. *Wartość materjałow statystycznych, dotyczących stanu ludnóści byłego Królestwa Polskiego*. Warsaw, 1920.

Szwankowski, Eugeniusz. "Praga w latach 1814–1880," in *Dzieje Pragi*. Edited by Józef Kazimierski et al., pp. 161–74. Warsaw, 1970.

———. *Ulice i place Warszawy*. Warsaw, 1963.

———. *Warszawa, rozwój urbanistyczny i architektoniczny*. Warsaw, 1952.

Wandycz, Piotr. *The Lands of Partitioned Poland, 1795–1918*. Seattle, Wash., 1974.

"Warszawa." *S. Orgelbranda encyklopedja powszechna z ilustracjami i mapami*. 1893–1903 ed.

Wasiutyński, Bohdan. *Ludność żydowska w Królestwie Polskiem*. Warsaw, 1911.

———. *Ludność żydowska w Polsce w wiekach XIX i XX: studjum statystyczne*. Warsaw, 1930.

Wróbel, Piotr. "Jewish Warsaw before the First World War." *Polin: A Journal of Polish-Jewish Studies*, 3 (1988), 156–87.

Wynot, Edward D. *Warsaw between the World Wars: Profile of the Capital City in a Developing Country*. Boulder, Colo., 1983.

Z dziejów Gminy Starozakonnych w Warszawie w XIX stuleciu. Vol. 1, *Szkolnictwo* (Only volume published) Warsaw, 1907.
Załęski, A. et al. "Warszawa." *Słownik geograficzny Królestwa Polskiego i innych krajów słowiańskich.* Warsaw, 1880–1904.
Załęski, Antoni. *Towarzystwo warszawskie: listy do przyjaciółki przez Baronessę XYZ.* 2nd ed. Edited by Ryszard Kołodziejczyk. Warsaw, 1971.
Żarnowska, Anna. *Klasa robotnicza Królestwa Polskiego 1870–1914.* Warsaw, 1974.
Żurawicka, Janina. *Inteligencja warszawska w końcu XIX wieku.* Warsaw, 1978.
Zyzniewski, Stanley John. "Russian Policy in the Congress Kingdom of Poland, 1863–1881." Unpublished Ph.D. dissertation, Harvard University, 1956.

Index

Acculturation, Jewish, 3, 21, 24, 31–38, 107–08, 121–22, 124
Aleksev, Sergei, 89, 104
Algemeyner yidisher arbeterbund in Lite, Rusland un Poyln, see Jewish Bund
Anti–Semitism, Polish, 3, 5, 33, 35, 38, 39, 59, 86–69, 72, 79, 83, 88–89, 93–96, 101–08
Anti–Semitism, Russian, see Union of the Russian People
Apukhtin, Aleksandr, 17–18
Assimilation and assimilationists, Jewish, 3, 10, 18, 21, 24, 29–38, 55–57, 59, 61, 63, 67, 73–75, 79, 83–88, 90–96, 99–101, 104–05, 121–22, 124
Association for Polish Culture (Towarzystwo Kultury Polskiej), 102
Association for Scholarly Courses (Towarzystwo Kursów Naukowych), 18

Balicki, Zygmunt, 72
Baranowski, Ignacy, 100
Baudouin de Courtenay, Jay, 103
Berg, Fedor, 11
Bloch, Jan, 36, 56–57
Boycott, Polish anti–Jewish (1912), 101–04
Budget, 12–13; Table 1–1
Bund, see Jewish Bund

Censorship, 66–67, 69–71
Censuses, 1882 and 1897, 21–26, 28–36, 40–49, 53–62, 117–18; Tables 2–1 to 2–5, 3–1, 4–1 to 4–6
Citadel, see Warsaw Citadel
Churches, see Warsaw churches
City Credit Association (Towarzystwo Kredytowe Miejskie), 102
Commerce and trade, 52, 54–59, 64
Constitutional Democrats, 85, 98, 101
Conversion, Jewish, 35–37, 57, 123
Craft industry, see Industry
Crime, 15–16, 48

Dmowski, Roman, 71–72, 82–83, 87–95, 103–04, 106–07
Duma Elections: first, 84–86; second, 87–88; third, 88–89; fourth, 89–101, 103–05, 108–09

Education, Jewish, 18–20, 61
Education, Polish, 16–20, 61
Eisenbaum, Antoni, 73
Emancipation, Jewish, 10, 79
Employment, Jewish, 51–64; Tables 4–1 to 4–6
Employment, Polish, 51–64; Tables 4–1 to 4–6
Ethnic identity and change, 2–4, 21, 24, 28–38, 107–08, 137–38

Factory industry, see Industry
Finkelstein, Noah and Nehemiah, 75
Flying University (Latają̨cy Uniwersytet), 18

General Jewish Labor Union in Lithuania, Russia, and Poland, see Jewish Bund
German culture and the Jews, 32, 35–37, 107, 123
Germans in Warsaw, 9, 31, 51, 57, 60
Glatsztern, Hilary, 75
Gmina Żydowska (Starozakonnych) w Warszawie, see Kehile in Warsaw
Government service, 54, 57, 60–63
Grosser, Bronisław, 34, 63
Grünbaum, Isaac, 38
Gurko, Iosif, 11

Hartglas, Apolinary, 33
Hasidim and Hasidism, 31–32, 57, 87, 121
Haskalah, 35–36
Housing, 13–14, 39–49

Illegitimacy, 28, 120
Imperial University of Warsaw (Imperatorskii Varshavskii Universitet), 17
In-migration, 22–26, 32, 34; Table 2–2
Industry, 51–52, 54–50; see also Jews in industry
Infant and child mortality, 26–28, 120
Intelligentsia, Jewish, 60–63, 84
Intelligentsia, Polish, 60–63, 69
Iwaszkiewicz, Janusz, 61–62
Jabłonowski, Roman, 103
Jabłonowski, Władysław, 93
Jackan, Samuel, 62, 75–76

Index

January Insurrection, 1863, 2, 8, 10. 11, 78–79
Jagiełło, Eugeniusz, 97–98, 100, 103
Jelenski, Jan, 30, 69, 80
Jewish acculturation, see Acculturation, Jewish
Jewish assimilation, see Assimilation, Jewish
Jewish Bund, 75, 82–83, 87–88, 93, 97
Jewish communal board, see Kehile board
Jewish conversion, see Conversion, Jewish
Jewish education, see Education, Jewish
Jewish Electoral Committee in Duma elections: first, 86; second, 87–88; fourth, 92, 96–100
Jewish emancipation, see Emancipation, Jewish
Jewish employment, see Employment, Jewish
Jewish intelligentsia, see Intelligentsia, Jewish
Jewish languages, see Languages of the Jews
Jewish nationalism, see Nationalism, Jewish
Jewish periodical press, 66–68, 73–77, 128
    Individual titles:
    Dostrzegacz Nadwiślański, 73
    Fraynd, Der, 38, 75, 97
    Głos Żydowski, 66, 77
    Ha-Zefirah, 73–75
    Haynt, 62, 75–76, 130, 136
    Izraelita, 30, 35, 66, 73–75, 77, 92–93, 96, 96, 99, 130
    Jutrzenka, 73
    Moment, Der, 62, 75–76, 130
    Przegląd Codzienny, 77
    Varshoyer Yudishe Tsaytung, 75
    Veg, Der, 75, 77
    Yidishes Tageblat, 75, 77
    Yud, Der, 75
    Życie Żydowskie, 66, 77
Jews in Industry, 55–56, 58, 64; see also Industry; Polonization of the economy

Kehile in Warsaw, 18–19, 29–30, 61, 83, 86, 90
Kempner, Stanisław, 66, 72, 82
Kieniewicz, Stefan, 109
Kirszrot, Jan, 33, 63
Kozicki, Stanisław, 72
Kraushar, Aleksander, 35, 66
Kronenberg family, 36, 56–57
Krzywicki, Ludwik, 14, 44, 49, 60, 87–88, 97

Kucharzewski, Jan, 92–100, 194–95, 108–09

Languages of the Jews, 3, 11, 17–20, 31–37, 67, 73–77, 122–24; Table 2–5
Latający Universytet, see Flying University
Lewental, Salomon (Franciszek Salezy), 36, 66, 123
Lipsztadt, Aleksander, 100
Litvaks, 32, 34–35, 63, 101, 107, 122–23; see also Russian culture and the Jews

Main School (Szkoła Główna), 17
Marchlewski, Julian, 56
Maskilim, 31–32, 123
Medem, Vladimir, 56
Misnagdim, 31–32, 57

Natanson, Kazimierz, 63, 91
Natanson, Ludwik, 29–30, 63, 70
Natanson family, 56, 63
National Concentration in Duma elections: second, 87–88; fourth, 91–100
National Democracy (Stronnictowo Narodowo–Demokratyczne), 71–72, 79–83, 85–98, 100–08; see also Nationalism, Polish
National Democratic Secession (Secesja), 89, 91, 100
Nationalism, Jewish, 19, 35, 67, 75, 78, 83–84, 89–91, 94, 105; see also Zionism
Nationalism, Polish, 1, 3, 5, 19, 50, 59, 64, 67, 71–72, 78, 82, 104–09; see also National Democratic Party
Neighborhood and sections, see Warsaw neighborhoods and sections
Newspapers, see Jewish periodical press; Polish periodical press
Nicholas I, Tsar, 8
1905 Revolution, see Revolution of 1905
Nowodworski, Franciszek, 86–88, 91
Nussbaum, Hilary, 55, 121

Oberpolitseimeister, 12, 14–16, 61, 102
Okhrana, 102
Orthodox in Warsaw, see Russian Orthodox in Warsaw
Orzeszkowa, Eliza, 79–80, 84
Paderewski, Ignacy, 90
Parks, places, and squares, see Warsaw parks, places, and squares
Peltin, Samuel (Peltyn), 74
Peretz, Isaac Leib, 61–62, 73, 75–76, 109
Periodical press, Jewish, see Jewish periodical press

Periodical press, Polish, see Polish periodical press
Pogrom of 1881 in Warsaw, 29–30, 42, 80
Poliakevitch tobacco factory, 56
Polish education, see Education, Polish
Polish employment, see Employment, Polish
Polish intelligentsia, see Intelligentsia, Polish
Polish nationalism, see Nationalism, Polish
Polish periodical Press, 66–72, 77, 128
    Individual titles:
    Czerwony Sztandar, 72
    Dzwon Polski, 86
    Gazeta Handlowa, 128
    Gazeta Poranna 2 grosze, 72, 94, 98, 102
    Głos, 69, 79
    Goniec, 69, 71, 88–90, 92
    Kurjer Codzienny, 72
    Kurjer Polski, 72
    Kurjer Poranny, 69, 72, 90, 92
    Kurjer Warszawski, 36, 38, 69–70, 72, 76, 90–94, 96, 98–101
    Nowa Gazeta, 72, 90, 95–97, 100, 128
    Prawda, 69, 79
    Rola, 69, 80
    Slowo, 69, 72, 94
    Tygodnik Illustrowany, 69–70, 101
Polish Progressive Party (Polska Patia Postępowa), 87, 91
Polish Progressive Union (Polski Związek Postępowy), 91
Polish Socialist Party (Polska Partia Socjalistyczna), 72, 81–82, 93, 97, 103
Polonization of the economy, 50, 59, 63–64; see also Commerce and trade; Industry; Jews in industry
Polska Partia Postępowa, see Polish Progressive Party
Polska Partia Socjalistyczna, see Polish Socialist Party
Polski Związek Postępowy, see Polish Progressive Union
Population, 1–2, 7–9, 21–38; Tables 2–1 to 2–5; see also In–migration; Infant and child mortality; Sex and age ratios
Positivism, 79, 131
Professions, 54, 57, 60–63
Progressive Alliance in Duma elections: second, 87–88
Progressive Democratic Union (Związek Postępowo–Demokratyczny), 72, 72, 85–87, 91, 105
Protestants in Warsaw, 9, 24, 31, 57
Prus, Boleslaw, 14–16, 43, 67, 69, 84
Prylucki, Zevi, 62, 75

Public works, services, sanitation, 12–15, 47

Realist Party (Stronnictwo Polityki Realnej), 72, 82, 87, 91, 94, 97

Religious composition, 2, 4, 9, 21, 24–25, 28, 40–49; Tables 2–3, 3–1, 3–2

Residential distribution, 9, 39–49

Revolution of 1905, 2, 16, 19, 22, 71, 80–81

Roman Catholic periodical press, 72

Russian culture and the Jews, 32, 34–37, 107; see also Litvaks

Russian military in Warsaw, 11–12, 20, 22, 48, 54, 57

Russian Orthodox and Orthodox churches in Warsaw, 24, 31, 41, 47

Russians in Warsaw, 8–12, 17, 31, 48, 51, 60–62, 84–85, 89, 104

Russification, 2,8, 11–12, 16–20, 24, 60–62, 78

Sadzewicz, Antoni, 72
Schoenaich, Wladyslaw, 27
Secesja, see National Democratic Secession
Segregation, Residential, see Residential distribution
Sex and age ratios, 25–26; Table 2–4
Shatzky, Jacob, 29–30
Sholem Aleichem, 73, 76
Singer, Bernard, 34, 37, 45–46, 53, 76, 100
Singer, Isaac Bashevis, 16, 39, 44–46, 76
Skalon, Georgii, 11, 81
Słonimski, Antoni, 41
Słonimski, Hayyim Selig, 74
Social Democratic Party (Socjaldemokracja Królestwa Polskiego i Litwy), 72, 82, 87–88, 93, 100, 103
Socialism, 3, 72, 80–84, 105; see also Jewish Bund, Polish Socialist Party, Social Democratic Party
Society for Lodging Houses, Cheap Kitchens and Tea Rooms, and Work Houses (Tomarzystwo Domów Nocległowych, Tanich Kuchni–Herbaciarni i Domów Pracy), 14
Socjaldemokracja Królestwa Polskiego i Litwy, see Social Democratic Party
Soiuz Russkogo Naroda, see Union of the Russian People
Sokolow, Nahum, 31, 62, 74, 92
Starynekevich, Sokrates, 12
Streets, see Warsaw streets
Stronnictwo Narodowo–Demokratyczne, see National Democratic Party
Stronnictwo Polityki Realnej, see Realist Party

Suburbs, see Warsaw suburbs
Suligowski, Adolf, 43
Świętochowski, Aleksander, 79, 82, 84, 87–88, 102
Synagogues in Warsaw, see Warsaw synagogues
Szkola Główna, see Main School
Towarzystwo Domow Nocległowych, Tanich Kuchni–Herbarciarni i Domów Pracy, see Society for Lodging Houses, Cheap Kitchens and Tea Rooms, and Work Houses
Towarzystwo Kredytowe Miejskie, see City Credit Association
Towarzystwo Kultury Polskiej, see Association for Polish Culture
Towarzystwo Kursów Naukowych, see Association for Scholarly Courses
Trade, see Commerce and trade
Tyszkiewicz, Władysław, 86

Union of the Russian People, 85, 89, 104
Urban self–government, 89, 95–96

Vináver, Maksim, 98, 101
Vonliarliarskii, Nikolai, 81

Warsaw budget, see Budget
Warsaw Catholic churches:
    Cathedral of St. John, 41
    Church of St. Florian, 47
    Church of the Holy Cross, 42, 80
Warsaw Citadel, 8, 12, 45, 49, 80
Warsaw neighborhoods and sections:
    Center, 40–42, 52
    New City (Nowe Miasto), 7, 40–42
    Northwest, 9, 45–46, 48–49, 52
    Powiśle, 43, 48, 52
    Praga, 7, 9, 15, 22, 40, 46–47, 49
    South, 42–43, 49
    Southwest, 43–45
Warsaw parks, places, and squares:
    Alexander Park, 36
    Botanical Gardens, 42
    Grzybów Place, 44, 52
    Iron Gate Square, 41, 52
    Krochmalna Square, 16, 39, 44
    Łazienki Park, 42
    Mirowski Place, 45, 52
    Muranów Place, 56

Saxon Gardens, 37, 40–42
Saxon Place, 41
Square of the Three Crosses (Alexander Place), 42
Ujazdowski Park, 42
Warsaw streets:
Bielańska, 37
Danilowiczowska, 35
Dzielna, 46
Dzika, 46
Elektoralna, 100
Franciszkańska, 49, 52
Gęsia, 46, 49, 52
Górczewska, 48
Grzybowska, 44, 49
Hoża, 42
Jerozolimskie, 42, 44, 49
Karmelicka, 49
Koszykowa, 42
Karkowskie Przedmieście, 15, 40–43
Leszno, 44, 49
Marszałkowska, 25, 37, 40, 42, 44, 49, 52
Mila, 37, 46
Muranowska, 37
Nalewki, 37, 45–46, 49, 52, 56
Nowogrodzka, 42
Nowolipia, 49, 56
Nowolipki, 49
Nowomila, 46
Nowy Świat, 15, 40, 42–43, 52
Okopowa, 46
Pańska, 49
Pawia, 46, 49
Piękna, 42
Sadowa, 42
Senatorska, 40
Śliska, 49
Świętojerska, 49
Tlomacka, 18
Twarda, 49
Ujazdowskie, 42–44, 48
Tlomacka, 18
Twarda, 49
Ujazdowskie, 42–44, 48

Wilcza, 42
Wspólna, 42
Żabia, 49
Żelazna, 44
Żorawia, 42
Warsaw suburbs, 7, 15, 22, 47–49
Individual suburbs:
Bródno, 22, 48
Czyste, 22, 44, 48–49
Marymont, 49
Mlociny, 22, 48
Mokotów, 22, 48–49
Ochota, 44, 49
Saska Kępa, 47
Wierzbno, 49
Wola, 44, 48–49, 52
Warsaw synagogues:
Daniłowiczowska Street, 35
Tłomacka Street, 18
Warsaw–Vienna railway station, 44, 52
Wasercug, Józef, 74
Wawelberg, Hipolit, 48
Wernick, Fritz, 39–40, 46–47

Zalewski (Zaleski, Witold), 29–30, 121
Żeromski, Stefan, 42, 69
Zionism, 3, 74, 77, 83, 87–88, 92; see also Nationalism, Jewish
Zwiazek Postepowo–Demokratyczny, see Progressive Democratic Union